WITHDRAWN
IOWA STATE UNIVERSITY
LIBRARY

D1451313

VISUAL BASIC DESIGN PATTERNS

WITHDRAWN
IOWA STATE UNIVERSITY
LIBRARY

WITHDRAWN
IOWA STATE UNIVERSITY
LIBRARY

VISUAL BASIC DESIGN PATTERNS

VB 6.0 and VB.NET

James W. Cooper

Addison-Wesley

Boston • San Francisco • New York • Toronto • Montreal
London • Munich • Paris • Madrid
Capetown • Sydney • Tokyo • Singapore • Mexico City

Many of the designations used by manufacturers and sellers to distinguish their products are claimed as trademarks. Where those designations appear in this book, and Addison-Wesley was aware of a trademark claim, the designations have been printed with initial capital letters or in all capitals.

The author and publisher have taken care in the preparation of this book, but make no expressed or implied warranty of any kind and assume no responsibility for errors or omissions. No liability is assumed for incidental or consequential damages in connection with or arising out of the use of the information or programs contained herein.

The publisher offers discounts on this book when ordered in quantity for special sales. For more information, please contact:

Pearson Education Corporate Sales Division
201 W. 103rd Street
Indianapolis, IN 46290
(800) 428-5331
corpsales@pearsoned.com

Library of Congress Cataloging-in-Publication Data

Cooper, James William, 1943–
    Visual Basic design patterns : VB 6.0 and VB.NET / James W. Cooper.
      p.   cm.
    Includes bibliographical references and index.
    ISBN 0-201-70265-7 (pbk. : alk. paper)
     1. Microsoft Visual BASIC. 2. BASIC (Computer program language) I. Title

QA76.73.B3 C6655 2001
005.13'3—dc21   2001041322

Copyright © 2002 by Pearson Education, Inc.

All rights reserved. No part of this publication may be reproduced, stored in a retrieval system, or transmitted, in any form, or by any means, electronic, mechanical, photocopying, recording, or otherwise, without the prior consent of the publisher. Printed in the United States of America. Published simultaneously in Canada.

For information on obtaining permission for use of material from this work, please submit a written request to:

Pearson Education, Inc.
Rights and Contracts Department
75 Arlington Street, Suite 300
Boston, MA 02116
Fax: (617) 848-7047

ISBN: 0-201-70265-7
Text printed on recycled paper
1 2 3 4 5 6 7 8 9 10—CRS—0504030201
First printing, November 2001

CONTENTS

PREFACE

This is a practical book that tells you how to write Visual Basic (VB6 and VB.NET) programs using some of the most common design patterns. It also serves as a quick introduction to programming in the new VB.NET version of the VB language. The pattern discussions are structured as a series of short chapters, each describing a design pattern and giving one or more complete working, visual-example programs that use that pattern. Each chapter also includes UML diagrams illustrating how the classes interact.

This book is not a "companion" book to the well-known *Design Patterns* text by the "Gang of Four." Instead, it is a tutorial for people who want to learn what design patterns are about and how to use them in their work. You do not have to have read *Design Patterns* to read this book, but when you are done here you may well want to read or reread it to gain additional insights.

In this book you will learn that design patterns are frequently used ways of organizing objects in your programs to make them easier to write and modify. You'll also see that by familiarizing yourself with them, you've gained some valuable vocabulary for discussing how your programs are constructed.

People come to appreciate design patterns in different ways—from the highly theoretical to the intensely practical—and when they finally see the great power of these patterns, an Aha! moment occurs. Usually this moment means that you suddenly have an internal picture of how that pattern can help you in your work.

In this book, we try to help you form that conceptual idea, or *gestalt*, by describing the pattern in as many ways as possible. The book is organized into six main sections: an introductory description, an introduction to VB.NET, and descriptions of patterns, grouped as creational, structural, and behavioral.

For each pattern, we start with a brief verbal description and then build simple example programs. Each of these examples is a visual program that you can run and examine to make the pattern as concrete a concept as possible. All of the example programs and their variations are on the companion CD-ROM, where you run them, change them, and see how the variations you create work.

We show that you can use design patterns effectively in VB6 and then show the same patterns in VB.NET (also called VB7). Since each of the examples consists of a number of VB files for each of the classes we use in that example, we also provide a VB project file for each example and place each example in a separate subdirectory to prevent any confusion. We place the VB.NET examples in a separate directory under each pattern. This book is based on the Beta-2 release of VB.Net. Any changes between this version and the final product will probably not be great. Consult the Addison-Wesley Web site for updates to any example code.

If you leaf through the book you'll see screen shots of the programs we developed to illustrate the design patterns, providing yet another way to reinforce your learning of these patterns. In addition, you'll see UML diagrams of these programs, illustrating the interactions between classes in yet another way. UML diagrams are just simple box-and-arrow illustrations of classes and their inheritance structure, where arrows point to parent classes, and dotted arrows point to interfaces. And if you're not yet familiar with UML, we provide a simple introduction in the second chapter.

When you finish this book you'll be comfortable with the basics of design patterns and will be able to start using them in your day-to-day Visual Basic programming work.

James W. Cooper
Nantucket, MA
Wilton, CT
Maui, HI
October, 2001

ACKNOWLEDGMENTS

I'd like to thank Bob Mack and Alan Marwick for their support and interest, as well as all the readers who sent me comments and suggestions, including David Holt, Conrad Frix, Brian Livingston, Tim Romano, Eric Cote, Romek Pawlikowski, Robert Cooley, David Wade, John Barrett, Kevin Downs, Dan Green, and Bill McClaren. I'd especially like to thank the reviewers, including Michael Deignan and Daniel Moth. I also appreciate the work that Mike Gold at Microgold Software put in to get a beta copy of WithClass to me.

Finally, I could never have written this without the continuing, unflagging support of my wife, Vicki.

PART 1

Object-Oriented Programming in VB

The first section of this book introduces the concepts of object-oriented programming in general, and in VB in particular. We cover how you draw UML diagrams to represent these programs and their objects and show how to build your own controls using VB6. We introduce inheritance and interfaces and then take you through the fundamentals of programming in VB.NET. Then we show you how you can simplify programming using these techniques in this powerful new language.

Once you have learned these introductory concepts, you'll be all set to make use of the design patterns we cover in the remaining three sections of the book.

CHAPTER 1

What Are Design Patterns?

Sitting at your desk in front of your workstation, you stare into space, trying to figure out how to write a new program feature. You know intuitively what must be done, what data and what objects come into play, but you have this underlying feeling that there is a more elegant and general way to write this program.

In fact, you probably don't write any code until you can build a picture in your mind of what the code does and how the pieces of the code interact. The more that you can picture this "organic whole," or *gestalt,* the more likely you are to feel comfortable that you have developed the best solution to the problem. If you don't grasp this whole right away, you may keep staring out the window for a time, even though the basic solution to the problem is quite obvious.

In one sense you feel that the more elegant solution will be more reusable and more maintainable, but even if you are the sole likely programmer, you feel reassured once you have designed a solution that is relatively elegant and that doesn't expose too many internal inelegancies.

One of the main reasons that computer science researchers began to recognize design patterns is to satisfy this need for elegant, but simple, reusable solutions. The term "design patterns" sounds a bit formal to the uninitiated and can be somewhat offputting when you first encounter it. But, in fact, design patterns are just convenient ways of reusing object-oriented code between projects and between programmers. The idea behind design patterns is simple—write down and catalog common interactions between objects that programmers have frequently found useful.

One of the frequently cited patterns from early literature on programming frameworks is the Model-View-Controller framework for Smalltalk (Krasner and Pope 1988), which divided the user interface problem into three parts, as shown in Figure 1-1. The parts were referred to as a *data model,* which contains the computational parts of the program; the *view,* which presented the user interface; and the *controller,* which interacted between the user and the view.

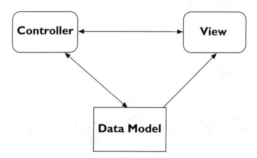

Figure 1-1   The Model-View-Controller framework

Each of these aspects of the problem is a separate object, and each has its own rules for managing its data. Communication among the user, the GUI, and the data should be carefully controlled, and this separation of functions accomplished that very nicely. Three objects talking to each other using this restrained set of connections is an example of a powerful design pattern.

In other words, design patterns describe how objects communicate without becoming entangled in each other's data models and methods. Keeping this separation has always been an objective of good OO programming, and if you have been trying to keep objects minding their own business, you are probably using some of the common design patterns already.

Design patterns began to be recognized more formally in the early 1990s by Erich Gamma (1992), who described patterns incorporated in the GUI application framework, ET++. The culmination of these discussions and a number of technical meetings was the publication of the parent book in this series, *Design Patterns—Elements of Reusable Software,* by Gamma, Helm, Johnson, and Vlissides (1995). This book, commonly referred to as the Gang of Four, or "GoF," book, has had a powerful impact on those seeking to understand how to use design patterns and has become an all-time bestseller. It describes 23 commonly occurring and generally useful patterns and comments on how and when you might apply them. We will refer to this groundbreaking book as *Design Patterns* throughout this book.

Since the publication of the original *Design Patterns* text, there have been a number of other useful books published. One closely related book is *The Design Patterns Smalltalk Companion* (Alpert, Brown, and Woolf 1998), which covers the same 23 patterns from the Smalltalk point of view. We'll refer to this book throughout as the *Smalltalk Companion.* Finally, we recently published *Java Design Patterns Java: A Tutorial,* which illustrates all of these patterns in Java.

Defining Design Patterns

We all talk about the way we do things in our jobs, hobbies, and home life, and we recognize repeating patterns all the time.

- Sticky buns are like dinner rolls, but I add brown sugar and nut filling to them.
- Her front garden is like mine, but I grow astilbe in my garden.
- This end table is constructed like that one, but in this one, there are doors instead of drawers.

We see the same thing in programming when we tell a colleague how we accomplished a tricky bit of programming so he doesn't have to recreate it from scratch. We simply recognize effective ways for objects to communicate while maintaining their own separate existences.

Some useful definitions of design patterns have emerged as the literature in this field has expanded.

- "Design patterns are recurring solutions to design problems you see over and over." (*The Smalltalk Companion*)
- "Design patterns constitute a set of rules describing how to accomplish certain tasks in the realm of software development." (Pree 1994)
- "Design patterns focus more on reuse of recurring architectural design themes, while frameworks focus on detailed design and implementation." (Coplien and Schmidt 1995)
- "A pattern addresses a recurring design problem that arises in specific design situations and presents a solution to it." (Buschmann et al. 1996)
- "Patterns identify and specify abstractions that are above the level of single classes and instances, or of components." (Gamma et al. 1993)

But while it is helpful to draw analogies to architecture, cabinet making, and logic, design patterns are not just about the design of objects but about the *interaction* between objects. One possible view of some of these patterns is to consider them as *communication patterns*.

Some other patterns deal not just with object communication but with strategies for object inheritance and containment. It is the design of simple, but elegant, methods of interaction that makes many design patterns so important.

Design patterns can exist at many levels from very low-level specific solutions to broadly generalized system issues. There are now hundreds of patterns in the literature. They have been discussed in articles and at conferences of all levels of granularity. Some are examples that apply widely, and a few writers have ascribed pattern behavior to class groupings that apply to just a single problem (Kurata 1998).

It has become apparent that you don't just *write* a design pattern off the top of your head. In fact, most such patterns are *discovered* rather than written. The process of looking for these patterns is called "pattern mining," and it is worthy of a book of its own.

The 23 design patterns selected for inclusion in the original *Design Patterns* book were those that had several known applications and that were on a middle level of generality, where they could easily cross application areas and encompass several objects.

The authors divided these patterns into three types: creational, structural, and behavioral.

- *Creational patterns* create objects for you rather than having you instantiate objects directly. This gives your program more flexibility in deciding which objects need to be created for a given case.
- *Structural patterns* help you compose groups of objects into larger structures, such as complex user interfaces or accounting data.
- *Behavioral patterns* help you define the communication between objects in your system and how the flow is controlled in a complex program.

We'll be looking at Visual Basic versions of these patterns in the chapters that follow, and we will provide at least one complete VB6 and VB.NET program for each of the 23 patterns. This way you can examine the code snippets we provide and also run, edit, and modify the complete working programs on the accompanying CD-ROM. You'll find a list of all the programs on the CD-ROM at the end of each pattern description.

The Learning Process

We have found that regardless of the language, learning design patterns is a multiple-step process.

1. Acceptance
2. Recognition
3. Internalization

First, you accept the premise that design patterns are important in your work. Then, you recognize that you need to read about design patterns in order to know when you might use them. Finally, you internalize the patterns in sufficient detail that you know which ones might help you solve a given design problem.

For some lucky people, design patterns are obvious tools, and these people can grasp their essential utility just by reading summaries of the patterns. For many of the rest of us, there is a slow induction period after we've read about a pattern followed by the proverbial "Aha!" when we see how we can apply them in our work. This book helps to take you to that final stage of internalization by providing complete, working programs that you can try out for yourself.

The examples in *Design Patterns* are brief and are in C++ or, in some cases, Smalltalk. If you are working in another language, it is helpful to have the pattern examples in your language of choice. This book attempts to fill that need for Visual Basic programmers.

Studying Design Patterns

There are several alternate ways to become familiar with these patterns. In each approach, you should read this book and the parent *Design Patterns* book in one order or the other. We also strongly urge you to read the *Smalltalk Companion* for completeness, since it provides alternative descriptions of each of the patterns. Finally, there are a number of Web sites on learning and discussing design patterns for you to peruse.

Notes on Object-Oriented Approaches

The fundamental reason for using design patterns is to keep classes separated and prevent them from having to know too much about one another. Equally important, using these patterns helps you avoid reinventing the wheel and allows you to describe your programming approach succinctly in terms other programmers can easily understand.

There are a number of strategies that OO programmers use to achieve this separation, among them encapsulation and inheritance. Nearly all languages that have OO capabilities support inheritance. A class that inherits from a parent class has access to all of the methods of that parent class. It also has access to all of its nonprivate variables. However, by starting your inheritance hierarchy with a complete, working class, you may be unduly restricting yourself as well as carrying along specific method implementation baggage. Instead, *Design Patterns* suggests that you always

Program to an interface and not to an implementation.

Putting this more succinctly, you should define the top of any class hierarchy with an *abstract* class or an *interface*, which implements no methods but simply defines the methods that class will support. Then in all of your derived classes you have more freedom to implement these methods as most suit your purposes.

The other major concept you should recognize is that of *object composition*. This is simply the construction of objects that contain others: encapsulation of several objects inside another one. While many beginning OO programmers use inheritance to solve every problem, as you begin to write more elaborate programs, you will begin to appreciate the merits of object composition. Your new object can have the interface that is best for what you want to accomplish without having all the methods of the parent classes. Thus, the second major precept suggested by *Design Patterns* is

Favor object composition over inheritance.

And, again, VB easily supports the inclusion of classes within other classes, so you find that we are exactly on track for how we will be able to implement rather sophisticated OO techniques in VB.

VB Design Patterns

Each of the 23 patterns in *Design Patterns* is discussed, at least one working program example for that pattern is supplied. All of the programs have some sort of visual interface to make them that much more immediate to you. All of them also use class, interfaces, and object composition, but the programs themselves are of necessity quite simple so that the coding doesn't obscure the fundamental elegance of the patterns we are describing.

We present each of the patterns both in VB.NET and (except one) in VB6. In most cases we present the VB6 version first and then show how the patterns become even easier to implement in VB.NET (VB7).

However, even though VB is our target language, this isn't specifically a book on the VB language. There are lots of features in VB that we don't cover, but we do cover most of what is central to VB. You will find, however, that this is a fairly useful tutorial in object-oriented programming in VB and provides good overview of how to program in VB.NET.

How This Book Is Organized

We take up each of the 23 patterns, grouped into the general categories of creational, structural, and behavioral patterns. Many of the patterns stand more or less independently, but we do take advantage of already discussed patterns from time to time. For example, we use the Factory and Command patterns extensively after introducing them, and we use the Mediator pattern several times after we introduce it. We use the Memento again in the State pattern, the

Chain of Responsibility in the Interpreter pattern discussion, and the Singleton pattern in the Flyweight pattern discussion. In no case do we use a pattern before we have introduced it formally.

We also take some advantage of the sophistication of later patterns to introduce new features of VB.NET. For example, the Listbox, DataGrid, and TreeView are introduced in the Adapter and Bridge patterns. We show how to paint graphics objects in the Abstract Factory. We introduce the Iterator and IEnumeration interfaces in the Iterator and in the Composite, where we also take up formatting. We use exceptions in the Singleton pattern and discuss ADO database connections in the Façade pattern. And we show how to use VB.NET timers in the Proxy pattern.

CHAPTER 2

UML Diagrams

We have illustrated the patterns in this book with diagrams drawn using Unified Modeling Language (UML). This simple diagramming style was developed from work done by Grady Booch, James Rumbaugh, and Ivar Jacobson, which resulted in a merging of ideas into a single specification and, eventually, a standard. You can read details of how to use UML in any number of books such as those by Booch et al. (1998), Fowler and Scott (1997), and Grand (1998). We'll outline the basics you'll need in this introduction.

Basic UML diagrams consist of boxes representing classes. Let's consider the following class (which has very little actual function).

```
'Class Person
Private age As Integer
Private personName As String
'-----
Public Sub init(nm As String)
  personName = nm
End Sub
'-----
Public Function makeJob() As String
  makeJob = "hired"
End Function
'-----
Private Sub splitNames()

End Sub
'-----
Public Function getAge() As Integer
 getAge = age
End Function
'-----
Private Function getJob() As String

End Function
```

We can represent this class in UML, as shown in Figure 2-1.

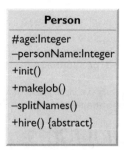

Figure 2-1   The Person class, showing private, protected, and public variables, and static and abstract methods

The top part of the box contains the class name and package name (if any). The second compartment lists the class's variables, and the bottom compartment lists its methods. The symbols in front of the names indicate that member's visibility, where "+" means public, "–" means private, and "#" means protected. Static methods are shown underlined. Abstract methods may be shown in italics or, as shown in Figure 2-1, with an "{abstract}" label.

You can also show all of the type information in a UML diagram where that is helpful, as illustrated in Figure 2-2a.

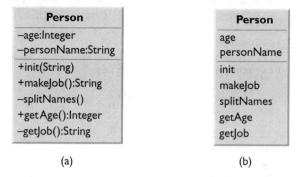

Figure 2-2(a)(b)   The Person class UML diagram shown both with and without the method types

UML does not require that you show all of the attributes of a class, and it is usual only to show the ones of interest to the discussion at hand. For example, in Figure 2-2b, we have omitted some of the method details.

Inheritance

Let's consider a VB7 version of Person that has public, protected, and private variables and methods, and an Employee class derived from it. We will also make the getJob method abstract in the base Person class, which means we indicate it with the MustOverride keyword.

```
Public MustInherit Class Person
    'Class Person
    Private age As Short
    Protected personName As String
    '-----
    Public Sub init(ByRef nm As String)
        personName = nm
    End Sub
    '-----
    Public Function makeJob() As String
        makeJob = "hired"
    End Function
    '-----
    Private Sub splitNames()

    End Sub
    '-----
    Public Function getAge() As Short
        getAge = age
    End Function
    '-----
    Public MustOverride Function getJob() As String
End Class
```

We now derive the Employee class from it, and fill in some code for the getJob method.

```
Public Class Employee
    Inherits Person
    Public Overrides Function getJob() As System.String
        Return "Worker"
    End Function
End Class
```

You represent inheritance using a solid line and a hollow triangular arrow. For the simple Employee class that is a subclass of Person, we represent this in UML, as shown in Figure 2-3.

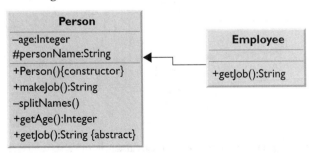

Figure 2-3   The UML diagram showing Employee derived from Person

Note that the name of the Employee class is not in italics because it is now a concrete class and because it includes a concrete method for the formerly abstract *getJob* method. While it has been conventional to show the inheritance with the arrow pointing *up* to the superclass, UML does not require this, and sometimes a different layout is clearer or uses space more efficiently.

Interfaces

An interface looks much like inheritance, except that the arrow has a dotted line tail, as shown in Figure 2-4. The name *<<interface>>* may also be shown, enclosed in double angle brackets, or *guillamets*.

Figure 2-4   ExitCommand implements the Command interface.

Composition

Much of the time, a useful representation of a class hierarchy must include how objects are contained in other objects. For example, a small company might include one Employee and one Person (perhaps a contractor).

```
Public Class Company
  Private emp as Employee
  Private pers as Person
End Class
```

We represent this in UML, as shown in Figure 2-5.

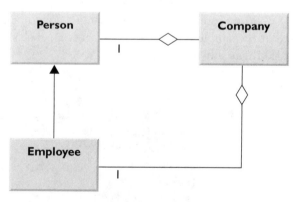

Figure 2-5   Company contains instances of Person and Employee.

The lines between classes show that there can be 0 to 1 instances of Person in Company and 0 to 1 instances of Employee in Company. The diamonds indicate the aggregation of classes within Company.

If there can be many instances of a class inside another, such as the array of Employees shown here

```
Public Class Company
   Private emp() as Employee
   Private pers
End Class
```

we represent that object composition as a single line with either a "*" on it or "0, *" on it, as shown in Figure 2-6.

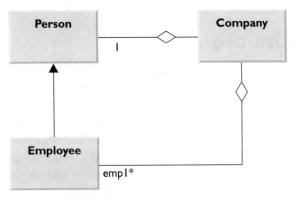

Figure 2-6   Company contains any number of instances of Employee.

Some writers have used hollow and solid diamond arrowheads to indicate containment of aggregates and circle arrowheads for single object composition, but this is not required.

Annotation

You will also find it convenient to annotate your UML or insert comments to explain which class calls a method in which other class. You can place a comment anywhere you want in a UML diagram. Comments may be enclosed in a box with a turned corner or just entered as text. Text comments are usually shown along an arrow line, indicating the nature of the method that is called, as shown in Figure 2-7.

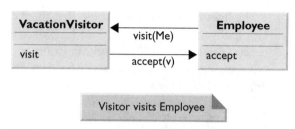

Figure 2-7   A comment is often shown in a box with a turned-down corner.

UML is quite a powerful way of representing object relationships in programs, and there are more diagram features in the full specification. However, the preceding brief discussion covers the markup methods we use in this text.

WithClass UML Diagrams

All of the UML programs in this book were drawn using the WithClass program from MicroGold. This program reads in the actual compiled classes and generates the UML class diagrams we show here. We have edited many of these class diagrams to show only the most important methods and relationships. However, the complete WithClass diagram files for each design pattern are stored in that pattern's directory. Thus, you can run your demo copy of With-Class on the enclosed CD and read it and investigate the detailed UML diagram starting with the same drawings you see here in the book.

Visual Basic Project Files

All of the programs in this book were written using Visual Basic 6.0 and VB.NET, using the project file feature. Each subdirectory of the CD-ROM contains the project file for that project so you can load the project and compile it as we did.

CHAPTER 3

Using Classes and Objects in VB

The original versions of Visual Basic (1.0 through 3.0) did not contain much in the way of object-oriented features, and many programmers' habits were formed by the features of these early versions. However, starting with Visual Basic 4.0, you could create Class modules as well as Form modules, and use them as objects. In this chapter we'll illustrate more of the advantages of using class modules. In the following chapter we'll extend these concepts for the more fully object-oriented VB.NET.

A Simple Temperature Conversion Program

Suppose we wanted to write a visual program to convert temperatures between the Celsius and Fahrenheit temperature scales. You may remember that water freezes at 0° on the Celsius scale and boils at 100°, whereas on the Fahrenheit scale, water freezes at 32° and boils at 212°. From these numbers you can quickly deduce the conversion formula that you may have forgotten.

The difference between freezing and boiling on one scale is 100° and on the other 180° or 100/180 or 5/9. The Fahrenheit scale is "offset" by 32, since water freezes at 32° on its scale. Thus,

$$C = (F - 32) * 5/9$$

and

$$F = 9/5 * C + 32$$

In our visual program, we'll allow the user to enter a temperature and select the scale to convert it, as we see in Figure 3-1.

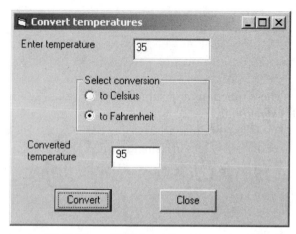

Figure 3-1   Converting 35° Celsius to 95° Fahrenheit with our visual interface

Using the very nice visual builder provided in VB, we can draw the user interface in a few seconds and simply implement routines to be called when the two buttons are pressed.

```
Private Sub btConvert_Click()
Dim enterTemp As Single, newTemp As Single

 enterTemp = Val(txTemperature.Text)

 If opFahr.Value Then
    newTemp = 9 * (enterTemp / 5) + 32
 Else
    newTemp = 5 * (enterTemp - 32) / 9
 End If

 lbNewtemp.Caption = Str$(newTemp)
End Sub
'------
Private Sub Closit_Click()
 End
End Sub
```

The preceding program is extremely straightforward and easy to understand and is typical of how many VB programs operate. However, it has some disadvantages that we might want to improve on.

The most significant problem is that the user interface and the data handling are combined in a single program module, rather than being handled separately. It is usually a good idea to keep the data manipulation and the interface manipulation separate so that changing interface logic doesn't impact the computation logic and vice versa.

Building a Temperature Class

As we noted in the previous chapter, a *class* in VB is a module that can contain both public and private functions and subroutines and can hold data values as well. It is logically the same as a Form, except that it has no visual aspects to it. These functions and subroutines in a class are frequently referred to collectively as *methods*.

Class modules are also like Basic Types or C structs that allow you to keep a set of data values in a single named place and fetch those values using get and set functions, which we then refer to as accessor methods.

You create a class module from the VB integrated development environment (IDE) using the menu item Project | Add class module. Then, you select the Properties window (using function key F4) and enter the module's name. In this example, we'll call the class module clsTemp.

What we want to do is to move all of the computation and conversion between temperature scales into this new clsTemp class module. One way to design this module is to rewrite the calling programs that will use the class module first. In the code sample below, we create an instance of the clsTemp class and use it to do whatever conversions are needed.

```
Private Sub btConvert_Click()
 Dim enterTemp As Single, newTemp As Single
 Dim clTemp As New clsTemp  'create class instance

 If opFahr.Value Then
    clTemp.setCels txTemperature
    lbNewtemp.Caption = Str$(clTemp.getFahr)
 Else
    clTemp.setFahr txTemperature
    lbNewtemp.Caption = Str$(clTemp.getCels)
 End If
```

Note that to create a working copy of a class (called an *instance*) you have to use the *new* keyword with the Dim statement.

```
Dim clTemp As New clsTemp     'create class instance
```

If you simply declare a variable without the New keyword,

```
Dim clTemp as clsTemp
```

you have created a pointer to a class instance but have not initialized an actual instance until you actually create one using New. You can set the value of the pointer you created using the Set keyword.

```
Set clTemp = New clsTemp     'create instance of clsTemp
```

In this program, we have two set methods—setCels and setFahr—and two get methods—getCels and getFahr.

These methods put values into the class and retrieve other values from the class. The actual class is just this.

```
Private temperature As Single

Public Sub setFahr(tx As String)
     temperature = 5 * (Val(tx) - 32) / 9
End Sub

Public Sub setCels(tx As String)
     temperature = Val(tx)
End Sub

Public Function getFahr() As Single
     getFahr = 9 * (temperature / 5) + 32
End Function

Public Function getCels() As Single
     getCels = temperature
End Function
```

Note that the temperature variable is declared as *private,* so it cannot be "seen" or accessed from outside the class. You can only put data into the class and get it back out using the four accessor methods. The main point to this code rearrangement is that the outer calling program does not have to know how the data are stored and how they are retrieved: that is only known inside the class. In this class we always store data in Celsius form and convert on the way in and out as needed. We could also do validity checks for legal strings on the way in, but since the Val function returns zeros and no error for illegal strings, we don't have to in this case.

The other important feature of the class is that it actually *holds data.* You can put data into it, and it will return it at any later time. This class only holds the one temperature value, but classes can contain quite complex sets of data values.

We could easily modify this class to get temperature values out in other scales without still ever requiring that the user of the class know anything about how the data are stored or how the conversions are performed.

Converting to Kelvin

Absolute zero on the Celsius scale is defined as −273.16° degrees. This is the coldest possible temperature, since it is the point at which all molecular motion stops. We can add a function

```
Public Function getKelvin() As Single
    getKelvin = temperature + 273.16
End Function
```

without any changes to the visual client at all. What would the setKelvin method look like?

Putting the Decisions into the Temperature Class

Now we are still making decisions within the user interface about which methods of the temperature class. It would be even better if all that complexity could disappear into the clsTemp class. It would be nice if we just could write our Conversion button click method as

```
Private Sub btConvert_Click()
Dim clTemp As New clsTemp

'put the entered value and conversion request
'into the class
clTemp.setEnterTemp txTemperature.Text, opFahr.Value

'and get out the requested conversion
lbNewtemp.Caption = clTemp.getTempString

End Sub
```

This removes the decision-making process to the temperature class and reduces the calling interface program to just two lines of code.

The class that handles all this becomes somewhat more complex, however, but then it keeps track of what data as been passed in and what conversion must be done.

```
Private temperature As Single    'always in Celsius
Private toFahr As Boolean        'conversion to F requested

Public Sub setEnterTemp(ByVal tx As String, _
        ByVal isCelsius As Boolean)
'convert to Celsius and save
 If Not isCelsius Then
   makeCel tx                    'convert and save
   toFahr = False
 Else
   temperature = Val(tx)    'just save temperature
   toFahr = True
 End If
End Sub
'------
Private Sub makeCel(tx As String)
```

```
    temperature = 5 * (Val(tx) - 32) / 9
End Sub
```

Now, the isCelsius Boolean tells the class whether to convert and whether conversion is required on fetching the temperature value. The output routine is simply the following.

```
Public Function getTempString() As String
  getTempString = Str$(getTempVal)
End Function
'------
Public Function getTempVal() As Single
 Dim outTemp As Single
  If toFahr Then           'should we convert to F?
   outTemp = makeFahr      'yes
  Else
   outTemp = temperature 'no
  End If
  getTempVal = outTemp      'return temp value
End Function
'------
Private Function makeFahr() As Single
 Dim t As Single
 'convert t to Fahrenheit
  t = 9 * (temperature / 5) + 32
  makeFahr = t
End Function
```

In this class we have both public and private methods. The public ones are callable from other modules, such as the user interface form module. The private ones, makeFahr and makeCel, are used internally and operate on the temperature variable.

Note that we now also have the opportunity to return the output temperature as either a string or a single floating point value and could thus vary the output format as needed.

Using Classes for Format and Value Conversion

It is convenient in many cases to have a method for converting between formats and representations of data. You can use a class to handle and hide the details of such conversions. For example, you might enter an elapsed time in minutes and seconds with or without the colon.

```
315.20
3:15.20
315.2
```

Since all styles are likely, you'd like a class to parse the legal possibilities and keep the data in a standard format within. Figure 3-2 shows how the entries "112" and "102.3" are parsed.

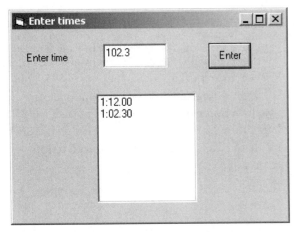

Figure 3-2   A simple parsing program that uses the Times class

The accessor functions for our Times class include the following.

```
setText (tx as String)
setSingle (t as Single)
getSingle as Single
getFormatted as String
getSeconds as Single
```

Parsing is quite simple and depends primarily on looking for a colon. If there is no colon, then values greater than 99 are treated as minutes.

```
Public Function setText(ByVal tx As String) As Boolean
  Dim i As Integer, mins As Long, secs As Single
   errflag = False
   i = InStr(tx, ":")
   If i > 0 Then
   mins = Val(Left$(tx, i - 1))
    secs = Val(Right$(tx, Len(tx) - i))
    If secs > 59.99 Then
      errflag = True
    End If
    t = mins * 100 + secs
  Else
   mins = Val(tx) \ 100
   secs = Val(tx) - (100 * mins)
   If secs > 59.99 Then
```

```
     errflag = True
     t = NT
  Else
    setSingle Val(tx)
  End If
 End If
 setText = errflag
End Function
```

Since illegal time values might also be entered, we test for cases like 89.22 and set an error flag.

Depending on the kind of time measurements these represent, you might also have some non-numeric entries such as NT for no time or in the case of athletic times, SC for scratch or DQ for disqualified. All of these are best managed inside the class. Thus, you never need to know what numeric representations of these values are used internally.

```
Private Const tmNT As Integer = 10000, tmDQ As Integer = 20000
Private Const tmSCRATCH As Integer = 30000
```

Some of these are processed in the code represented by Figure 3-3.

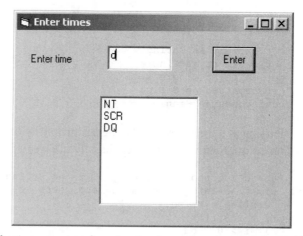

Figure 3-3   The time entry interface, showing the parsing of symbols for No Time, Scratch, and Disqualification

Handling Unreasonable Values

A class is also a good place to encapsulate error handling. For example, it might be that times greater than some threshold value are unlikely and might actually be times that were entered without a decimal point. If large times are unlikely, then a number such as 123473 could be assumed to be 12:34.73.

```
Public Sub setSingle(tv As Single)
t = tv
If tv > minVal And tv <> tmNT Then
   t = tv / 100
End If
End Sub
```

The cutoff value minVal may vary with the domain of times being considered and thus should be a variable. While classes do not have a Form_Load event like Forms do, they do have and initialize events where you can set up default values for variables.

```
Private Sub Class_Initialize()
      minVal = 10000
End Sub
```

To set up the Initialize event in the IDE, click on the left drop-down in the editor title bar so that Class is selected and select Initialize from the right drop-down as shown in Figure 3-4.

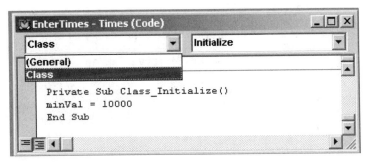

Figure 3-4   Selecting the Class Initialize method

A String Tokenizer Class

A number of languages provide a simple method for dividing strings into tokens separated by a specified character. While VB does not provide a class for this feature, we can write one quite easily using the little-known Split function. The goal of the Tokenizer class will be to pass in a string and obtain the successive string tokens back one at a time. For example, if we had the simple string

```
Now is the time
```

our tokenizer should return four tokens.

```
Now
is
```

```
the
time
```

The critical part of this class is that it holds the initial string and remembers which token is to be returned next.

We could write this class using the Instr function, or we could use the Split function, which approximates the Tokenizer but returns an array of substrings instead of having a class interface. The class we want to write will have a nextToken method that returns string tokens or a zero length string when we reach the end of the series of tokens.

The whole class is shown here.

```
'String tokenizer class
Private s As String, i As Integer
Private sep As String      'token separator
Private stokens() As String 'array of tokens
Public Sub init(ByVal st As String)
 s = st
 setSeparator " "
End Sub
Private Sub Class_Initialize()
 sep = " "    'default is a space separator
End Sub
Public Sub setSeparator(ByVal sp As String)
  sep = sp
  stokens = Split(s, sp)
  i = -1
End Sub
Public Function nextToken() As String
 Dim tok As String
 If i < UBound(stokens) Then
   i = i + 1
   tok = stokens(i)
 Else
   tok = ""
 End If
 nextToken = tok      'return token
End Function
```

The class is illustrated in use in Figure 3-5.

This is the code that uses the Tokenizer class.

```
Private Sub Tokenize_Click()
 Dim tok As New Tokenizer
 Dim s As String

 tok.init txString.Text  'set the string from the input
 lsTokens.Clear          'clear the list box
 s = tok.nextToken       'get a token
```

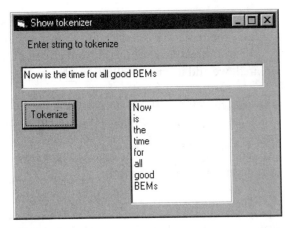

Figure 3-5   The tokenizer in use

```
While Len(s) > 0        'as long as not of zero length
   lsTokens.AddItem s   'add into the list
   s = tok.nextToken    'and look for next token
Wend
End Sub
```

Classes as Objects

The primary difference between ordinary procedural programming and object-oriented (OO) programming is the presence of classes. A class is just a module as we have just shown, that has both public and private methods and that can contain data. However, classes are also unique in that there can be any number of *instances* of a class, each containing different data. We frequently refer to these instances as objects. We'll see some examples of single and multiple instances following.

Suppose we have a file of results from a swimming event stored in a text data file. Such a file might look, in part, like this.

```
1 Emily Fenn              17   WRAT      4:59.54
2 Kathryn Miller          16   WYW       5:01.35
3 Melissa Sckolnik        17   WYW       5:01.58
4 Sarah Bowman            16   CDEV      5:02.44
5 Caitlin Klick           17   MBM       5:02.59
6 Caitlin Healey          16   MBM       5:03.62
```

The columns represent place, names, age, club, and time. If we wrote a program to display these swimmers and their times, we'd need to read in and parse this file. For each swimmer, we'd have a first and last name, an age, a club, and a

time. An efficient way to keep the data for each swimmer grouped together is to
design a Swimmer class and create an instance for each swimmer.

Here is how we read the file and create these instances. As each instance is
created, we add it into a Collection object.

```
Private swimmers As New Collection

Private Sub Form_Load()
Dim f As Integer, S As String
Dim sw As Swimmer
Dim i As Integer

f = FreeFile
'read in data file and create swimmer instances
Open App.Path & "\500free.txt" For Input As #f
While Not EOF(f)
  Line Input #f, S
  Set sw = New Swimmer      'create instances
  sw.init S                 'load in data
  swimmers.Add sw           'add to collection
Wend
Close #f
'put names of swimmers in list box
For i = 1 To swimmers.Count
  Set sw = swimmers(i)
  lsSwimmers.AddItem sw.getName
Next i
End Sub
```

The Swimmer class itself parses each line of data from the file and stores it for
retrieval using getXXX accessor functions.

```
Private frname As String, lname As String
Private club As String
Private age As Integer
Private tms As New Times
Private place As Integer
'------
Public Sub init(dataline As String)
Dim tok As New Tokenizer

tok.init dataline              'initilaize string tokenizer
place = Val(tok.nextToken)     'get lane number
frname = tok.nextToken         'get first name
lname = tok.nextToken          'get last name
age = Val(tok.nextToken)       'get age
club = tok.nextToken           'get club
tms.setText tok.nextToken      'get and parse time
End Sub
'------
```

```
Public Function getTime() As String
 getTime = tms.getFormatted
End Function
'------
Public Function getName() As String
 'combine first and last names and return together
 getName = frname & " " & lname
End Function
'------
Public Function getAge() As Integer
 getAge = age
End Function
'------
Public Function getClub() As String
 getClub = club
End Function
```

Class Containment

Each instance of the Swimmer class contains an instance of the Tokenizer that it uses to parse the input string and an instance of the Times class we wrote previously to parse the time and return it in formatted form to the calling program. Having a class contain other classes is a very common ploy in OO programming and is one of the main ways we can build up more complicated programs from rather simple components.

The program that displays these swimmers is shown in Figure 3-6.

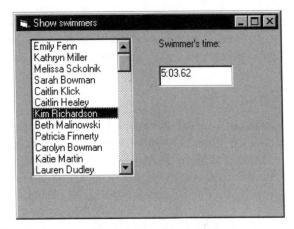

Figure 3-6   A list of swimmers and their times, using containment

When you click on any swimmer, her time is shown in the box on the right. The code for showing that time is extremely easy to write, since all the data are in the swimmer class.

```
Private Sub lsSwimmers_Click()
 Dim i As Integer
 Dim sw As Swimmer
 i = lsSwimmers.ListIndex         'get index of list
 If i >= 0 Then
   Set sw = swimmers(i)           'get that swimmer
   lbTime.Caption = sw.getTime    'display that time
 End If
End Sub
```

Class Initialization

As we showed previously, you can use the Class_Initialize event to set up default values for some class variables. However, if you want to set up some values that are specific for each instance (such as our swimmer's names and times), we need a standard way to do this. In other languages, classes have special methods called *constructors* that you can use to pass in useful data at the same time you create the instance. Since VB6 classes lack these methods, we introduce the convention of an *init* method that we'll use to pass in instance specific data.

In our preceding Swimmer class, note that we have an init method that in turn calls the init method of the Tokenizer class.

```
Public Sub init(dataline As String)
Dim tok As New Tokenizer

tok.init dataline          'initialize string tokenizer
```

Other languages, including VB7, also allow classes to have a series of constructors that each have different arguments. Since this is not a feature of VB6, we'll use various setXXX methods instead.

Classes and Properties

Classes in VB can have Property methods as well as public and private functions and subs. These correspond to the kinds of properties you associate with Forms, but they can store and fetch any kinds of values you care to use. For example, rather than having methods called getAge and setAge, you could have a single Age property that then corresponds to a Property Let and a Property Get method.

```
Property Get age() As Integer
 age = sAge  'return the current age
End Property
'------
Property Let age(ag As Integer)
 sAge = ag   'save a new age
End Property
```

To use these properties, you refer to the Let property on the left side of an equals sign and the Get property on the right side.

```
myAge = sw.Age       'Get this swimmer's age
sw.Age = 12          'Set a new age for this swimmer
```

Properties are somewhat vestigial, since they really applied more to Forms, but many programmers find them quite useful. They do not provide any features not already available using get and set methods, and both generate equally efficient code.

In the revised version of our SwimmerTimes display program, we convert all of the get and set methods to properties and then allow users to vary the times of each swimmer by typing in new ones. Here is the Swimmer class.

```
Option Explicit
Private frname As String, lname As String
Private sClub As String
Private sAge As Integer
Private tms As New Times
Private place As Integer
'------
Public Sub init(dataline As String)
Dim tok As New Tokenizer

   tok.init dataline          'initilaize string tokenizer
   place = Val(tok.nextToken) 'get lane number
   frname = tok.nextToken     'get first name
   lname = tok.nextToken      'get last name
   sAge = Val(tok.nextToken)  'get age
   sClub = tok.nextToken      'get club
   tms.setText tok.nextToken  'get and parse time
End Sub
'------
Property Get time() As String
   time = tms.getFormatted
End Property
'------
Property Let time(tx As String)
   tms.setText tx
End Property
'------
Property Get Name() As String
   'combine first and last names and return together
   Name = frname & " " & lname
End Property
'------
Property Get age() As Integer
   age = sAge   'return the current age
End Property
'------
```

```
Property Let age(ag As Integer)
 sAge = ag    'save a new age
End Property
'------
Property Get Club() As String
 Club = sClub
End Property
```

Then when the txTime text entry field loses focus, we can store a new time as follows.

```
Private Sub txTime_Change()
 Dim i As Integer
 Dim sw As Swimmer
 i = lsSwimmers.ListIndex        'get index of list
 If i >= 0 Then
   Set sw = swimmers(i)          'get that swimmer
   sw.time = txTime.Text   'store that time
 End If
End Sub
```

Another Interface Example—The Voltmeter

Suppose that you need to interface a digital voltmeter to your computer. We'll assume that the meter can connect to your serial port and that you send it a string command and get the measured voltage back as a string. We'll also assume that you can set various measurement ranges such as millivolts, volts, and tens of volts. The methods for accessing this voltmeter might look like this.

```
'The Voltmeter class
Public Sub setRange(ByVal maxVal As Single)
  'set maximum voltage to measure
End Sub
'------
Public Function getVoltage() As Single
 'get the voltage and convert it to a Single
End Function
```

The nice visual data-gathering program you then write for this voltmeter works fine, until you suddenly need to make another simultaneous set of measurements. You discover that the model of voltmeter that you wrote the program for is no longer available and that the new model has different commands. It might even have a different interface (IEEE-488 or USB, for instance).

This is an ideal time to think about program interfaces. The simple two-method interface we specified previously should work for any voltmeter, and the rest of the program should run without change. All you need to do is write a class for the new voltmeter that implements the same interface. Then your data-gathering program only needs to be told which meter to use and it will run completely unchanged, as we show here.

```
Private Sub OK_Click()
  If opPe.Value Then
     Set vm = New PE2345
  Else
     Set vm = New HP1234
  End If
  vm.getVoltage
End Sub
```

Further, should your data needs expand so that there are still more meters, you can quickly write more classes that implement this same Voltmeter interface. This is the advantage of OO programming in a nutshell: Only the individual classes have detailed knowledge of how they work. The only external knowledge is contained in the interfaces.

A vbFile Class

File handling in VB is for the most part awkward and primitive for historical reasons. The statements for opening files have this form.

```
f = FreeFile
Open "file.txt" for Input as #f
```

And those for reading data from files have this form.

```
Input #f, s
Line Input #f, sLine
```

There is no simple statement for checking for the existence of a file, and the file rename and delete have counterintuitive names.

```
Exists = len(dir$(filename))>0    'file exists
Name file1 as file2               'Rename file
Kill filename                     'Delete file
```

None of these statements are at all object oriented. There ought to be objects that encapsulate some of this awkwardness and keep the file handles suitably hidden.

VB6 introduced the Scripting.FileSystemObject as a way to handle files in a presumably more object-oriented way. However, these objects are not fully realized and a bit difficult to use. Thus, we might do well to create our own vbFile object with convenient methods. These methods could include the following.

```
Public Function OpenForRead(Filename As String) As Boolean
Public Function fEof() As Boolean
Public Function readLine() As String
Public Function readToken() As String
Public Sub closeFile()
Public Function exists() As Boolean
Public Function delete() As Boolean
Public Function OpenForWrite(fname As String) As Boolean
Public Sub writeText(s As String)
Public Sub writeLine(s As String)
Public Sub setFilename(fname As String)
Public Function getFilename() As String
```

A typical implementation of a few of these methods includes the following.

```
Public Function OpenForRead(Filename As String) As Boolean
 'open file for reading
 f = FreeFile               'get a free handle
 File_name = Filename       'save the filename

 On Error GoTo nofile       'trap errors
 Open Filename For Input As #f
     opened = True          'set true if open successful
oexit:
     OpenForRead = opened   'return to caller
Exit Function
'--error handling--
nofile:
   end_file = True          'set end of file flag
   errDesc = Err.Description 'save error messae
   opened = False           'no file open
   Resume oexit             'and resume
End Function
'------
Public Function fEof() As Boolean
 'return end of file
 If opened Then
  fEof = EOF(f)
 Else
  fEof = True     'if not opened then end file is true
 End If
End Function
'------
Public Function readLine() As String
 Dim s As String
 'read one line from a text file
 If opened Then
   Line Input #f, s
   readLine = s
 Else
   readLine = ""
 End If
End Function
```

With these useful methods, we can write a simple program to read a file and display it in a list box.

```
Dim fl As New vbFile
cDlg.ShowOpen    'use common dialog open

fl.OpenForRead cDlg.Filename
'read in up to end of file
sline = fl.readLine
While Not fl.fEof
  lsFiles.AddItem sline
  sline = fl.readLine
Wend
fl.closeFile
```

Now, the implementation of this vbFile object can change as VB evolves. However, by concealing the details, we can vary the implementation in the future. We'll see another implementation of this class when we discuss VB.NET.

Programming Style in Visual Basic

You can develop any of a number of readable programming styles for VB. The one we use here is partly influenced by Microsoft's Hungarian notation (named after its originator, Charles Simonyi) and partly on styles developed for Java.

We favor using names for VB controls such as buttons and list boxes that have prefixes that make their purpose clear, and we will use them whenever there is more than one of them on a single form.

Control	Prefix	Example
Buttons	bt	btCompute
List boxes	ls	lsSwimmers
Radio (option buttons)	op	opFSex
Combo boxes	cb	cbCountry
Menus	mnu	mnuFile
Text boxes	tx	TxTime

We will name classes in ways that describe their purpose and only precede them with clsXXX if there is any ambiguity. We will not generally create new names for labels, frames, and forms when they are never referred to directly in the code. Even though VB is case insensitive, we otherwise will begin class names with capital letters and instances of classes with lowercase letters. We will also spell instances and classes with a mixture of lowercase and capital letters to make their purpose clearer.

```
swimmerTime
```

Summary

In this chapter, we've introduced VB classes and shown how they can contain public and private methods and can contain data. Each class can have many instances and each could contain different data values. Classes can also have Property methods for setting and fetching data. These Property methods provide a simpler syntax over the usual getXXX and setXX accessor methods but have no other substantial advantages.

CHAPTER 4

Object-Oriented Programming

Object-oriented programming is a little different from earlier kinds of programming because it introduces programming constructs called objects, which contain both procedures and data. In this chapter we'll begin to understand what objects are and why they make programming easier and less prone to errors.

A *procedural* program is written in the style you are probably most familiar with: one in which there are arithmetic and logical statements, variables, functions, and subroutines. Data are declared somewhere at the top of a module or a procedure, and more data are passed in and out of various functions and procedures using argument lists.

This style of programming has been successfully utilized for a very long time as programming goes, but it does have some drawbacks. For example, you must be sure that the data are passed correctly between procedures, making sure that it is of the correct size and type. Thus, the procedures and their calling arguments may need to be revised frequently as a new function is added to the program during development.

Object-oriented programming differs in that a group of procedures are grouped around a set of related data to construct an *object*. An object is thus a collection of data and the subroutines or *methods* that operate on it. Objects are usually designed to mimic actual physical entities that the program deals with: customers, orders, accounts, graphical widgets, and so on.

More to the point, most of *how* the data are manipulated inside an object is invisible to the user and only of concern inside the object. You may be able to put data inside an object, and you may be able to ask the data to perform computations, but how it performs them and on exactly what internal data representation are invisible to you as you create and use that object.

Of course, a class (in VB) is actually just a template for an object. If you design a class that represents a Customer, you haven't created an object. An object is an *instance* of the Customer class, and there can, of course, be many such objects, all of type Customer. Creating a specific variable of a particular class type is referred to as *instantiating* that class.

Because objects contain data, you can regard them as having *states*. If you wrote a module of related functions, you probably would not have their behavior dependent on a variable somewhere, even if it is in the same module. However, when you write a class or object, you *expect* the various methods within the class to make reference to the data contained in that class and behave accordingly. For example, you might create a File object that can be open or closed, or at the end-of-file or not.

Once someone creates a complete, working object, it is less likely that other programmers will modify it. Instead, they will simply derive new objects based on it. We discuss the concept of deriving new objects in Chapter 5.

As we have noted, objects are really a lot like C structures or Pascal records, except that they hold both functions and data. However, objects are just the structures or data types. In order to use them in programs, we have to create variables with that data type. We call these variables *instances* of the object.

Building VB Objects

Let's take a very simple example. Suppose we want to design an object for measuring distance. Now, our first thought might have been to simply write a little subroutine to execute the measurement and then perform the measurement each time by calling this subroutine.

But in VB, we can write our code as a series of objects. So rather than writing subroutines, we do the following.

- Create a TapeMeasure *class.*
- Create *instances* of that class, each with a different size.
- Ask each instance to draw itself.

In VB, objects are represented as *class* modules. Each VB class is an object that can have as many instances as you like. When you write a VB program, the entire program is one or more classes. The main class represents the running program itself, and it must have the same name as the program file. In our example, the program is called Measurer.cls, and the main class is called Measure.frm.

Classes in VB contain data and functions, which are called *methods*. Both the data and the methods can have either a public or a private modifier, which determines whether program code outside the class can access them. Usually we make all data values private and write public methods to store data and retrieve it from the class. This keeps programs from changing these internal data values accidentally by referring to them directly.

If we want users of the class to be able to use a method, we, of course, must make it public. If, on the other hand, we have functions or subs that are only used inside the class, we would make them private. A VB program can be made up of any number of .cls and .frm files.

Creating Instances of Objects

We use the **new** operator in VB to create an instance of a class. For example, to create an instance of the TapeMeasure class, we could write the following.

```
Dim tp as TapeMeasure 'variable of type TapeMeasure

'create instance of TapeMeasure
set tp = new TapeMeasure
```

Remember, while we can create new variables of the primitive types (such as Integer, Single, and so on) we must use the new operator to create instances of objects. The reason for this distinction is that objects take up some block of memory. In order to reserve that memory, we have to create an instance of the object, using the new operator.

A VB Measurement Program

In the following example, we see a complete TapeMeasure class, including its measure routine.

```
'Tape measure class
Private width As Single, factor As Single

Public Sub setUnits(units As String)
'allows units to be cm or feet
  Select Case LCase$(units)
     Case "c":              'centimeters
        factor = 1
     Case "i":              'inches
        factor = 2.54
    Case Else
        factor = 1
    End Select
End Sub

Public Function Measure() As Single
  width = Rnd * 100#
  Measure = width / factor
End Function
```

```
Public Function lastMeasure() As Single
  lastMeasure = width / factor
End Function
```

The calling program is the Measurer form, which is merely the following.

```
Dim tp As New TapeMeasure

Private Sub btMeasure_Click()
txMeasure.Text = Str$(tp.Measure)
End Sub

Private Sub opCM_Click()
tp.setUnits "c"
txMeasure.Text = Str$(tp.lastMeasure)
End Sub

Private Sub opFt_Click()
tp.setUnits "f"
txMeasure.Text = Str$(tp.lastMeasure)
End Sub
```

Methods Inside Objects

As we noted previously, functions inside a class are referred to as *methods*. These functions can be public, meaning that you can access them from outside the class, or private, meaning that they can only be accessed from inside the class.

Variables

In object-oriented programming, you usually make all of the variables in a class private, as we did previously with width and factor. Then you set the values of these variables either as part of the constructor or using additional *set* and *get* functions. This protects these variables from accidental access from outside the class and allows you to add data integrity checks in the *set* functions to make sure that the data are valid.

We could, of course, have made the TapeMeasure's factor variable public and set it directly.

```
tp.factor = 2.54;
```

However, this gives the class no protection from erroneous data such as this.

```
tp.factor = -50;
```

So instead, we use *accessor* functions such as setUnits to make sure that the data values we send the class are valid.

```
tp.setUnits "c"
```

Then within the class we would write this accessor function with some error checking.

Likewise, since the TapeMeasure class saves the last measurement it makes, you can always read it back by calling a lastMeasure method.

Passing Arguments by Reference and by Value

By default, all variables are passed into methods by *reference*. In other words, the original data can be accessed and change within any class method.

```
Public Sub setTemp(t As Single)
  t = 5                 'changes t in the calling program
End Sub
```

To avoid this happening by accident, you should make a habit of prefixing your arguments with ByVal, which copies the value into the subroutine.

```
Public Sub setTemp(ByVal t as Single)
        t = 5   'has no affect on calling program
End Sub
```

Object-Oriented Jargon

Object-oriented programs are often said to have these three major properties.

- *Encapsulation.* We hide as much of what is going on inside methods in the object.
- *Polymorphism.* Many different objects might have methods with identical names, such as our Measure method. While they may do the same thing, the way each is implemented can vary widely. In addition, there can be several methods within a single object with the same name but different sets of arguments. In VB, a class cannot have multiple methods with the same name but different arguments as in other more polymorphic languages, but related classes can have methods with the same name and arguments that do different things.
- *Inheritance.* Objects can inherit properties and methods from other objects, allowing you to build up complex programs from simple base

objects. VB6 only supports a subset of inheritance, using interfaces and implementations, as we see in the next chapter. VB.Net is more fully object oriented, and we examine it in Chapters 7 and 8. Nonetheless, even with these limitations, we can use VB6's OO features to write some very sophisticated programs, as you will see shortly.

CHAPTER 5

Building Your Own VB Control

One of the great strengths of VB is its powerful visual builder (IDE) environment. It is easy to build complex and sophisticated user interfaces by just dragging a few components onto a form and writing a little code to control their interactions. However, if no control does exactly what you want, it appears at first to be quite difficult (or impossible) to create a new control with these new properties. In this chapter we carry the idea of OO programming a little further by showing how easy it is to derive a new ActiveX control from the existing ones in VB6. We'll show you how to do this in VB.NET in Chapter 7.

A Highlighted Text Field

Suppose we would like to build a text entry field that always highlights all the text when it receives the focus. This can be desirable whenever you want to make sure that a single key press will replace the previous text with new text. In fact, it seems that what we want to do is derive a new class from the TextBox. However, VB6 doesn't allow us to do this directly because it doesn't support inheritance.

However, you'll soon discover that the Gang of Four's maxim applies here.

Favor object composition over inheritance.

And object composition is just another word for encapsulation or containment. Thus, if we can create a new class that *contains* the TextBox but highlights the text whenever the control gets the focus, we'll have what we want.

We'll start by using the VB IDE to create the ActiveX control. Select File | New Project and select ActiveX Control from the menu, as shown in Figure 5-1.

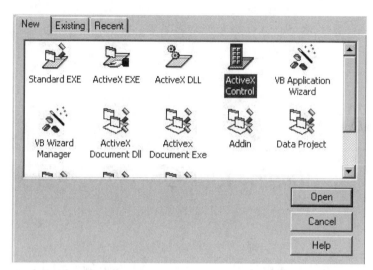

Figure 5-1   Selecting ActiveX Control creation from the VB Project menu

This brings up a gray form without borders called a UserControl that provides the canvas on which to create your control, as shown in Figure 5-2.

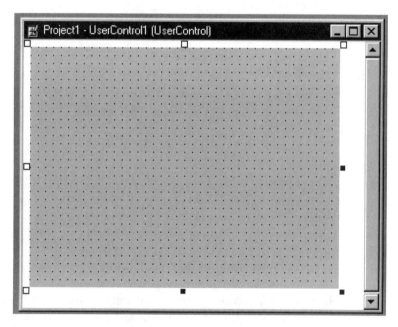

Figure 5-2   The UserControl canvas

First, change the name from UserControl1 (which is hardly mnemonic) to HiText by pressing F4 and changing the name in the Properties window. Then, drop a TextBox onto the form in the upper left corner, and resize the gray background to match the size of the text box, as illustrated in Figure 5-3.

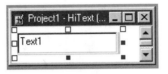

Figure 5-3   The Text box inside the UserControl

Now, let's add just a little code. Select the GotFocus event for the txEntry box you just added and add the code.

```
Private Sub txEntry_GotFocus()
Dim s As String
        s = Text1.Text
        txEntry.SelStart = 0            'Start highlight
        txEntry.SelLength = Len(s)      'end highlight
End Sub
```

Resizing a User Control

The last important part of a user control is that it must resize during the design mode. Select the HiText UserControl, and select the Resize event. Enter the following code.

```
Private Sub UserControl_Resize()
  txEntry.Width = Width      'design time resize of width
  txEntry.Height = Height    'and height
End Sub
```

Testing Your HiText Controls

Now, to test this control, close its design window. Then, select File | Add project to add a second project with which to test your new control. On the Controls toolbar, you will find a new icon representing the HiText control, as shown in Figure 5-4.

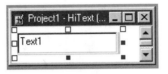

Figure 5-4   The HiText control icon in the Controls toolbar

This icon will only be active if the design window is closed for the HiText control. Click on this new icon, and put an instance of the control onto the Form panel of the new project you just created. Then add a button labeled Clear, as shown in Figure 5-5.

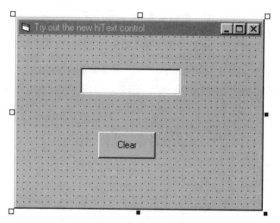

Figure 5-5   The test project for our HiText control

If you try to resize the HiText control, you'll see that the included TextBox resizes with it in design mode.

Now, if you run the test form, you will be able to type text into the HiText box. Then, if you press the Tab key twice, you will move the focus down to the button and back to the HiText control. When it receives the focus, it will display the text highlighted, as shown in Figure 5-6.

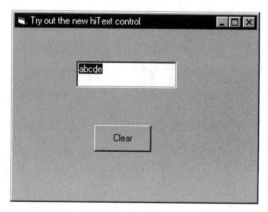

Figure 5-6   The HiText control in action

Adding Properties and Methods to User Controls

You can add any property you want to your new user control, and these properties will appear in the Properties box if you create both a Let and a Get property. For example, you might want to be able to change the Backcolor of the TextBox. Just add the following code.

```
Property Let Backcolor(c As ColorConstants)
  txEntry.Backcolor = c
  PropertyChanged "BackColor"
End Property
'------
Property Get Backcolor() As ColorConstants
  Backcolor = Text1.Backcolor
End Property
```

Note that you must add the PropertyChanged method call whenever you change a property of a user control. This passes this information to theVB engine to make sure that the screen is refreshed as needed.

In the same way, you can add methods to your user control, and they will appear in the syntax completion drop-down for any instance of that control. For example, the TextBox control lacks a Clear method. However, we can easily add one to our new control.

```
Public Sub Clear()
  txEntry.Text = ""
End Sub
```

Now that we've added that convenient Clear method, we can connect it to the Clear button.

```
Private Sub Clearit_Click()
  hiText1.Clear
End Sub
```

And clicking the button will clear our new text box.

Compiling a User Control

Once you have your test program and user control working, you can compile both of them by selecting File | Make Project Group. This will produce an .EXE file for your test program and an .OCX file for your user control. Then, if you want to use this control in further programs, you will find that VB has automatically registered it, and you can find it under Project | Components to add to any new project.

Summary

Building a user control like this helps you see how encapsulation can be used to create new objects that have the properties you need. The only disadvantage of this approach is that you must add all of the properties to the control manually rather than having them inherited, as could occur in VB7, which allows inheritance. However, in many cases encapsulation is very effective, since you have only a few properties to pass through from the outer control interface to the enclosed control interfaces. And if the new control contains more than one basic control, this is the only possible approach.

Programs on the CD-ROM

`\ActiveX\htx.vbg`	Highlight control project group for both DLL and example

CHAPTER 6

Inheritance and Interfaces

As you begin to work more with classes, you soon come across programming cases where you have classes that are similar to others you are already using in this program or another one. It seems a shame to just copy all that code over again and have a lot of objects that are separate but very alike.

In languages like Java and VB.NET, you can derive new classes from existing classes and change only those methods that differ in the new class, with the unchanged parent methods called automatically. VB6 does not support this level of inheritance, but it does provide interfaces and implementations that allow you to produce related classes with only a small amount of effort.

Interfaces

In VB, you can create a class containing only definitions of the methods and no actual code. This is called an *interface* definition. Then you can create other classes that *implement* that interface, and they all can be treated as if they were instances of the parent interface, even though they implement the methods differently.

For example, you could create an interface called Command that has the following methods.

```
Public Sub Execute()

End Sub
'------
Public Sub init(nm As String)

End Sub
```

Then you could create a number of Command objects, such as ExitCommand, that implement the Command interface. To do this, you create a class called ExitCommand, and insert this line.

```
Implements Command
```

Then, from the left drop-down you select the Command interface, and from the right drop-down you create instances of the Execute and init methods. You can now fill in these methods with whatever code is appropriate.

```
Private Sub Command_Execute()
'do something
End Sub
'------
Private Sub Command_init(nm As String)
'initialize something
End Sub
```

The advantage of this approach is that the ExitCommand class is now also of the type Command, and all of the classes that implement the Command interface can be treated as instances of the Command class. To see how this can be helpful, let's consider a program for simulating investment growth.

An Investment Simulator

Our investment simulation program will present us with a mixture of stocks and bonds, and we can look at their growth during any time interval. We will assume that the bonds are all tax-free municipal bonds and that all the stocks have positive growth rates.

The program starts with a list of seven stocks and bonds and an investment nest egg of $10,000 to use. You can invest in any combination of stocks and bonds at any rate until all your money is invested. The initial program state is shown in Figure 6-1.

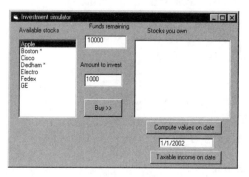

Figure 6-1   An investment simulator at the start

You select investments by highlighting them, selecting a purchase amount, and clicking on the Buy button.

Once you have selected some stocks, you can enter any future date and compute the total stock value and the total taxable income. For simplicity, we assume that the stock income is all taxable and that the bond income is all non-taxable. A typical investment result is shown in Figure 6-2.

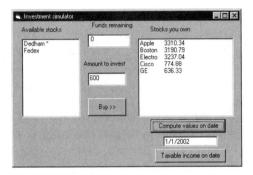

Figure 6-2   A typical investment result

The taxable income display is shown in Figure 6-3.

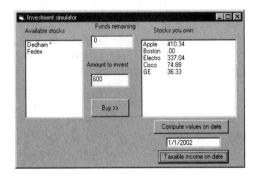

Figure 6-3   Taxable income results

Writing the Simulator

The most important class in the simulator represents a stock. This class has an init method that sets the name and type (stock or bond) and an invest method that determines the date and how much was invested.

```
Private stockName As String      'name
Private isMuniBond As Boolean    'true of muni bond
Private investment As Single     'amount invested
Private invDate As Date          'date of investment
Private rate As Single           'growth rate
```

```
'------
Public Sub init(nm As String, muniBond As Boolean)
  stockName = nm            'save the name
  isMuniBond = muniBond     'and whether a bond
  If isMuniBond Then
    rate = 0.05             'low fixed rate for bonds
  Else
    rate = Rnd / 10         'random rate for stocks
  End If
End Sub
'-----
Public Sub invest(amt As Single)
  invDate = CVDate(Date$) 'remember date
  investment = amt          'and amount invested
End Sub
```

Then, when we ask for the amount of the investment or the taxable amount earned, we compute them based on the days elapsed since the investment.

```
Public Function getName() As String
  getName = stockName      'return the stock name
End Function
'------
Public Function getValue(toDate As Date) As Single
  Dim diff, value As Single
  'compute the value of the investment
  diff = DateDiff("d", invDate, toDate)
  value = (diff / 365) * rate * investment + investment
  getValue = value          'and return it
End Function
'------
Public Function getTaxable(toDate As Date) As Single
  If isMuniBond Then
    getTaxable = 0           'no taxable income
  Else
    'return the taxable income
    getTaxable = getValue(toDate) - investment
  End If
End Function
```

Indicators for Using an Interface

There are two places in the preceding code where we have to ask what kind of investment this is. One is when we decide on the rate and the other is when we decide on the taxable return. Whenever you see decisions like this inside classes, you should treat them as a yellow caution flag indicating that there might be a better way. Why should a class have to make such decisions? Would it be better if each class represented only one type of investment? If we did create a Stock and a Bond class, the program would become more complicated because our display of list data assumes the data are all of type stock.

```
Private Sub Taxable_Click()
 Dim i As Integer, dt As Date
 Dim stk as Stock
 lsOwn.Clear
 dt = CVDate(txDate.Text)
 For i = 1 To stocksOwned.Count
   Set stk = stocksOwned(i)
   lsOwn.AddItem stk.getName & vbTab & _
      Format$(stk.getTaxable(dt), "####.00")
 Next i
End Sub
```

Instead, we'll create a new class called Equity and derive the Stock and Bond classes from it. Here is our empty Equity interface.

```
Public Sub init(nm As String)
End Sub
'------
Public Sub invest(amt As Single)
End Sub
'------
Public Function getName() As String
End Function
'------
Public Function getValue(toDate As Date) As Single
End Function
'------
Public Function getTaxable(toDate As Date) As Single
End Function
'------
Public Function isBond() As Boolean
End Function
```

Now, our Stock class just becomes the following.

```
Implements Equity
Private stockName As String      'stock name
Private investment As Single     'amount invested
Private invDate As Date          'investment date
Private rate As Single           'rate of return
'------
Private Function Equity_getName() As String
   Equity_getName = stockName     'return the name
End Function
'------
Private Function Equity_getTaxable(toDate As Date) As Single
  'compute the taxable include
  Equity_getTaxable = Equity_getValue(toDate) - investment
End Function
'------
Private Function Equity_getValue(toDate As Date) As Single
  Dim diff, value As Single
  'compute the total value of the investment to date
  diff = DateDiff("d", invDate, toDate)
```

```
   value = (diff / 365) * rate * investment + investment
   Equity_getValue = value
End Function
'------
Private Sub Equity_init(nm As String)
   stockName = nm      'initialize the name
   rate = Rnd / 10     'and a rate
End Sub
'------
Private Sub Equity_invest(amt As Single)
   invDate = CVDate(Date$)    'set the date
   investment = amt           'and the amount
End Sub
'------
Private Function Equity_isBond() As Boolean
   Equity_isBond = False  'is not a bond
End Function
```

The Bond class is pretty similar, except for the getTaxable, init, and isBond methods.

```
Implements Equity
Private stockName As String
Private investment As Single
Private invDate As Date
Private rate As Single
'------
Private Function Equity_getName() As String
   Equity_getName = stockName
End Function
'------
Private Function Equity_getTaxable(toDate As Date) As Single
   Equity_getTaxable = 0
End Function
'------
Private Function Equity_getValue(toDate As Date) As Single
   Dim diff, value As Single

   diff = DateDiff("d", invDate, toDate)
   value = (diff / 365) * rate * investment + investment
   Equity_getValue = value
End Function
'------
Private Sub Equity_init(nm As String)
   stockName = nm
   rate = 0.05
End Sub
'------
Private Sub Equity_invest(amt As Single)
   invDate = CVDate(Date$)
   investment = amt
End Sub
'------
```

```
Private Function Equity_isBond() As Boolean
  Equity_isBond = True
End Function
```

However, by making both Stocks and Bonds implement the Equity interface, we can treat them all as Equities, since they have the same methods, rather
than having to decide which kind is which.

```
Private Sub Taxable_Click()
Dim i As Integer, dt As Date
Dim stk as Equity
'Show the list of taxable incomes
 lsOwn.Clear
 dt = CVDate(txDate.Text)
 For i = 1 To stocksOwned.Count
   Set stk = stocksOwned(i)
   lsOwn.AddItem stk.getName & vbTab & _
       Format$(stk.getTaxable(dt), "####.00")
 Next i
End Sub
```

Reusing Common Methods

A quick glance at the preceding code shows that the Stock and Bond classes
have some duplicated code. One way to prevent this from happening is to put
some methods in the base class and then call them from the derived classes.
While the initial idea was to make the interface module just a series of empty
methods, VB6 does not require this, and they can indeed have code in them.

For example, we could rewrite the basic Equity class to contain another
method that actually computes the interest and is called by the derived classes.

```
'Class Equity with calcValue added
Public Sub init(nm As String)
End Sub
'------
Public Sub invest(amt As Single)
End Sub
'------
Public Function getName() As String
End Function
'------
Public Function getValue(toDate As Date) As Single
End Function
'------
Public Function getTaxable(toDate As Date) As Single
End Function
'------
Public Function isBond() As Boolean
End Function
```

```
'------
Public Function calcValue(invDate As Date, toDate As Date, _
        rate As Single, investment As Single)
 Dim diff, value As Single

  diff = DateDiff("d", invDate, toDate)
  value = (diff / 365) * rate * investment + investment
  calcValue = value
End Function
```

Now, since we don't have real inheritance in VB6, we can't call this from the derived classes directly, but we can insert an instance of the Equity class *inside* the Stock and Bond classes and call its calcValue method. This simplifies the Stock class to the following.

```
Implements Equity
Private stockName As String        'stock name
Private investment As Single       'amount invested
Private invDate As Date            'date of investment
Private rate As Single             'rate of return
Private eq As New Equity           'instance of base Equity class
'------
Private Function Equity_getName() As String
   Equity_getName = stockName
End Function
'------
Private Function Equity_getTaxable(toDate As Date) As Single
   Equity_getTaxable = Equity_getValue(toDate) - investment
End Function
'------
Private Function Equity_getValue(toDate As Date) As Single
'compute using method in base Equity class
   Equity_getValue = eq.calcValue(invDate, toDate, rate, _
                      investment)
End Function
'------
Private Sub Equity_init(nm As String)
   stockName = nm
   rate = Rnd / 10
End Sub
'------
Private Sub Equity_invest(amt As Single)
   invDate = CVDate(Date$)
   investment = amt
End Sub
'------
Private Function Equity_isBond() As Boolean
   Equity_isBond = False
End Function
```

Now, since the calcValue method is part of the interface, you have to include an empty method by that name in the Stock and Bond classes as well so the classes can compile without error.

```
Private Function Equity_calcValue(invDate As Date, _
        toDate As Date, rate As Single, _
        investment As Single) As Variant
        'never used in child classes
End Function
```

You could avoid this by creating an ancillary class that contains the computation method and creating an instance of it in the Stock and Bond classes, but this does lead to more clutter of extra classes.

Hidden Interfaces

Another way of accomplishing the same thing in this particular case is to give Stock and Bond the same public interfaces without using an Equity interface at all. Since all the operations in this simple program take place through a Collection, we can obtain a collection item and call its public methods without ever knowing which type of equity it actually is. For example, the following code will work for a collection Stocks containing a mixture of Stock and Bond objects.

```
For i = 1 To stocks.Count
  sname = stocks(i).getName
  lsStocks.AddItem sname
Next i
```

You should recognize, however, that this special case only occurs because we never need to get the objects back out as any particular type. In the cases we develop in the chapters that follow, this will seldom be the case.

Summary

In this chapter, we've shown how to construct an interface and a set of classes that implement it. We can then refer to all the derived classes as if they were an instance of the interface class and simplify our code considerably.

Programs on the **CD-ROM**

\Inheritance\Basic	Investment simulator

CHAPTER 7

Introduction to VB.NET

VB.NET or VB7 has much the same basic syntax as earlier versions of Visual Basic, but it is in many ways a completely new language. Unlike previous versions of VB, VB7 is completely object oriented, and many common operations are implemented a little differently because of this difference. For these reasons, it is best to consider VB.NET a language for developing new .NET applications, rather than as a new compiler for programs you have already written. Because of the awkward typography of VB.NET, we'll use the name VB7 to mean the same thing as VB.NET when we refer to it within the text. We'll maintain the VB.NET name in subheads. We'll see some of the advantages of VB7 in this chapter, and in later chapters we'll see how it makes some of the design patterns that much easier to construct useful object-oriented VB programs.

Syntax Differences in VB.NET

The major differences you will find in this version of VB is that all calls to subroutines and class methods must be enclosed in parentheses. In VB6, we could write the following.

```
Dim myCol As New Collection
MyCol.Add "Mine"
```

However, in VB7 you must enclose the arguments in parentheses:

```
Dim myCol As New ArrayList
MyCol.Add ("Mine")
```

One other significant difference—and for most people an improvement—is that arguments passed into subroutines are by default passed by *value* instead of by *reference*. In other words, you can operate on the variable within the subroutine without inadvertently changing its value in the calling program. Thus, the ByVal modifier is now the default. In fact, the development environment inserts it automatically in most cases. If you want to change the value in the calling program, you can still declare an argument using the ByRef modifier instead.

Three other keywords have also been removed or significantly changed from VB6: Set, Variant, and Wend. In fact, the development environment simply removes the Set verb from the beginning of any line where you use it.

Table 7-1   Some syntax differences between VB6 and VB7.

VB6	VB7
`Set q = New Collection`	`q = New Collection`
`Dim y as Variant`	`Dim y as Object`

`While x < 10`
`  x = x + 1`
`Wend`
	`While x < 10`
	`  x = x + 1`
	`End While`

`Dim x as Integer, y as integer`	`Dim x, y As Integer`

`ReDim X(30) As  Single`	`Dim X(30) as Single`
	`X = New Single(40)`
	`or`
	`ReDim X(40)`

The Dim statement now allows you to list several variables of the same type in a single statement.

```
Dim x, y As Integer
```

But you can also list variables of different types in a single statement.

```
Dim X as Integer, Y As Single
```

You can also, of course, list them on separate lines.

```
Dim X as Integer            'legal in both vb6 and vb7
Dim Y as Single
```

These changes are summarized in Table 7-1.

In addition, the string functions Instr, Left, and Right have been supplemented by the more versatile indexOf and substring methods of the String class.

Note that string indexes are *zero based* when using these new methods (see Table 7-2).

Table 7-2 String functions in VB6 and 7 compared with String methods.

VB6 or VB7	VB7
`Instr(s, ",")`	`s.indexOf(",")`
`Left(s, 2)`	`s.substring(0,2)`
`Right(s, 4)`	`s.substring(s.Length() -4)`

Improved Function Syntax

One of the awkward bugaboos in VB has been the need to refer to the function name in returning a value from a function.

```
Public Function Squarit(x as Single)
   Squarit = x * x
End Function
```

In VB7, this restriction is finally lifted, and you can simply use the return statement, as is common in many other languages.

```
Public Function Squarit(x as Single)
    Return x * x
End Function
```

This makes functions much simpler to type and use.

Variable Declarations and Scoping

VB7 normally requires that you declare all variables with a Dim statement before you use them. While it is possible to turn this off, it is certainly unwise because of the additional error checking protection it provides.

In addition, VB7 allows you to declare a variable and assign a value to it at the same time:

```
Dim age As Integer = 12
```

In fact, this changes the whole style of programming and variable declaration, because you can declare a variable right where you use it instead of at the top of the subroutine. In the following example we sort the elements of the array a.

```
For i = 1 To UBound(a)
    Dim j As Integer
    For j = i + 1 To UBound(a)
        If (a(i) > a(j)) Then
            Dim temp As Single
            temp = a(i)
            a(i) = a(j)
            a(j) = temp
        End If
    Next j
Next i
'error! temp no longer exists
Console.WriteLine("temp=" + temp)
```

We declare a variable j inside the outer loop, and a variable temp inside the inner loop. These variables only have existence inside that block and are "forgotten" by the compiler at the end of that block. Thus, you cannot refer to the variable j outside the j-loop and cannot refer to the temp variable outside the inner loop. The Console.WriteLine statement results in a compiler error, since temp no longer exists outside the inner loop.

You cannot declare a variable at two different block levels in VB7. Thus, if you declare a variable in an outer loop, you can't redeclare a new version of it in an inner block enclosed by that outer block.

```
Dim temp As Single   'outer declaration

For i = 1 To UBound(a)
    Dim j As Integer
    For j = i + 1 To UBound(a)
        If (a(i) > a(j)) Then
            'error! temp already longer exists
            Dim temp As Single
            temp = a(i)
            a(i) = a(j)
            a(j) = temp
        End If
    Next j
Next i
```

However, you can declare the same variable over again in a new block once the program has exited from the previous block.

```
For i = 1 To UBound(a)
        Dim j As Integer 'legal
        For j = i + 1 To UBound(a)
        'some code
        Next j
    Next i
    Dim j As Integer 'legal
```

Objects in VB.NET

In VB7, everything is treated as an object. While in VB6, you can create class instances that behave as objects. Objects contain data and have methods that operate on them. In VB7, this is true of every kind of variable.

Strings are objects, as we just illustrated. They have methods such as these.

```
Substring
ToLowerCase
ToUpperCase
IndexOf
Insert
```

However, strings do not at the moment have methods for converting to numerical values. Instead, you can use the VB Cint, CSng and CDbl functions for this purpose.

Integers and Single and Double variables are also objects, and they have methods as well.

```
Dim s as String
Dim x as Single

x =  12.3
s = x.ToString          'convert to String
x = CSng(s)             'convert to Single
```

Note that conversion between strings and numerical types is better done using these methods rather than using the Val and Str functions. If you want to format a number as a particular kind of string, each numeric type has a Format method.

```
Dim s as String
Dim x as Single
x = 12.34

s = Single.Format(x, "##.000")
```

Compiler Options

If you are familiar with VB6, you probably know about the compiler Option Explicit directive. This requires that you declare all variables with Dim statements before using them. VB7 introduces the Option Strict On statement. Option Strict forces a higher level of compiler checking, and restricts automatic conversion between wider and narrower variable types. The default setting in VB7 is Option Explicit, but you can turn on Option Strict for a whole project by right clicking on the Project name in the Project Explorer window. Then select Build and select On from the Option Strict drop-down selector as shown in Figure 7-1.

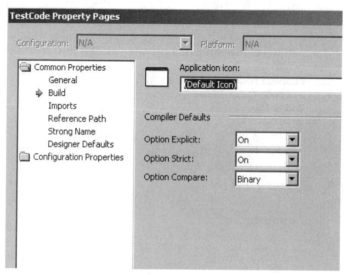

Figure 7-1   Setting Option Strict in the Property pages dialog

Numbers in VB.NET

All numbers without decimal points are assumed to be of type Integer or Int32 (a 32-bit signed integer), and all numbers with decimal points are assumed to be of type Double.

Normally the VB.NET compiler is set to Option Explicit, which prevents most undeclared type conversions, except to wider types. You can always convert from integer to single or double. However, if you want to convert a single to an integer, you must specifically indicate that this is what you want to do, using the CInt, CSng, CDbl, CLng, CDate, and CStr functions.

```
Dim k As Integer = CInt(time)
Dim time as Single = CSng("3.3")
```

The Currency type is no longer available in VB7. Instead, you can use the Decimal type, which provides a high precision.

VB7 also provides the Convert class, which has a number of shared methods for converting between types.

```
Dim k As Integer = Convert.ToInt32(s)
```

Properties in VB6 and VB.NET

Visual Basic provides a construct called *properties* that is analogous to the getXxx and setXxx methods of other languages. In VB6, you can specify a property by name and define its Get and Let methods. These two methods allow you to set the value of a private variable and return the value of that variable.

```
Property Get fred() As String
   fred = fredName
End Property

Property Let fred(s As String)
   fredName = s
End Property
```

Of course, you can do pre- and postprocessing of these data to validate them or convert them from other forms as needed.

In VB7, these properties are combined into a single routine.

```
Property Fred() As String
    Get
        Return fredName
    End Get
    Set
        fredName = value
    End Set
End Property
```

Note the special keyword *value*. We use it in VB7 to indicate the value being passed *in* to a property. So if we write the following

```
Abc.Fred = "dog"
```

then the string *value* will contain "dog" when the property Set code is executed.

In both systems, the purpose is to provide a simple interface to get and set values from a class without knowing how the data are actually stored. You use these properties in common assignment statements. If "Fred" is a property of the Boy class, then you can write statements like this.

```
Dim kid as Boy
Kid.fred = "smart"
```

And you can write this.

```
Dim brain as string
Brain = kid.fred
```

In general, the Property system provides an alternate syntax to the getFred and setFred functions that you could write just as easily. While the syntax differs, there is no obvious advantage except that many native VB objects have properties rather than get and set methods. In this book we will not make much use of properties because they are not a significant advantage in coding object-oriented programs.

Shorthand Equals Syntax

VB7 adopts the shorthand equals syntax we find in C, C++, C#, and Java. It allows you to add, subtract, multiply, or divide a variable by a constant without typing its name twice.

```
Dim i As Integer = 5
        i += 5   'add 5 to i
        i -= 8   'subtract 8 from i
        i *= 4   'multiply i by 4
```

You can use this approach to save typing, but the code generated is undoubtedly the same as if you had written the code out in the old way

```
i = i + 5
i = i - 8
i = i * 4
```

The same applies to division, but you seldom see it because it is awkward to read.

Managed Languages and Garbage Collection

VB.NET and C# are both *managed* languages. This has two major implications. First, both are compiled to an intermediate low-level language, and a common language runtime (CLR) is used to execute this compiled code, perhaps first compiling it further. So not only do VB7 and C# share the same runtime libraries, they are to a large degree two sides of the same coin and two aspects of the same language system. The differences are that VB7 is more Visual Basic-like and a bit easier to learn and use. C# on the other hand is more C++ and Java-like, and it may appeal more to programmers already experienced in those languages.

The other major implication is that managed languages are *garbage collected*. Garbage-collected languages take care of releasing unused memory: You never have to be concerned with this. As soon as the garbage-collection system detects that there are no more active references to a variable, array, or object, the memory is released back to the system. So you no longer need to worry as much about running out of memory because you allocated memory and never released it. Of course, it is still possible to write memory-eating code, but for the most part you do not have to worry about memory allocation and release problems.

Classes in VB.NET

Classes are a very important part of VB7. Almost every important program consists of one or more classes. The distinction between classes and forms has disappeared in VB7, and most programs are all classes. Since nearly everything is a class, the number of names of class objects can get to be pretty overwhelming. They have therefore been grouped into various functional libraries that you must specifically mention in order to use the functions in these libraries.

Under the covers these libraries are each individual DLLs. However, you need only refer to them by their base names, using the Imports statement, and the functions in that library are available to you.

```
Imports System.IO      'Use File namespace classes
```

Logically, each of these libraries represents a different *namespace*. Each namespace is a separate group of class and method names that the compiler will recognize after you import that name space. You can import namespaces that contain identically named classes or methods, but you will only be notified of a conflict if you try to use a class or method that is duplicated in more than one namespace.

You can specify which namespaces you want to import into every class in your project using the Property pages dialog, as shown in Figure 7-2.

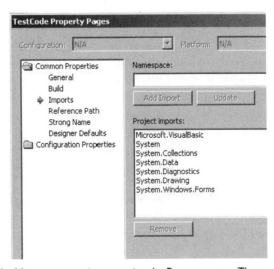

Fig 7-2   Setting the Namespaces to import using the Property pages. The names shown are set by default.

The most common namespace is the System namespace, and it is imported by default without your needing to declare it. It contains many of the most fundamental classes and methods that VB7 uses for access to basic classes, such as Application, Array, Console, Exceptions, Objects, and standard objects, such as Byte, Boolean, Single and Double, and String. In the simplest VB7 program we can simply write "hello" out to the console without ever bringing up a window or form.

```
'Simple VB Hello World program
Public Class cMain
    Shared Sub Main()     'entry point is Main
        'Write text to the console
        Console.WriteLine ("Hello VB World")
    End Sub
End Class
```

This program just writes the text "Hello VB World" to a command (DOS) window. The entry point of any program must be a Sub Main subroutine, and in a class module, it must be declared Shared. The only other type of module in VB7 is the Module type. Here the program can be written like this.

```
'Simple VB Hello World program
Public Module cMain
    Sub Main()     'entry point is Main
        'Write text to the console
        Console.WriteLine ("Hello VB World")
    End Sub
End Module
```

The programs are pretty much identical, except that a Module has all public (and shared) methods and the Sub Main need not be declared as Shared. Modules are analogous to the Modules in earlier versions of VB and are the ones that Vb would have created with a .bas file type. They have the advantage that all of the methods and constants declared in a Module are public and can be referenced throughout the program. However, unlike classes, they provide no way to hide information or algorithms, and we will not use them further in this book.

In VB6, the class name was usually declared the filename, although you could change a class's Name property. In VB7, the Class keyword allows you to declare the class name irrespective of the filename, and in fact, you must declare a class name for each class. The default file extensions for VB6 classes was .cls and for forms .frm. In VB7, you can use any filename or extension you want, but the default file extension is .vb.

Building a VB7 Application

Let's start by creating a simple console application: one without any windows that just runs from the command line. Start the Visual Studio.NET program, and select File|New Project. From the selection box, choose Console application, as shown in Figure 7-3.

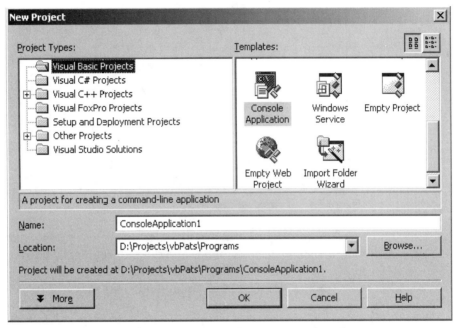

Figure 7-3   The New Project selection window. Selecting a console application

This will bring up a module, with the Sub Main already filled in. You can type in the rest of the code as follows.

```
Module cMain
    Sub Main()
        'write text to the console
        Console.WriteLine("Hello VB world")
    End Sub
End Module
```

You can compile this and run it by pressing F5. If you change the program's main module name from Module1 to cMain, as we did here, you will also have to change the name of the Startup module. To do this, in the right-hand Solution Explorer window, right-click on the project name and select Properties from the pop-up menu. This will appear as in Figure 7-4.

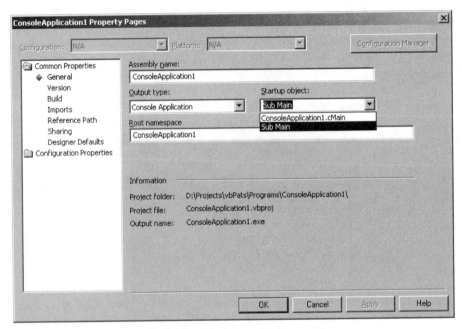

Figure 7-4 The property page for the project

You can change the startup object in the drop-down menu to the correct new name. When you compile and run the program by pressing F5, a DOS window will appear and print out the message "Hello VB World" and exit.

You can also delete the module and insert a class instead.

```
Public Class cMain
    Shared Sub Main()
        Console.WriteLine("Hello classy VB world")
    End Sub
End Class
```

This will compile and run in just the same way.

The Simplest Window Program in VB.NET

It is just about as simple to write a program that brings up a window. In fact, you can create most of it using the Windows Designer. To do this, start Visual Studio.NET and select File|New project, and then select Windows Application. The default name (and filename) is WindowsApplication1, but you can change this before you close the New dialog box. This brings up a single form project, initially called Form1.vb. You can then use the Toolbox to insert controls, just as you could in VB6.

The Windows Designer for a simple form with two labels, one text field and one button, is shown in Figure 7-5.

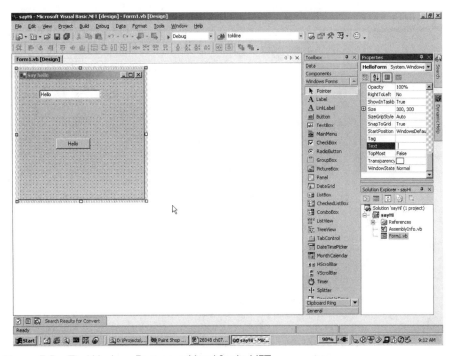

Figure 7-5 The Windows Designer in Visual Studio.NET

You can draw the controls on the form and double click on the controls to enter code. In this simple form, we click on the "Say hello" button, and it copies the text from the text field to the blank label we named lbHi and clears the text field.

```
Protected Sub SayHello_Click(ByVal sender As Object, _
                    ByVal e As System.EventArgs)
     lbhi.Text() = txhi.Text
     txhi.Text = ""
End Sub
```

The code it generates is a little different. Note that the Click routine passes in the sender object and an event object that you can query for further information. The running program is shown in Figure 7-6.

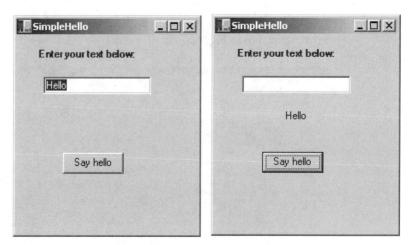

Figure 7-6   The SimpleHello form before and after clicking the Say Hello button

While we only had to write the two lines of code inside the preceding subroutine, it is instructive to see how different the rest of the code is for this program.

Inheritance

Next, we see the most stunning change in VB7- inheritance.

```
Public Class HelloForm
      Inherits System.Windows.Forms.Form
```

The form we create is a child class of the Form class, rather than being an instance of it as was the case in previous versions of VB. This has some very powerful implications. You can create visual objects and override some of their properties so each behaves a little differently. We'll see some examples of this shortly.

The code the designer generates for the controls is illuminating. No longer is the code for the control creation buried in an interpreter of Form module declarations you can't easily change. Instead, it is right there in the open for you to change if you want. Note, however, that if you change this code manually instead of using the property page, the window designer may not work anymore. That is why this section is initially collapsed inside a "[+]" box line on the code display.

Essentially, each control is declared as a variable and added to a container. Here are the control declarations.

```
Friend WithEvents txHi As System.Windows.Forms.TextBox
Friend WithEvents lbHi As System.Windows.Forms.Label
Friend WithEvents Button1 As System.Windows.Forms.Button
```

```
        'Required by the Windows Form Designer
        Private components As System.ComponentModel.Container
        <System.Diagnostics.DebuggerStepThrough()>
Private Sub InitializeComponent()
        Me.txHi = New System.Windows.Forms.TextBox()
        Me.lbHi = New System.Windows.Forms.Label()
        Me.Button1 = New System.Windows.Forms.Button()
        Me.SuspendLayout()
        '
        'txHi
        '
        Me.txHi.Location = New System.Drawing.Point(48, 24)
        Me.txHi.Name = "txHi"
        Me.txHi.Size = New System.Drawing.Size(144, 20)
        Me.txHi.TabIndex = 0
        Me.txHi.Text = "Hello"
        '
        'lbHi
        '
        Me.lbHi.Font = New System.Drawing.Font(
            "Microsoft Sans Serif", 14.25!,
            System.Drawing.FontStyle.Regular,
            System.Drawing.GraphicsUnit.Point, CType(0, Byte))
        Me.lbHi.ForeColor = System.Drawing.Color.FromArgb(
            CType(0, Byte), CType(0, Byte), CType(192, Byte))
        Me.lbHi.Location = New System.Drawing.Point(48, 64)
        Me.lbHi.Name = "lbHi"
        Me.lbHi.Size = New System.Drawing.Size(152, 24)
        Me.lbHi.TabIndex = 1
        '
        'SayHello
        '
        Me.SayHello.Location =
            New System.Drawing.Point(88, 136)
        Me.SayHello.Name = "SayHello"
        Me.SayHello.Size = New System.Drawing.Size(80, 24)
        Me.SayHello.TabIndex = 2
        Me.SayHello.Text = "Hello"
        '
        'Form1
        '
        Me.AutoScaleBaseSize = New System.Drawing.Size(5, 13)
        Me.ClientSize = New System.Drawing.Size(292, 273)
        Me.Controls.AddRange(
        New System.Windows.Forms.Control()
                    {Me.Button1, Me.lbHi, Me.txHi})
        Me.Name = "Form1"
        Me.Text = "Say hello"
        Me.ResumeLayout(False)


    End Sub
```

Note that the SayHello button is declared using the WithEvents modifier. This means that there can be a direct connection between the button and the subroutine SayHello_Click.

Constructors

All classes now have specific *constructors* that are called when you create an instance of a class. These constructors are always named New. This applies to form classes as well as nonvisual classes. Here is the constructor for our simple hello window.

```
Public Sub New()
  MyBase.New()
 'This call is required by the Windows Form Designer.
  InitializeComponent()
 'Add any initialization after the InitializeComponent() call
End Sub
```

Note the MyBase.New method call. This calls the constructor of the parent class and initializes it. Code to accomplish this is generated even if you leave this line out.

Many times, we'll need to initialize variables or other classes as part of our program startup. The place we would insert that code is at the bottom of the New method shown above. However, since the New method is usually hidden inside the collapsed +-sign area, we'll adopt the convention that our New method will always call an init() method and place that call at the bottom of the New method. Then we can place the init method in plain sight. Here is a trivial example:

```
    Private Sub init()
        lbHi.Text = "..."
    End Sub
#Region " Windows Form Designer generated code "

Public Sub New()
    MyBase.New()
        'This call is required by the Windows Form Designer.
        InitializeComponent()
'Add any initialization after the InitializeComponent() call
        init()
End Sub
```

When you create your own classes, you can create New methods to initialize them and can pass arguments into the class to initialize class parameters to specific values. Suppose you wanted to create a StringTokenizer class like the one we defined in Chapter 3.

The VB7 String class has a Split method that is analogous to VB6's Split function that returns an array of strings. The difference is that you pass it an array of characters for the possible separators instead of a String.

```
sarray = s.Split(sep.ToCharArray)
```

We'll use this method in our VB7 tokenizer class.

Here we use real constructors instead of the init() method. Our constructor will copy the string into an internal variable and create a default value for the token separator.

```
Public Class StringTokenizer
    Private s As String
    Private i As Integer
    Private sep As String     'token separator
    Private sArray() As String
    '------
    Public Sub New(ByVal st As String)
        s = st            'copy in string
        set_Separator(" ")          'default separator
    End Sub
    '------
    Public Sub New(ByVal st As String, _
            ByVal sepr As String)
        s = st
        set_Separator(sepr) 'creates the array
    End Sub
    '-----
    Private Sub set_separator(ByVal sp As String)
        sep = sp       'copy separator
        'and create the array
        sarray = s.Split(sep.ToCharArray)
        i = 0
    End Sub
    '------
    Public Sub setSeparator(ByVal sp As String)
        set_separator(sp)
    End Sub
    '------
    Public Function nextToken() As String
        Dim j As Integer
        j = i
        i = i + 1
        If j < sarray.Length Then
            Return sarray(j)
        Else
            Return ""
        End If
    End Function
End Class
```

Our calling program simply creates an instance of the tokenizer and prints out the tokens as a console application.

```
'illustrates use of tokenizer
Public Class TokTest
    Shared Sub Main()
        Dim s As String
        Dim tok As New StringTokenizer("Hello VB World")
        s = tok.nextToken()
        While (s <> "")
            Console.writeLine(s)
            s = tok.nextToken()
        End While
    End Sub
End Class
```

Note that VB7 allows you to declare variables and initialize them in the same statement.

```
Dim tok As New StringTokenizer("Hello VB World")
```

Drawing and Graphics in VB.NET

In VB7, controls are repainted by the Windows system, and you can override the OnPaint event to do your own drawing. The PaintEventArgs object is passed into the subroutine by the underlying system, and you can obtain the graphics surface to draw on from that object. To do drawing, you must create an instance of a Pen object and define its color and, optionally, its width. This is illustrated here for a black pen with a default width of 1.

```
Protected Overrides Sub OnPaint(ByVal e as PaintEventArgs)
  Dim g as Graphics = e.Graphics
  Dim rpen As new Pen(Color.Black)
  g.drawLine(rpen, 10,20,70,80)
End Sub
```

The Overrides keyword is a critical part of the VB inheritance system. Using this keyword tells the compiler that you are overriding the same method in a parent class.

Tooltips and Cursors

A Tooltip is a message that appears when you allow the mouse cursor to hover over a control. In VB6, each control had a Tooltip property. In VB7, you create an instance of the Tooltip object for each form, and add the controls to it along with the message you wish to display.

```
Dim tips As New ToolTip()
tips.SetToolTip(Button1, "Click to Execute")
```

A cursor is the visual indication of the mouse position. Its default image is an arrow. There can only be one cursor displayed on a form and you set it using the shared Current property of the Cursor object. You can select the type of cursor from the public shared constants in the Cursors object:

```
Cursor.Current = Cursors.WaitCursor
Cursor.Current = Cursors.Default
```

The usual list of constant cursor names includes:

```
Cursors.Arrow
Cursors.Cross
Cursors.Default
Cursors.Ibeam
Cursors.No
Cursors.SizeAll
Cursors.UpArrow
Cursors.WaitCursor
```

and so forth.

Overloading

In VB7, as well as other object-oriented languages, you can have several class methods with the same name as long as they have different calling arguments or *signatures*. For example, we might want to create an instance of the StringTokenizer where we define both the string and the separator.

```
tok = New StringTokenizer("apples, pears", ",")
```

If we want to implement this constructor, we *overload* the constructor and the compiler will know we have two methods with the same name, but different arguments. Here are the two constructors.

```
Public Sub New(st as String, sepr as String)
  s = st
  sep = sepr
End Sub
'------
Public Sub New(st As String)
 s = st          'copy in string
 sep = " "       'default separator
End Sub
```

VB allows us to overload any other method as long as we provide arguments that allow the compiler to distinguish between the various overloaded (or *polymorphic*) methods. You can use the OverLoads keyword to point out that you have two or more methods with the same name, but different arguments for any Sub of Function you create. However, you do not use OverLoads with New methods, and the compiler flags the use of the Overloads keyword with New methods as an error.

Inheritance

The most powerful new feature in VB7 is the ability to create classes that are derived from existing classes. In new derived classes, we only have to specify the methods that are new or changed. All the others are provided automatically from the base class from which we inherit. To see how this works, let's consider writing a simple Rectangle class that draws itself on a form window. This class has only two methods, the constructor and the draw method.

```
Namespace VBPatterns
Public Class Rectangle
    Private x, y, h, w As Integer
    Protected rpen As Pen
    '------
Public Sub New(ByVal x_ As Integer, _
               ByVal y_ As Integer, _
               ByVal h_ As Integer, _
               ByVal w_ As Integer)
    x = x_
    y = y_
    h = h_
    w = w_
    rpen = New Pen(Color.Black)
  End Sub
  '--------
  Public Sub draw(ByVal g As Graphics)
      g.DrawRectangle(rpen, x, y, w, h)
  End Sub
 End Class
End Namespace
```

Namespaces

We mentioned the System namespaces previously. VB7 creates a Namespace for each project equal to the name of the project itself. You see this default name-space being generated in Figure 7-4. You can change this namespace on the property page or make it blank so that the project is not in a namespace. How-ever, you can create namespaces of your own, and the Rectangle class provides a good example of a reason for doing so. There already is a Rectangle class in the System.Drawing namespace that this program imports. Rather than renaming the class to avoid this name overlap or "collision," we can just put the whole

Rectangle class in its own namespace by wrapping the class inside a namespace declaration, as we just showed.

Then, when we declare the variable in the main Form window, we declare it as a member of that namespace.

```
Public Class Rect_Form
    Inherits System.Windows.Forms.Form

    Private rect As VBPatterns.Rectangle
```

In this main Form window's init method (which we call from within New as before), we create an instance of our Rectangle class.

```
Private Sub init()
    rect = New VBPatterns.Rectangle(20, 50, 100, 200)
End Sub
```

Then we override the OnPaint event to do the drawing and pass the graphics surface on to the Rectangle instance.

```
Protected Overrides Sub OnPaint( _
        ByVal e As PaintEventArgs)
    Dim g As Graphics
    g = e.Graphics
    rect.draw(g)
End Sub
```

This gives us the display we see in Figure 7-7.

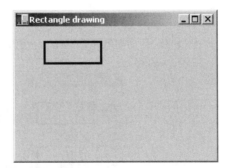

Figure 7-7   The Rectangle drawing program

Creating a Square from a Rectangle

A square is just a special case of a rectangle, and we can derive a Square class from the Rectangle class without writing much new code. Here is the entire class.

```
Namespace VBPatterns
    Public Class Square
        Inherits Rectangle
        Public Sub New(ByVal x As Integer, _
            ByVal y As Integer, ByVal w As Integer)
            MyBase.New(x, y, w, w)
        End Sub
    End Class
End Namespace
```

This Square class contains only a constructor, which passes the square dimensions on to the underlying Rectangle class by calling the constructor of the parent Rectangle class. The Rectangle class creates the pen and does the actual drawing. Note that there is no draw method at all for the Square class. If you don't specify a new method, the parent class's method is used automatically.

The program that draws both a rectangle and a square has a simple constructor where instances of these objects are created. It calls the init method below:

```
Private Sub init()
        rect = New VBPatterns.Rectangle(20, 50, 100, 200)
        sq = New VBPatterns.Square(70, 80, 50)
    End Sub
```

The program also has an OnPaint routine, where they are drawn.

```
Protected Overrides Sub OnPaint( _
            ByVal e As PaintEventArgs)
    Dim g As Graphics
    g = e.Graphics
    rect.draw(g)
    sq.draw(g)
End Sub
```

The display for the square and rectangle is shown in Figure 7-8.

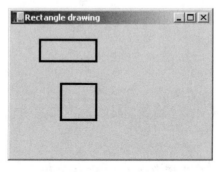

Figure 7-8   The rectangle class and the square class derived from it

Public, Private, and Protected

In VB6, you could declare variables and class methods as either public or private. A public method is accessible from other classes, and a private method is accessible only inside that class. Usually, you make all class variables private and write getXxx and seXxx accessor functions to set or obtain their values. It is generally a bad idea to allow variables inside a class to be accessed directly from outside the class, since this violates the principle of *encapsulation*. In other words, the class is the only place where the actual data representation should be known, and you should be able to change the algorithms inside a class without anyone outside the class being any the wiser.

VB7 introduces the *protected* keyword as well. Both variables and methods can be protected. Protected variables can be accessed within the class and from any subclasses you derive from it. Similarly, protected methods are only accessible from that class and its derived classes. They are not publicly accessible from outside the class.

Overriding Methods in Derived Classes

Suppose we want to derive a new class called DoubleRect from Rectangle that draws a rectangle in two colors offset by a few pixels. In the constructor, we create a red pen for doing this drawing.

```
Namespace VBPatterns
    Public Class DoubleRect
        Inherits Rectangle
        Private redPen As Pen
        '-----
        Public Sub New(ByVal x As Integer, _
                ByVal y As Integer, ByVal w As Integer, _
                ByVal h As Integer)
          MyBase.New(x, y, w, h)
          redPen = New Pen(Color.FromARGB(255, _
                Color.Red), 2)
        End Sub
```

This means that our new class DoubleRect must have its own draw method. Now the base class has a draw method, and we really should create a method with the same name, since we want all these classes to behave the same. However, this draw method will use the parent class's draw method but add more drawing of its own. In other words, the draw method will be overridden, and we must specifically declare that fact to satisfy the VB compiler.

```
Public Overrides Sub draw(ByVal g As Graphics)
    MyBase.draw(g)
    g.drawRectangle(redPen, x + 4, y + 4, w, h)
End Sub
```

Note that we want to use the coordinates and size of the rectangle that was specified in the constructor. We could keep our own copy of these parameters in the DoubleRect class, or we could change the protection mode of these variables in the base Rectangle class to protected from private.

```
Protected x, y, h, w As Integer
```

We also must tell the compiler that we want to allow the Rectangle's draw method to be overridden by declaring it as overridable.

```
Public Overridable Sub draw(ByVal g As Graphics)
    g.DrawRectangle(rpen, x, y, w, h)
End Sub
```

The final rectangle drawing window is shown in Figure 7-9.

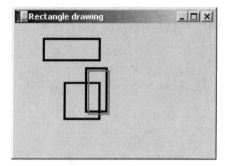

Figure 7-9   The Rectangle, Square, and DoubleRect classes

Overloading and Shadowing

VB7 provides the keyword Shadows in addition to Overloads. A method or property which overloads the member of the base class simply replaces that particular method name in the derived class. If you have several overloaded versions of that method name, the overloaded one is the only one replaced.

Let's consider the simple class BaseClass shown here:

```
Public Class BaseClass
    Private data As Single
    '-----
    Public Sub setData(ByVal x As Single)
        data = x
    End Sub
```

```
    '-----
    Public Sub setData()
        data = 12.2
    End Sub
End Class
```

In this class there are two overloaded versions of the setData method, one which requires an argument and one which uses a default internal value. You can also write the same class using the Overloads keyword:

```
Public Class BaseClass
    Private data As Single
    Private Const defaultv As Single = 12.2
    '-----
    Public Overloads Sub setData(ByVal x As Single)
        data = x
    End Sub
    '-----
    Public Overloads Sub setData()
        data = defaultv
    End Sub
End Class
```

These have the same meaning and compile to the same code.

Now let's consider a class derived from this one which has a new version of the setData method:

```
Public Class DerivedClass
    Inherits BaseClass
    '-----
    Public Overloads Sub setData(ByVal x As Single)
        MyBase.setData(x + 12)
    End Sub
End Class
```

This class has two setData methods: the one that is declared above and the one that is inherited from the BaseClass class. So we can write

```
Dim cl As New DerivedClass()
        cl.setData()
        cl.setData(14)
```

On the other hand, if we use the Shadows keyword, then all other overloaded methods of that name in the base class become inaccessible in the derived class.

```
Public Class DerivedClass
    Inherits BaseClass
    '-----
    Public Shadows Sub setData(ByVal x As Single)
        MyBase.setData(x + 12)
    End Sub
End Class
```

Then the only version of the setData method that exists in the DerivedClass is
the one shown, and the one with no arguments is an error:

```
Dim cl As New DerivedClass()
        cl.setData()    'now is illegal
        cl.setData(14) 'is legal
```

Overriding Windows Controls

In VB7 we can finally make new Windows controls based on existing ones,
using inheritance. Earlier we created a Textbox control that highlighted all the
text when you tabbed into it. In VB6, we did this by writing a new DLL in
which the Textbox was enclosed in a Usercontrol and where we passed all the
useful events on to the Textbox. In VB7, we can create that new control by just
deriving a new class from the Textbox class.

We'll start by using the Windows Designer to create a window with two
text boxes on it. Then we'll go to the Project|Add User Control menu and add
an object called HiTextBox.vb. We'll change this to inherit from TextBox
instead of UserControl.

```
public class HTextBox
        Inherits Textbox
```

Then, before we make further changes, we compile the program. The new
HiTextBox control will appear at the bottom of the Toolbox on the left of the
development environment. You can create visual instances of the HiTextBox on
any windows form you create. This is shown in Figure 7-10.

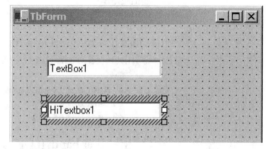

Figure 7-10   The Toolbox, showing the new control we created and an instance of the HiTextBox
on the Windows Designer pane of a new form

Now we can modify this class and insert the code to do the highlighting.

```
'A text box that highlights when you tab into it

Public Class HiTextBox
    Inherits System.windows.forms.TextBox
    Private Sub init()
        AddHandler Enter, _
            New System.EventHandler(AddressOf Me.HT_Enter)
    End Sub

    '------------
    'Enter event handler is inside the class
    Protected Sub HT_Enter(ByVal sender As System.Object, _
            ByVal e As System.EventArgs)
        Me.SelectionStart = 0
        Me.SelectionLength = Me.Text.Length
    End Sub

End Class
```

And that's the whole process. We have derived a new Windows control in about ten lines of code. That's pretty powerful. You can see the resulting program in Figure 7-11. If you run this program, you might at first think that the ordinary TextBox and the HiTextBox behave the same because tabbing between them highlights both. This is the "autohighlight" feature of the VB7 textbox. However, if you *click* inside the TextBox and the HiTextBox and tab back and forth, you will see in Figure 7-11 that only our derived HiTextBox continues to highlight.

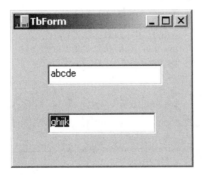

Figure 7-11   A new derived HiTextBox control and a regular TextBox control

Interfaces

VB7 also continues to support interfaces much like VB6 did. However, the syntax has changed somewhat. Now an Interface is a special kind of class.

```
Public Interface MultiChoice
    'an interface to any group of components
    'that can return zero or more selected items
    'the names are returned in an Arraylist
    Function getSelected() As ArrayList
    Sub clear()              'clear all selected
    Function getWindow() As Panel
End Interface
```

When you implement the methods of an Interface in concrete classes, you must declare that the class implements that interface.

```
Public Class ListChoice
    Implements MultiChoice
```

And you must also declare that each method of the class implements it as well.

```
Public Function getSelected() As ArrayList _
        Implements MultiChoice.getSelected

 End Function
'--------
'clear all selected items
Public Sub clear()  implements MultiChoice.clear
End Sub
'--------
Public Function getWindow() As Panel _
        Implements MultiChoice.getWindow
    return pnl
End Function
```

You can easily insert these methods correctly from the Visual Studio code designer as you can see in Figure 7-12.

Figure 7-12   Using the IDE to create the methods to implement the MultiChoice interface.

Note that all interfaces must be declared as "Public" or you will get a confusing compiler error about attempting to access Friend classes. We'll show how to use this interface when we discuss the Builder pattern.

Summary

We've seen the shape of most of the new features in VB7 in this chapter. In addition to some syntax changes, VB7 adds inheritance, constructors, and the ability to overload methods to provide alternate versions. This leads to the ability to create new derived versions even of Windows controls. In the chapters that follow, we'll show you how you can write design patterns in both VB6 and VB7.

Programs on the CD-ROM

\IntroVBNet\Hello1	The console "Hello" application using the Module approach
\IntroVBNet\Hello2	The console "Hello" application using the Class approach
\IntroVBNet\HiText	A subclassed text box
\IntroVBNet\SayHello	A Simple Hello program
\IntroVBNet\Tokenizer	A string tokenizer

CHAPTER 8

Arrays, Files, and Exceptions in VB.Net

VB7 makes some significant changes in the ways you handle arrays and files and completely changes error handling. All of these changes make your programming a lot easier than it was before.

Arrays

In VB7, all arrays are zero based. This is actually the same as in previous versions of Basic, but it was seldom emphasized. In VB6, if you wrote the following

```
Dim x(10) As Single
```

then you assumed that the x array had elements from 1 to 10, but it actually always included a zero element as well. In other words, the x array actually had 11 elements. This remains true in VB7.

However, we can also now move through arrays to be in line with the style used in C, C++, C#, and Java.

```
Dim Max as Integer
Max = 10
Dim x(Max)

For j = 0 to Max-1
 x(j) = j
Next j
```

However, you can still use

```
For j = 1 to Max
```

as you always could.

All array variables have a length property so you can find out how large the array is.

```
Dim z(20) As Single
Dim j As Integer

For j = 0  To z.Length — 1
     z(j) = j
Next j
```

But *beware!* The construction

```
For j = 0  To z.Length — 1
```

actually moves through 21 elements. If you declare

```
Dim z(20) As Single
```

it contains elements from 0 to 20, or 21 in all. So the value of

```
z.length
```

is 21, and moving from 0 to z.length –1 is moving through 21 elements. And, if you were to write

```
For j = 0  To z.Length
```

You would pass the upper bound of the array. It is safer to write

```
For j = 0 to Ubound(z) — 1
```

Arrays in VB7 are dynamic, and you can reallocate space at any time. To create a reference to an array and allocate it later within the class, use the New syntax.

```
'Declare at the class level
   Dim x() As Single
'allocate within any method
   x = New Single(20) {}
```

Note the unusual use of curly braces following the type and size. This means that you are creating a new array object. This syntax applies because you can also specify the contents of the array in the same declaration:

```
Dim a() As Single
a = New Single() {1, 3, 4, 5}
```

You can also use the ReDim statement with or without Preserve to change the size of a declared array. However, you should note that ReDim no longer allows an "As" clause, since the array type cannot be changed during ReDim.

```
ReDim x(40)
ReDim Preserve x(50)
```

Collection Objects

The System.Collections namespace contains a number of useful variable-length array objects you can use to add and obtain items in several ways.

ArrayLists

Since arrays are zero-based, VB7 introduces the ArrayList object to replace the Collection object, which was always 1-based. The ArrayList is essentially a variable-length array that you can add items to as needed. The basic ArrayList methods are about the same as for Collections, although there are quite a few more methods you can also use.

```
Dim i, j As Integer
 'create ArrayList
Dim arl As New ArrayList() 'constructor
 'add to it
 For j = 0 To 9
     Arl.Add(j)
 Next j
```

Like the Collection object, the ArrayList has a Count property and an Item property that allows you to obtain elements from it by index. And like the Collection, this property can be omitted, treating the ArrayList just as if it were an array.

```
'print out contents
For i = 0 To arl.Count - 1
    Console.writeLine(arl.Item(i))
    Console.writeLine(arl(i))
Next i
```

You can also use the methods of the ArrayList shown in Table 8-1.

Hashtables

A Hashtable is a variable-length array where every entry can be referred to by a key value. Typically, keys are strings of some sort, but that can be any sort of object. Keys must be unique for each element, although the elements themselves

Table 8-1   ArrayList Methods

Clear	Clears the contents of the ArrayList
Contains(object)	Returns true if the ArrayList contains that value
CopyTo(array)	Copies entire ArrayList into a one-dimensional array
IndexOf(object)	Returns the first index of the value
Insert(index, object)	Inserts the element at the specified index
Remove(object)	Removes element from list
RemoveAt(index)	Removes element from specified position
Sort	Sort ArrayList

need not be unique. Hashtables are used to allow rapid access to one of a large and unsorted set of entries and can also be used by reversing the key and the entry values to create a list where each entry is guaranteed to be unique. The most important Hashtable methods are Add and the Item fetch.

```
Dim hash As New Hashtable()
  Dim fredObject As New Object()
  Dim obj As Object
  hash.Add("Fred", fredObject)
  obj = hash.Item("Fred")
```

Hashtables also have a count property, and you can obtain an enumeration of the keys or of the values.

SortedLists

The SortedList class is most like the VB6 Collection class. It maintains two internal arrays, so you can obtain the elements either by zero-based index or by alphabetic key.

```
Dim sList As New SortedList()
  slist.Add("Fred", fredObject)
  slist.Add("Sam", obj)
  Dim newObj As Object
  newObj = slist.GetByIndex(0)      'by index
  newObj = slist.Item("Sam")        'by key
```

You will also find the Stack and Queue objects in this namespace. They behave much as you'd expect, and you can find their methods in the system help documentation.

Exceptions

Error handling in VB7 is accomplished using *exceptions* instead of the awkward On Error Goto syntax, which is no longer supported. The thrust of exception handling is that you enclose the statements that could cause errors in a Try block and then catch any errors using a Catch statement.

```
Try
   'Statements
 Catch e as Exception
   'do these if an error occurs
 Finally
   'do these anyway
End Try
```

Typically, you use this approach to test for errors around file handling statements, although you can also catch array index out-of-range statements and a large number of other error conditions. The way this works is that the statements in the Try block are executed, and if there is no error, control passes to the Finally statements, if any, and then on out of the block. If errors occur, control passes to the Catch statement, where you can handle the errors, and then control passes on to the Finally statements and then on out of the block.

The following example shows testing for any exception. Since we are moving one element beyond the end of the ArrayList, an error will occur.

```
Try
    For i = 0 To ar.Count            'NOTE: one too many
        Console.write(ar.Item(i))
    Next i
Catch e As Exception
    Console.writeLine(e.Message)
    Console.writeLine(e.stackTrace)
End Try

Console.writeline("end of loop")
```

This code prints out the error message and the calling locations in the program and then goes on.

```
0123456789Index is out of range.  Must be non-negative and less
than size.
```

```
Parameter name: index
   at System.Collections.ArrayList.get_Item(Int32)
   at ArrayTest.Main()
end of loop
```

By contrast, if we do not catch the exception, we will get an error message from the runtime system, and the program will exit instead of going on.

```
Exception occurred: System.ArgumentOutOfRangeException: Index
is out of range.
Must be non-negative and less than size.
Parameter name: index
   at System.Collections.ArrayList.get_Item(Int32)
   at ArrayTest.Main()
   at _vbProject._main(System.String[])
```

Some of the more common exceptions are shown in Table 8-2.

Table 8-2   VB7 Exceptions

`AccessException`	Error in accessing a method or field of a class
`ArgumentException`	Argument to a method is not valid
`ArgumentNullException`	Argument is null
`ArithmeticException`	Overflow or underflow
`DivideByZeroException`	Division by zero
`IndexOutOfRangeException`	Array index out of range
`FileNotFoundException`	File not found
`EndOfStreamException`	Access beyond end of input stream (such as files)
`DirectoryNotFoundException`	Directory not found
`NullReferenceException`	The object variable has not been initialized to a real value

Multiple Exceptions

You can also catch a series of exceptions and handle them differently in the same Try block.

```
Try
    For i = 0 To ar.Count
        Dim k As Integer = CType(ar(i), Integer)
        Console.writeLine(i.toString & " " & k / i)
      Next i
Catch e As DivideByZeroException
    Console.writeLine(e.Message)
    Console.writeLine(e.stackTrace)
Catch e As IndexOutOfRangeException
    Console.writeLine(e.Message)
    Console.writeLine(e.stackTrace)
Catch e As Exception
    Console.writeLine("general exception" + e.Message)
    Console.writeLine(e.stackTrace)
End Try
```

This gives you the opportunity to recover from various errors in different ways.

Throwing Exceptions

You don't have to deal with exceptions exactly where they occur; you can pass them back to the calling program using the Throw statement. This causes the exception to be thrown in the calling program.

```
Try
    'some code
Catch e as Exception
    Throw e    'pass on to calling routine
End Try
```

File Handling

You can use some of the file handling functions you are used to in VB6; however, the syntax is rather different because of the requirement that all arguments be enclosed in parentheses. Thus, you will have to make major changes throughout your file handling code.

```
Input #f, s    'read a string from a file in VB6
```

becomes

```
Input(f, s)    'vb6 compatible string read from file
```

Further, VB7 has no Line Input statement at all. Therefore, it is usually easier to read and write file data using the new File and Stream methods provided in VB7.

The File Object

The File class provides some useful methods for testing for a file's existence as well as renaming and deleting a file. The File object contains only Shared methods. Thus, you call the File class methods without creating an instance. These are all *shared* methods in VB parlance. Other languages refer to them as *static* methods, since they work using the class rather than an object. We show some of the most common File methods in Table 8-3. For a complete list, consult the documentation and help files.

Table 8-3   File Methods

Static Method	Meaning
`File.Exists(filename)`	True if file exists
`File.Delete(filename)`	Delete the file
`File.AppendText(String)`	Append text
`File.getAttributes(String)`	Return FileAttributes object
`File.Copy(fromFile, toFile)`	Copy a file
`File.Move(fromFile, toFile)`	Move a file, deleting old copy
`File.OpenText(filename)`	Opens text file for reading
`File.OpenWrite(filename)`	Opens any file for reading

For example, if you want to delete a file using the File class you check for its existence and then delete it as follows:

```
If File.Exists("foo.txt") Then   'test existence
    File.Delete("foo.txt")       'delete it
End If
```

You can also use the File object to obtain a StreamReader or FileStream for reading and writing file data.

```
Dim ts As StreamReader
Dim fs As FileStream

ts = File.OpenText("foo.txt")  'open a text file for reading
fs = File.OpenRead("foo.data") 'open any file for reading
```

Reading a Text File

To read a text file, use the File object to obtain a StreamReader object. Then use the text stream's read methods.

```
Dim ts As StreamReader
ts = File.OpenText("foo.txt")   'open a text file

Dim s As String
s = ts.ReadLine()
```

Writing a Text File

To create and write a text file, use the CreateText method to get a StreamWriter object.

```
Dim sw As StreamWriter
sw = File.CreateText("foo.txt")
sw.WriteLine("Hello there")
```

If you want to append to an existing file, you can create a StreamWriter object directly with the Boolean argument for append set to true.

```
'appending
 sw = New StreamWriter("foo.txt", True)
```

Exceptions in File Handling

A large number of the most common exceptions occur in handling file input and output. You can get exceptions for illegal filenames, files that do not exist, directories that do not exist, illegal filename arguments, and file protection errors. Thus, the best way to handle file input and output is to enclose file manipulation code in Try blocks to assure yourself that all possible error conditions are caught and thus prevent embarrassing fatal errors. All of the methods of the various file classes show in their documentation which methods they throw. You can be sure that you will catch all of them if you catch only the general Exception object, but if you must take different actions for different exceptions, you can test for them separately.

For example, you might open text files in the following manner.

```
Try
      ts = File.OpenText("foo.txt")
Catch e As FileNotFoundException
      'print out any error
      Console.WriteLine(e.Message)
      errFlag = True
End Try
```

Testing for End of File

There are two useful ways to make sure that you do not pass the end of a text file: looking for a null exception and looking for the end of a data stream. When you read beyond the end of a file, no error occurs and no end of file exception is thrown. However, if you read a string after the end of a file, it will return as a Null value. VB7 does not provide an IsNull method, but you can easily force a Null Reference exception by trying to obtain the length of a string. If you try to execute a length method on a null string, the system will throw a null reference exception, and you can use this to detect the end of a file.

```
Public Function readLine() As String
'Read one line from the file
 Dim s As String
 Try
     s = ts.readLine         'read line from file
     lineLength = s.length   'use to catch null exception
 Catch e As Exception
   end_file = True           'set EOF flag if null
   s = ""                    'and return zero length string
 Finally
   readLine = s
 End Try
End Function
```

The other way for making sure you don't read past the end of a file is to peek ahead, using the Stream's Peek method. This returns the ASCII code for the next character or a −1 if no characters remain.

```
'example of alternate approach to detecting end of file
 Public Function readLineE() As String
    'Read one line from the file
    Dim s As String
    If ts.peek >= 0 Then       'look ahead
        s = ts.readLine        'read if more chars
        Return s
    Else
        end_file = True        'Set EOF flag if none left
        Return ""
    End If
 End Function
```

The FileInfo Class

The FileInfo class has all non-shared methods and operates on a particular file-name. You can use it to get information about a particular file:

Method	Meaning
`Attributes`	Gets FileAttribute object
`DirectoryName`	Gets file's path
`Extension`	Gets the file's extension
`Length`	Length of the file
`Name`	Gets the file's name
`Exists`	True if file exists
`Delete()`	Deletes the file
`OpenText()`	Creates a StreamReader for reading a text file
`AppendText()`	Creates a StreamWriter to append text to file
`OpenWrite()`	Creates a StreamWriter for output

For a complete list consult the documentation.

A vbFile Class

Earlier, we wrote a vbFile class for reading and writing text files a line at a time and a token at a time. We can reimplement this vbFile class for VB7 to have exactly the same methods but utilize the VB7 file handling classes. In essence we are reimplementing the vbFile interface for VB7. Since the syntax remains the same, we might declare formally that we are using the same interface, but since the syntax differs somewhat, we will just write a new class using that same interface.

The main difference is that we can include the filename and path in the constructor. In this example, we use the static File class to obtain the stream reader and writer objects. You can also use an instance of the FileInfo class in a similar fashion. That example is on the CDROM.

```
Public Sub New(ByVal filename As String)
    'Create new file instance
    File_name = filename      'save file name
    tokLine = ""              'initialize tokenizer
    sep = ","                 'and separator
End Sub
```

We can open a file for reading using either of two methods: one including the filename and one that uses a filename in the argument.

```
Public Overloads Function OpenForRead() As Boolean
            Return OpenForRead(file_name)
End Function
'----------------
Public Overloads Function OpenForRead(_
ByVal Filename As String) As Boolean
    'opens specified file
    file_name = Filename      'save file name
    errFlag = False           'clear errors
    end_File = False          'and end of file
    Try
        ts = fl.Opentext()      'open the file
    Catch e As Exception
        errDesc = e.Message   'save error message
        errFlag = True        'and flag
    End Try
    Return Not errFlag     'false if error
End Function
```

You can then read data from the text file as we just illustrated.

Likewise, the following methods allow you to open a file for writing and write lines of text to it.

```
Public Overloads Function OpenForWrite( _
            ByVal fname As String) As Boolean
    errFlag = False
    Try
        File_name = fname
        sw = File.CreateText(File_name) 'get StreamWriter
    Catch e As Exception
        errDesc = e.Message
        errFlag = True
    End Try
    OpenForWrite = Not errFlag
End Function
'--------------
Public Overloads Function OpenForWrite() As Boolean
    OpenForWrite = OpenForWrite(file_name)
End Function
'--------------
Public Sub writeText(ByVal s As String)
    sw.writeLine(s)                'write text to stream
End Sub
```

Since we have implemented the same methods in our new vbFile class as for the VB6 class, we can substitute the new one and use it with VB7 programs without changing the surrounding programs at all.

Programs on the CD-ROM

`\FilesArraysExceptions\Array`	Showcase use of arrays and ArrayList
`\FilesArraysExceptions\Exceptions`	Illustrates how to use exceptions
`\FilesArraysExceptions\FileObject`	Shows VB7 implementation of the vbFile class using the File object.
`\FilesArraysExceptions\FileStream`	Shows VB7 implementation of the vbFile class using the FileInfo object.

PART 2

Creational Patterns

With the foregoing description of objects, inheritance, and interfaces in hand, we are now ready to begin discussing design patterns in earnest. Recall that these are merely recipes for writing better object-oriented programs. We have divided them into the Gang of Four's three groups: creational, structural, and behavioral. We'll start out in this section with the creational patterns.

All of the creational patterns deal with ways to create instances of objects. This is important because your program should not depend on how objects are created and arranged. In VB6, of course, the simplest way to create an instance of an object is by using the *new* operator.

```
set fred1 = new Fred            'instance of Fred class
```

However, this really amounts to hard coding, depending on how you create the object within your program. In many cases, the exact nature of the object that is created could vary with the needs of the program, and abstracting the creation process into a special "creator" class can make your program more flexible and general.

The **Factory Method pattern** provides a simple decision-making class that returns one of several possible subclasses of an abstract base class, depending on the data that are provided. We'll start with the **Simple Factory pattern** as an introduction to factories and then introduce the Factory Method pattern as well.

The **Abstract Factory pattern** provides an interface to create and return one of several families of related objects.

The **Builder pattern** separates the construction of a complex object from its representation so that several different representations can be created, depending on the needs of the program.

The **Prototype pattern** starts with an instantiated class and copies or clones it to make new instances. These instances can then be further tailored using their public methods.

The **Singleton pattern** is a class of which there can be no more than one instance. It provides a single global point of access to that instance.

CHAPTER 9

The Simple Factory Pattern

One type of pattern that we see again and again in OO programs is the Simple Factory pattern. A Simple Factory pattern is one that returns an instance of one of several possible classes, depending on the data provided to it. Usually all of the classes it returns have a common parent class and common methods, but each of them performs a task differently and is optimized for different kinds of data. This Simple Factory is not, in fact, one of the 23 GoF patterns, but it serves here as an introduction to the somewhat more subtle Factory Method GoF pattern we'll discuss shortly.

How a Simple Factory Works

To understand the Simple Factory pattern, let's look at the diagram in Figure 9-1.

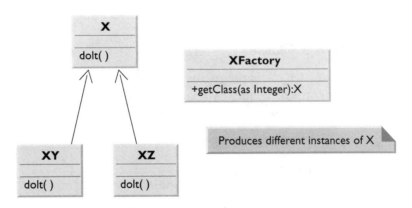

Figure 9-1   A Simple Factory pattern

In Figure 9-1, **X** is a base class, and classes **XY** and **XZ** are derived from it. The XFactory class decides which of these subclasses to return, depending on the arguments you give it. On the right, we define a *getClass* method to be one that passes in some value *abc* and that returns some instance of the class **x**. Which one it returns doesn't matter to the programmer, since they all have the same methods but different implementations. How it decides which one to return is entirely up to the factory. It could be some very complex function, but it is often quite simple.

Sample Code

Let's consider a simple VB6 case where we could use a Factory class. Suppose we have an entry form and we want to allow the user to enter his name either as "firstname lastname" or as "lastname, firstname." We'll make the further simplifying assumption that we will always be able to decide the name order by whether there is a comma between the last and first name.

This is a pretty simple sort of decision to make, and you could make it with a simple *if* statement in a single class, but let's use it here to illustrate how a factory works and what it can produce. We'll start by defining a simple interface that takes the name string in and allows you to fetch the names back.

```
Public Sub init(ByVal s As String)
End Sub
'-----
Public Function getFrName() As String
End Function
'-----
Public Function getLname() As String
End Function
```

The Two Derived Classes

Now we can write two very simple classes that implement that interface and split the name into two parts in the constructor. In the FNamer class, we make the simplifying assumption that everything before the last space is part of the first name.

```
'Class FNamer
Implements Namer
Private nm As String, lname As String, frname As String
'-----
Private Function Namer_getFrname() As String
Namer_getFrname = frname
End Function
```

```
'-----
Private Function Namer_getLname() As String
Namer_getLname = lname
End Function
'-----
Private Sub Namer_init(ByVal s As String)
Dim i As Integer
nm = s
i = InStr(nm, " ")                    'look for space
If i > 0 Then
  frname = Left$(nm, i - 1)       'separate names
  lname = Trim$(Right$(nm, Len(nm) - i))
Else
  lname = nm                'or put all in last name
  frname = ""
End If
End Sub
```

And in the LNamer class, we assume that a comma delimits the last name. In both classes, we also provide error recovery in case the space or comma does not exist.

```
'Class LNamer
Implements Namer
Private nm As String, lname As String, frname As String
'-----
Private Function Namer_getFrname() As String
Namer_getFrname = frname
End Function
'-----
Private Function Namer_getLname() As String
Namer_getLname = lname
End Function
'-----
Private Sub Namer_init(ByVal s As String)
Dim i As Integer
nm = s                     'save whole name
i = InStr(nm, ",")         'if comma, last is to left
If i > 0 Then
  lname = Left$(nm, i - 1)
  frname = Trim$(Right$(nm, Len(nm) - i))
Else
  lname = nm                'or put all in last name
  frname = ""
End If
End Sub
```

Building the Simple Factory

Now our Simple Factory class is easy to write and is part of the user interface. We just test for the existence of a comma and then return an instance of one class or the other.

```
Private nmer As Namer     'will be one kind or the other
'-----
Private Sub getName_Click()
Dim st As String, i As Integer
st = txNames.Text        'get the name from the entry field
i = InStr(st, ",")       'look for a comma
If i > 0 Then
  Set nmer = New lNamer  'create last name class
Else
  Set nmer = New Frnamer 'or fist name class
End If
nmer.init st
'put results in display fields
txFrName.Text = nmer.getFrName
txlName.Text = nmer.getLname
End Sub
```

Using the Factory

Let's see how we put this together. The complete class diagram is shown in Figure 9-2.

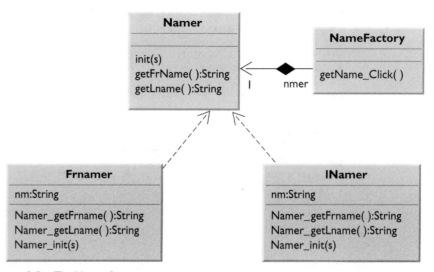

Figure 9-2   The Namer factory program

We have constructed a simple user interface that allows you to enter the names in either order and see the two names separately displayed. You can see this program in Figure 9-3.

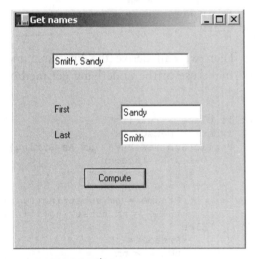

Figure 9-3   The Namer program executing

You type in a name and then click on the Compute button, and the divided name appears in the text fields below. The crux of this program is the compute method that fetches the text, obtains an instance of a Namer class, and displays the results.

And that's the fundamental principle of the Simple Factory pattern. You create an abstraction that decides which of several possible classes to return, and it returns one. Then you call the methods of that class instance without ever knowing which subclass you are actually using. This approach keeps the issues of data dependence separated from the classes' useful methods.

Writing the Factory Pattern in VB.NET

In VB7, we can get a fair amount of mileage out of using inheritance here. We can define a base class called NameClass that holds the first and last name in protected variables and define the two accessor functions to get the first and last name out of the variables.

```
Public Class NameClass
    Protected Lname, Frname As String
```

```
      Public Function getFirst() As String
          Return Frname
      End Function

      Public Function getLast() As String
          Return Lname
      End Function
End Class
```

Then we can derive the FirstFirst and LastFirst classes from this class and make use of the underlying get methods. The complete FirstFirst class is just this.

```
Public Class FirstFirst
    Inherits NameClass
    Public Sub New(ByVal nm As String)
        Dim i As Integer
        i = nm.indexOf(" ")
        If i > 0 Then
            Frname = nm.substring(0, i).trim()
            Lname = nm.substring(i + 1).trim()
        Else
            Frname = ""
            LName = nm
        End If
    End Sub
End Class
```

And the LastFirst class is entirely analogous. The factory class is quite similar but makes use of the constructors.

```
Public Class NameFactory

    Public Function getNamer( _
        ByVal nm As String) As NameClass
        Dim i As Integer

        i = nm.indexOf(",")
        If i > 0 Then
            Return New LastFirst(nm)
        Else
            Return New FirstFirst(nm)
        End If
    End Function
End Class
```

You can see the difference in how these classes relate in Figure 9-4.

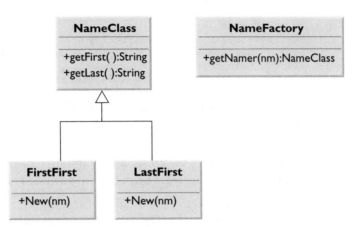

Figure 9-4   The VB7 Namer program, showing inheritance

Factory Patterns in Math Computation

Most people who use Factory patterns tend to think of them as tools for simplifying tangled programming classes. But it is perfectly possible to use them in programs that simply perform mathematical computations. For example, in the Fast Fourier Transform (FFT), you evaluate the following four equations repeatedly for a large number of point pairs over many passes through the array you are transforming. Because of the way the graphs of these computations are drawn, the following four equations constitute one instance of the FFT "butterfly." These are shown as Equations 1–4.

$$R_1 = R_1 + R_2 \cos(y) - I_2 \sin(y) \quad (1)$$
$$R_2 = R_1 - R_2 \cos(y) + I_2 \sin(y) \quad (2)$$
$$I_1 = I_1 + R_2 \sin(y) - I_2 \cos(y) \quad (3)$$
$$I_2 = I_1 - R_2 \sin(y) - I_2 \cos(y) \quad (4)$$

However, there are a number of times during each pass through the data where the angle y is zero. In this case, your complex math evaluation reduces to Equations (5–8).

$$R_1 = R_1 + R_2 \quad (5)$$
$$R_2 = R_1 - R_2 \quad (6)$$
$$I_1 = I_1 + I_2 \quad (7)$$
$$I_2 = I_1 - I_2 \quad (8)$$

Then we can make a simple factory class that decides which class instance to return. Since we are making Butterflies, we'll call our Factory a Cocoon.

```
'Class Cocoon
'get back right kind of Butterfly
Public Function getButterfly(y As Single) As Butterfly
 If y = 0 Then
    Set getButterfly = New addButterfly
 Else
    Set getButterfly = New trigButterfly
 End If
End Function
```

In this example, we create a new instance each time. Since there are only two kinds, we might create them both in advance and return them as needed.

```
'Class Cocoon1
Private addB As Butterfly, trigB As Butterfly
'-----
'create instances in advance
Private Sub Class_Initialize()
 Set addB = New addButterfly
 Set trigB = New trigButterfly
End Sub
'-----
'get back right kind of Butterfly
Public Function getButterfly(y As Single) As Butterfly
 If y = 0 Then
    Set getButterfly = addB
 Else
    Set getButterfly = trigB
 End If
End Function
```

THOUGHT QUESTIONS

1. Consider a personal checkbook management program like Quicken. It manages several bank accounts and investments and can handle your bill paying. Where could you use a Factory pattern in designing a program like that?

2. Suppose you are writing a program to assist homeowners in designing additions to their houses. What objects might a Factory be used to produce?

Programs on the CD-ROM

\Factory\Namer	The VB6 name factory
\Factory\Namer\vbNetNamer	The VB7 name factory
\Factory\FFT	A VB6 FFT example

CHAPTER 10

The Factory Method

We've just seen a couple of examples of the simplest of factories. The factory concept recurs all throughout object-oriented programming, and we find a few examples embedded in VB itself and in other design patterns (such as the Builder pattern). In these cases a single class acts as a traffic cop and decides which subclass of a single hierarchy will be instantiated.

The Factory Method pattern is a clever but subtle extension of this idea, where no single class makes the decision as to which subclass to instantiate. Instead, the superclass defers the decision to each subclass. This pattern does not actually have a decision point where one subclass is directly selected over another class. Instead, programs written to this pattern define an abstract class that creates objects but lets each subclass decide which object to create.

We can draw a pretty simple example from the way that swimmers are seeded into lanes in a swim meet. When swimmers compete in multiple heats in a given event, they are sorted to compete from slowest in the early heats to fastest in the last heat and arranged within a heat with the fastest swimmers in the center lanes. This is referred to as *straight seeding*.

Now, when swimmers swim in championships, they frequently swim the event twice. During preliminaries everyone competes, and the top 12 or 16 swimmers return to compete against each other at finals. In order to make the preliminaries more equitable, the top heats are *circle* seeded: The fastest three swimmers are in the center lane in the fastest three heats, the second fastest three swimmers are in the next to center lane in the top three heats, and so forth.

So, how do we build some objects to implement this seeding scheme and illustrate the Factory Method. First, let's design an abstract Events class.

```
Option Explicit
'Class Events
Private numLanes As Integer
```

```
Private swimmers As New Collection   'list of swimmers
'-----
Public Sub init(Filename As String, lanes As Integer)
End Sub
'-----
Public Function getSwimmers() As Collection
 Set getSwimmers = swimmers
End Function
'-----
Public Function isPrelim() As Boolean
End Function
'-----
Public Function isFinal() As Boolean
End Function
'-----
Public Function isTimedFinal() As Boolean
End Function
'-----
Public Function getSeeding() As Seeding
End Function
```

Grammatically, it would have been better to call this an "Event" class, but "Event" is a reserved word in VB6.

This defines the remaining methods simply without any necessity of filling them in. Then we can implement concrete classes from the Events class, called PrelimEvent and TimedFinalEvent. The only difference between these classes is that one returns one kind of seeding and the other returns a different kind of seeding.

We also define an abstract Seeding class with the following methods.

```
'Class Seeding
Private numLanes As Integer
Private laneOrder As Collection
Dim asw() As Swimmer
'-----
Public Function getSeeding() As Collection
End Function
'-----
Public Function getHeat() As Integer
End Function
'-----
Public Function getCount() As Integer
End Function
'-----
Public Sub seed()
End Sub
'-----
Public Function getSwimmers() As Collection
End Function
'-----
```

```
Public Function getHeats() As Integer
End Function
'-----
Private Function odd(n As Integer) As Boolean
  odd = (n \ 2) * 2 <> n
End Function
'-----
Public Function calcLaneOrder(lns As Integer) As Collection
  numLanes = lns
 'This function is implemented but not shown here
  ReDim lanes(numLanes) As Integer
End Function
'-----
Public Sub init(swmrs As Collection, lanes As Integer)
End Sub
'-----
Public Function sort(sw As Collection) As Collection
  ReDim asw(sw.count) As Swimmer
   'This function is implemented but not shown here
End Function
```

Note that we actually included code for the calcLaneOrder and sort functions but omit the code here for simplicity. The derived classes then each create an instance of the base Seeding class to call these functions.

We can then create two concrete seeding subclasses: StraightSeeding and CircleSeeding. The PrelimEvent class will return an instance of CircleSeeding, and the TimedFinalEvent class will return an instance of StraightSeeding. Thus, we see that we have two hierarchies: one of Events and one of Seedings. We see these two hierarchies illustrated in Figures 10-1 and 10-2.

In the Events hierarchy, you will see that both derived Events classes contain a *getSeeding* method. One of them returns an instance of StraightSeeding and the other an instance of CircleSeeding. So you see, there is no real factory decision point as we had in our simple example. Instead, the decision as to which Event class to instantiate is the one that determines which Seeding class will be instantiated.

While it looks like there is a one-to-one correspondence between the two class hierarchies, there needn't be. There could be many kinds of Events and only a few kinds of Seeding used.

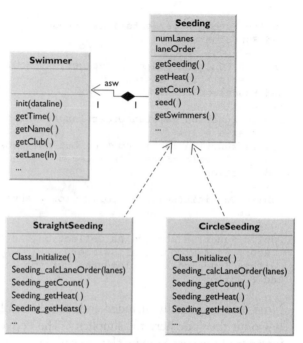

Figure 10-1   The class relations between Seeding classes

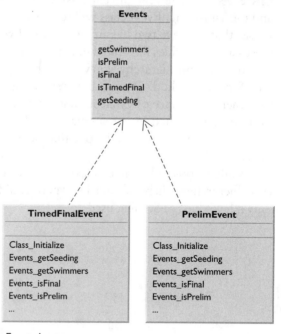

Figure 10-2   The Event classes

The Swimmer Class

We haven't said much about the Swimmer class, except that it contains a name, club age, seed time, and place to put the heat and lane after seeding. The Event class reads in the Swimmers from some database (a file in our example) and then passes that Collection to the Seeding class when you call the getSeeding method for that event.

The Events Classes

We have seen the previous abstract base Events class. In actual use, we use it to read in the swimmer data (here from a file) and pass it on to instances of the Swimmer class to parse.

```
Option Explicit
'Class Events
Private numLanes As Integer
Private swimmers As New Collection  'list of swimmers
'-----
Public Sub init(Filename As String, lanes As Integer)
Dim f As Integer, s As String
Dim sw As Swimmer
Dim fl As New vbFile
'read in the data file in the constructor
f = FreeFile
numLanes = lanes
Set swimmers = New Collection
  'read in swimmers from file
  Filename = App.Path & "\" & Filename
  fl.OpenForRead Filename
  s = fl.readLine

  While (Not fl.fEof)
    Set sw = New Swimmer    'create each swimmer
    sw.init s               'and initialize it
    swimmers.Add sw         'add to list
    s = fl.readLine            'read another
  Wend
 Close #f
End Sub
'-----
Public Function getSwimmers() As Collection
 Set getSwimmers = swimmers
End Function
'-----
Public Function isPrelim() As Boolean
End Function
'-----
Public Function isFinal() As Boolean
```

```
End Function
'-----
Public Function isTimedFinal() As Boolean
End Function
'-----
Public Function getSeeding() As Seeding
End Function
```

The base Event class has empty methods for whether the event is a prelim, final, or timed final event. We fill in the event in the derived classes.

Our PrelimEvent class just returns an instance of CircleSeeding.

```
'Class PrelimEvent
Implements Events
Private numLanes As Integer
Private swimmers As Collection
Private evnts As New Events
Private sd As Seeding
Private Sub Class_Initialize()
 Set evnts = New Events
End Sub
'-----
Private Function Events_getSeeding() As Seeding
 Set sd = New CircleSeeding
 sd.init swimmers, numLanes
 Set Events_getSeeding = sd
End Function
'-----
Private Function Events_getSwimmers() As Collection
 Set Events_getSwimmers = swimmers
End Function
'-----
Private Function Events_isFinal() As Boolean
 Events_isFinal = False
End Function
'-----
Private Function Events_isPrelim() As Boolean
 Events_isPrelim = True
End Function
'-----
Private Function Events_isTimedFinal() As Boolean
 Events_isTimedFinal = False
End Function
'-----
Private Sub Events_init(Filename As String, lanes As Integer)
 evnts.init Filename, lanes
 numLanes = lanes
 Set swimmers = evnts.getSwimmers
End Sub
```

The TimedFinalEvent returns an instance of StraightSeeding.

```
'Class PrelimEvent
Implements Events
Private numLanes As Integer
Private swimmers As Collection
Private evnts As New Events
Private sd As Seeding
Private Sub Class_Initialize()
 Set evnts = New Events
End Sub
'-----
Private Function Events_getSeeding() As Seeding
 Set sd = New CircleSeeding
 sd.init swimmers, numLanes
 Set Events_getSeeding = sd
End Function
```

In both cases our events classes contain an instance of the base Events class, which we use to read in the data files.

Straight Seeding

In actually writing this program, we'll discover that most of the work is done in straight seeding. The changes for circle seeding are pretty minimal. So we instantiate our StraightSeeding class and copy in the Collection of swimmers and the number of lanes.

```
Private Sub Seeding_seed()
Dim lastHeat As Integer, lastlanes As Integer
Dim heats As Integer, i As Integer, j As Integer
Dim swmr As Swimmer

Set sw = sd.sort(sw)
Set laneOrder = sd.calcLaneOrder(numLanes)
count = sw.count
lastHeat = count Mod numLanes
If (lastHeat < 3) And lastHeat > 0 Then
    lastHeat = 3    'last heat must have 3 or more
End If
count = sw.count
lastlanes = count - lastHeat
numheats = lastlanes / numLanes
If (lastHeat > 0) Then
    numheats = numheats + 1
End If
heats = numheats

'place heat and lane in each swimmer's object
  'details on CDROM
'Add in last partial heat
```

```
'details on CDROM
End Sub
```

This makes the entire array of seeded Swimmers available when you call the getSwimmers method.

Circle Seeding

The CircleSeeding class is derived from StraightSeeding, so it copies in the same data.

```
'Circle seeding method
Private Sub Seeding_seed()
Dim i As Integer, j As Integer, k As Integer
'get the lane order]
Set laneOrder = sd.calcLaneOrder(numLanes)
Set sw = sd.sort(sw)     'sort the swimmers
strSd.init sw, numLanes 'create Straight Seeding object
strSd.seed              'seed into straight order
numheats = strSd.getHeats    'get the total number of heats
   If (numheats >= 2) Then
       If (numheats >= 3) Then
           circlesd = 3        'seed either 3
       Else
           circlesd = 2        'or 2
       End If
       i = 1
       'copy seeding info into swimmers data
       'details on CDROM
   End If
End Sub
```

Since the circle seeding calls straight seeding, it copies the swimmer collection and lanes values. Then our call to strSd.seed does the straight seeding. This simplifies things because we will always need to seed the remaining heats by straight seeding. Then we seed the last two or three heats as just shown, and we are done with that type of seeding as well.

Our Seeding Program

In this example, we took a list of swimmers from the Web who competed in the 500-yard freestyle and the 100-yard freestyle and used them to build our TimedFinalEvent and PrelimEvent classes. You can see the results of these two seedings in Figure 10-3.

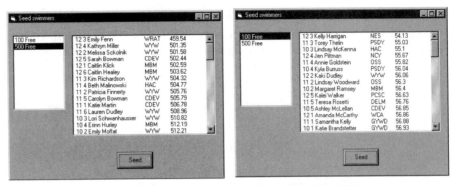

Figure 10-3 Straight seeding of the 500 free and circle seeding of the 100 free

Other Factories

Now one issue that we have skipped over is how the program that reads in the swimmer data decides which kind of event to generate. We finesse this here by simply creating the correct type of event when we read in the data. This code is in the Form_Load event.

```
Dim ev As Events

Set ev = New PrelimEvent       'create a Prelim/final event
ev.init "100free.txt", 6       'read in the data
Seedings.Add ev.getSeeding     'get the seeding and add to collection
lsEvents.AddItem "100 Free"

Set ev = New TimedFinalEvent   'create a new Timed final event
ev.init "500free.txt", 6       'read in the data
Seedings.Add ev.getSeeding     'get the seeeding
lsEvents.AddItem "500 Free"    'and add to collection
```

Clearly, this is an instance where an EventFactory may be needed to decide which kind of event to generate. This revisits the simple factory with which we began the discussion.

The Seeding Program in VB7

In VB7, we can make effective use of inheritance to make each of these classes substantially simpler. For example, the Events class is an abstract class where we fill in the methods in the derived TimedFinalEvent and PrelimEvent classes. In VB7, these classes differ in that we put the file reading methods in the base Seeding class and let them be used by the derived classes, whereas in VB6, we had to create an instance of the base Event class inside the TimedFinal and Prelim event classes and call its functions specifically. The basic abstract class for Events is now simply the following.

```
Public Class Events

    Protected numLanes As Integer
    Protected swmmers As Swimmers
    '-----
    Public Sub New(ByVal Filename As String, _
                        ByVal lanes As Integer)
        MyBase.New()
        Dim s As String
        Dim sw As Swimmer
        Dim fl As vbFile

        fl = New vbFile(filename)    'Open the file
        fl.OpenForRead()

        numLanes = lanes             'Remember lane number
        swmmers = New Swimmers()     'list of kids

        'read in swimmers from file
        s = fl.ReadLine

        While Not fl.feof
            sw = New Swimmer(s)      'create each swimmer
            swmmers.Add(sw)          'add to list
            s = fl.ReadLine          'read another
        End While
        fl.closeFile()
    End Sub
    '-----
    Public Function getSwimmers() As ArrayList
        Return swmmers
    End Function
    '-----
    Public Overridable Function isPrelim() As Boolean
    End Function
    '-----
    Public Overridable Function isFinal() As Boolean
    End Function
    '-----
    Public Overridable Function isTimedFinal() As Boolean
    End Function
    '-----
    Public Overridable Function getSeeding() As Seeding
    End Function
End Class
```

Then our TimedFinalEvent is derived from that and creates an instance of the StraightSeeding class.

```
Public Class TimedFinalEvent
    Inherits Events

    Public Sub New(ByVal Filename As String, _
            ByVal lanes As Integer)
        MyBase.New(Filename, lanes)
    End Sub
    '-----
    Public Overrides Function getSeeding() As Seeding
        Dim sd As Seeding
        'create seeding and execute it
        sd = New StraightSeeding(swmmers, numLanes)
        sd.seed()
        Return sd
    End Function
    '-----
    Public Overrides Function isFinal() As Boolean
        Return False
    End Function
    '-----
    Public Overrides Function isPrelim() As Boolean
        Return False
    End Function
    '-----
    Public Overrides Function isTimedFinal() As Boolean
        Return True
    End Function
End Class
```

The PrelimEvent class is basically the same, except that we create an instance of circle seeding and set the prelim and finals flags differently. Here is the getSeeding method.

```
Public Overrides Function getSeeding() As Seeding
        Return New CircleSeeding(swmmers, numLanes)
End Function
```

In a similar fashion, the base Seeding class contains the functions sort and getLaneOrder, and the derived classes for Straight and Circle seeding contain only the changed seed methods. You can see the class inheritance structure of this VB7 version in Figure 10-4.

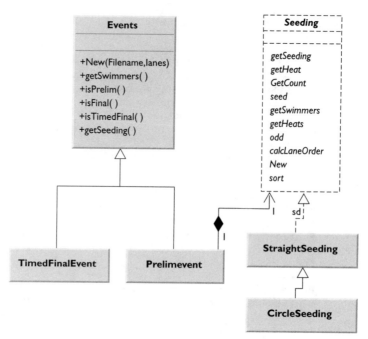

Figure 10-4   The VB7 Seeding program

When to Use a Factory Method

You should consider using a Factory method in the following situations.

- A class can't anticipate which kind of class of objects it must create.
- A class uses its subclasses to specify which objects it creates.
- You want to localize the knowledge of which class gets created.

There are several variations on the factory pattern to recognize.

1. The base class is abstract and the pattern must return a complete working class.

2. The base class contains default methods and these methods are called unless the default methods are insufficient.

3. Parameters are passed to the factory telling it which of several class types to return. In this case the classes may share the same method names but may do something quite different.

THOUGHT QUESTION

Seeding in track is carried out from inside to outside lanes. What classes would you need to develop to carry out tracklike seeding as well?

Programs on the CD-ROM

`\Factory\Seeder`	VB6 version of seeding program
`\Factory\Seeder\vbNetSeeder`	VB7 version of seeding program

CHAPTER 11

The Abstract Factory Pattern

The Abstract Factory pattern is one level of abstraction higher than the factory pattern. You can use this pattern when you want to return one of several related classes of objects, each of which can return several different objects on request. In other words, the Abstract Factory is a factory object that returns one of several groups of classes. You might even decide which class to return from that group using a Simple Factory.

Common thought experiment-style examples might include automobile factories. You would expect a Toyota factory to work exclusively with Toyota parts and a Ford factory to use Ford parts. You can consider each auto factory as an Abstract Factory and the parts the groups of related classes.

A GardenMaker Factory

Let's consider a practical example where you might want to use the abstract factory in your application. Suppose you are writing a program to plan the layout of gardens. These could be gardens consisting of annuals, vegetables, or perennials. However, no matter which kind of garden you are planning, you want to ask the same questions.

1. What are good border plants?

2. What are good center plants?

3. What plants do well in partial shade? (And probably a lot more plant questions that we won't get into here.)

We want a base VB6 Garden class that can answer these questions as class methods.

```
Public Function getCenter() As Plant
End Function
'-----
Public Function getBorder() As Plant
End Function
'-----
Public Function getShade() As Plant
End Function
```

Our Plant object just contains and returns the plant name.

```
'Class Plant
Private plantName As String
'-----
Public Sub init(nm As String)
   plantName = nm          'save the plant name
End Sub
'-----
Public Function getName() As String
   getName = plantName      'return the plant name
End Function
```

In *Design Patterns* terms, the Garden interface is the Abstract Factory. It defines the methods of concrete class that can return one of several classes. Here, we return central, border, and shade-loving plants as those three classes. The abstract factory could also return more specific garden information, such as soil pH or recommended moisture content.

In a real system, each type of garden would probably consult an elaborate database of plant information. In our simple example we'll return one kind of each plant. So, for example, for the vegetable garden we simply write the following.

```
'Class VeggieGarden
Implements Garden
Private pltShade as Plant, pltBorder as Plant
Private pltCenter As Plant
'-----
Private Sub Class_Initialize()
 Set pltShade = New Plant
 pltShade.init "Broccoli"
 Set pltBorder = New Plant
 pltBorder.init "Peas"
 Set pltCenter = New Plant
 pltCenter.init "Corn"
End Sub
'-----
Private Function Garden_getBorder() As Plant
  Set Garden_getBorder = pltBorder
End Function
'-----
Private Function Garden_getCenter() As Plant
```

```
      Set Garden_getCenter = pltCenter
End Function
'-----
Private Function Garden_getShade() As Plant
   Set Garden_getShade = pltShade
End Function
```

In a similar way, we can create Garden classes for PerennialGarden and AnnualGarden. Each of these concrete classes is known as a Concrete Factory, since it implements the methods outlined in the parent abstract class. Now we have a series of Garden objects, each of which returns one of several Plant objects. This is illustrated in the class diagram in Figure 11-1.

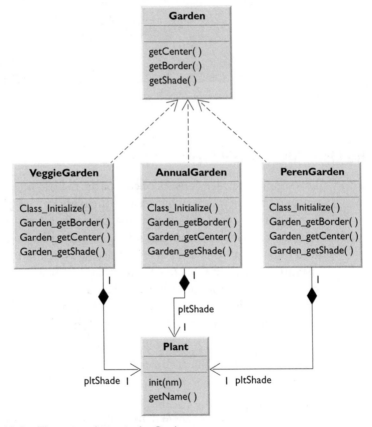

Figure 11-1   The major objects in the Gardener program

We can easily construct our Abstract Factory driver program to return one of these Garden objects based on the radio button that a user selects, as shown in the user interface in Figure 11-2.

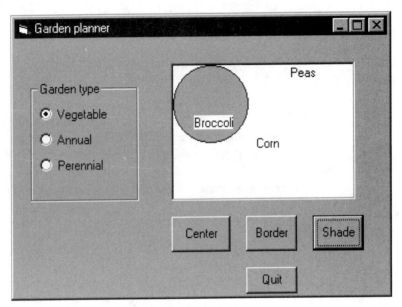

Figure 11-2   The user interface of the Gardener program

How the User Interface Works

This simple interface consists of two parts: the left side, which selects the garden type, and the right side, which selects the plant category. When you click on one of the garden types, this causes the program to return a type of garden that depends on which button you select. At first, you might think that we would need to perform some sort of test to decide which button was selected and then instantiate the right Concrete Factory class. However, a more elegant solution is to just listen for the radio button click and change the current garden. Then, when a user clicks on one of the plant type buttons, the plant type is returned from the current garden, and the name of that plant is displayed.

```
Private Sub opAnnual_Click()
   Set gden = New AnnualGarden    'select Annual garden
End Sub
'-----
Private Sub opPeren_Click()
   Set gden = New PerenGarden     'select Perennial garden
End Sub
'-----
Private Sub opVeggie_Click()
   Set gden = New VeggieGarden    'select vegetable garden
End Sub
```

Then, when we are called upon to draw a plant name on the garden display, we erase the old name by XORing it and then draw a new one in its place by getting the correct Plant from the current Garden.

```
'-----
Private Sub btCenter_Click()
  Set plt = gden.getCenter   'get the center plant
  drawCenter plt.getName     'and draw it's name
End Sub
'-----
Private Sub drawCenter(st As String)
  pcGarden.PSet (1200, 1000)
  pcGarden.Print oldCenter   'XOR out old name
  pcGarden.PSet (1200, 1000)
  pcGarden.Print st          'draw in new name
  oldCenter = st             'remember this name so we can erase
End Sub
```

Creating an Abstract Factory Using VB7

The same GardenMaker program differs substantially in VB7. While it is certainly possible to write Garden as an interface and have each of the derived gardens implement that interface, it is easier to have some of the methods in the base Garden class and the rest in the derived classes.

The other major differences in VB7 have to do with the event system. In VB7, you do not draw on the screen directly from your code. Instead, the screen is updated when the next OnPaint event occurs, and you must tell the paint routine what objects it can now paint.

Since each garden should know how to draw itself, it should have a draw method that draws the appropriate plant names on the garden screen. And since we provided push buttons to draw each of the types of plants, we need to set a Boolean that indicates that you can now draw each of these plant types.

We start with our simplified Plant class, where we pass in the name of the plant right in the constructor.

```
Public Class Plant
    Private plantName As String
    '-----
    Public Sub New(ByVal nm As String)
        MyBase.New()
        plantName = nm        'save the plant name
    End Sub
    '-----
    Public Function getName() As String
```

```
        getName = plantName     'return the plant name
    End Function
End Class
```

Then we create the basic Garden class, which contained the getShade, get-Center, and getBorder methods in the original implementation. We don't need these methods in this implementation because the Garden itself does the drawing.

```
Public Class Garden
    'protected objects are accessed by derived classes
    Protected pltShade, pltBorder, pltCenter As Plant
    Protected center, shade, border As Boolean

    'These are created in the constructor
    Private gbrush As SolidBrush
    Private gdFont As Font

    'Constructor creates brush and font fro drawing
    Public Sub New()
        MyBase.New()
        gBrush = New SolidBrush(Color.Black)
        gdFont = New Font("Arial", 10)
End Sub
'-----
```

The drawing is done in a simple draw method where we check if we should draw each kind of plant name and draw it if that Boolean is true.

```
Public Sub draw(ByVal g As Graphics)
        If border Then
            g.DrawString(pltBorder.getName, gdFont, _
                gbrush, 50, 150)
        End If
        If center Then
            g.DrawString(pltCenter.getName, gdFont, _
                gbrush, 100, 100)
        End If
        If shade Then
            g.DrawString(pltShade.getName, gdFont,_
                gbrush, 10, 50)
        End If
End Sub
```

Then we add three set methods to indicate that you can draw each plant.

```
    Public Sub showCenter()
        center = True
    End Sub
    '-----
    Public Sub showBorder()
        border = True
```

```
    End Sub
    '-----
    Public Sub showShade()
        shade = True
    End Sub
    '-----
    Public Sub clear()
        center = False
        border = False
        shade = False
    End Sub
```

Now the three derived classes for the three gardens are extremely simple, and they only contain calls to the constructors for the three plants. The following is the entire AnnualGarden class.

```
Public Class AnnualGarden
    Inherits Garden
    Public Sub New()
        MyBase.New()
        pltShade = New Plant("Coleus")
        pltBorder = New Plant("Alyssum")
        pltCenter = New Plant("Marigold")
    End Sub
End Class
```

Note that the plant names are now set in their constructors and that the three plant variables that we set are part of the base garden class.

The PictureBox

We draw the circle representing the shady area inside the PictureBox and draw the names of the plants inside this box as well. Thus, we need to add an OnPaint method not to the main GardenMaker window class but to the PictureBox it contains. One way to do this is by creating a subclass of PictureBox that contains the paint method including the circle drawing and tells the garden to draw itself.

```
Public Class GdPic
    Inherits System.Windows.Forms.PictureBox
    Private gden As Garden
    Private loaded As Boolean
    Private br As SolidBrush
    '-----
    Private Sub init()
        br = New SolidBrush(Color.Gray)
    End Sub
    '-----
    Public Sub setGarden(ByVal gd As Garden)
        gden = gd
```

```
                gden.clear()
                Refresh()
                loaded = True
            End Sub
            '-----
            Protected Overrides Sub OnPaint( _
                ByVal pe As System.Windows.Forms.PaintEventArgs)
                Dim g As Graphics = pe.Graphics
                'draw the circle
                g.FillEllipse(br, 5, 5, 100, 100)
                If loaded Then
                    'have the garden draw itself
                    gden.draw(g)
                End If
            End Sub
        End Class
```

Note that we do not have to erase the plant name text each time in VB7 because Paint is only called when the whole picture needs to be repainted.

Handling the RadioButton and Button Events

When one of the three radio buttons is clicked, you create a new garden of the correct type and pass it into the picture box class.

```
Private Sub opPerennial_CheckedChanged( _
            ByVal sender As System.Object, _
            ByVal e As System.EventArgs) _
            Handles opPerennial.CheckedChanged
        gden = New PerennialGarden()
        pbox.setGarden(gden)
End Sub
```

When you click on one of the buttons to show the plant names, you simply call that garden's method to show that plant name and then call the picture box's Refresh method to cause it to repaint.

```
Protected Sub ckBorder_CheckedChanged( _
            ByVal sender As Object, _
            ByVal e As System.EventArgs)
        gden.showBorder()
        pBox.refresh()
End Sub
```

The final VB7 Gardener class is shown in Figure 11-3, and the UML diagram in Figure 11-4.

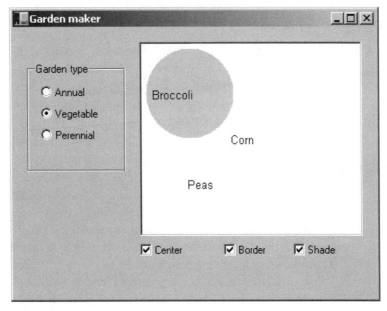

Figure 11-3   The VB7 Gardener program.

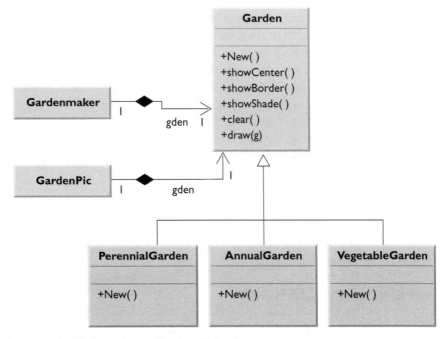

Figure 11-4   The UML diagram for the VB7 Gardener program.

Adding More Classes

One of the great strengths of the Abstract Factory is that you can add new subclasses very easily. For example, if you needed a GrassGarden or a WildFlower-Garden, you can subclass Garden and produce these classes. The only real change you'd need to make in any existing code is to add some way to choose these new kinds of gardens.

Consequences of Abstract Factory

One of the main purposes of the Abstract Factory is that it isolates the concrete classes that are generated. The actual class names of these classes are hidden in the factory and need not be known at the client level at all.

Because of the isolation of classes, you can change or interchange these product class families freely. Further, since you generate only one kind of concrete class, this system keeps you from inadvertently using classes from different families of products. However, it is some effort to add new class families, since you need to define new, unambiguous conditions that cause such a new family of classes to be returned.

While all of the classes that the Abstract Factory generates have the same base class, there is nothing to prevent some subclasses from having additional methods that differ from the methods of other classes. For example, a BonsaiGarden class might have a Height or WateringFrequency method that is not in other classes. This presents the same problem that occurs in any subclass: You don't know whether you can call a class method unless you know whether the subclass is one that allows those methods. This problem has the same two solutions as in any similar case: You can either define all of the methods in the base class, even if they don't always have an actual function, or, you can derive a new base interface that contains all the methods you need and subclass that for all of your garden types.

THOUGHT QUESTION

If you are writing a program to track investments, such as stocks, bonds, metal futures, derivatives, and the like, how might you use an Abstract Factory?

Programs on the CD-ROM

\AbstractFactory\GardenPlanner	VB6 version of Gardener program
\AbstractFactory\VBNet\Gardenmaker	VB7 version of Gardener program

CHAPTER 12

The Singleton Pattern

In this chapter, we'll take up the Singleton pattern. This pattern is grouped with the other creational patterns, although it is to some extent a pattern that limits the creation of classes rather than promoting such creation. Specifically, the Singleton assures that there is one and only one instance of a class, and it provides a global point of access to it. There are any number of cases in programming where you need to make sure that there can be one and only one instance of a class. For example, your system can have only one window manager or print spooler, or a single point of access to a database engine. Your PC might have several serial ports, but there can be only one instance of "COM1."

Creating Singleton Using a Static Method

The easiest way to make a class that can have only one instance is to use an external static variable that we set on the first instance and check for each time we create an instance of the class. Then we have the Class_Initialize method create a single instance or cause an error.

In this first example, we create a variable spool_counter in a publicly accessible module and refer to it throughout.

```
'Singleton PrintSpooler static constant
Public spool_counter As Integer
```

Within the PrintSpooler class we check that counter and either create an instance or cause an error.

```
'-----
Private Sub Class_Initialize()
 If spool_counter > 0 Then
```

```
      Err.Raise vbObjectError + 1                'raise error
  End If
  spool_counter = spool_counter + 1
End Sub
```

Although this ensures that you can have one instance, it does not provide global access to it. To do that, we must allow the class to create only one accessible instance and use a getSpooler method to return that instance.

```
'Class PrintSpooler
'-----
Private Sub Class_Initialize()
  If spool_counter = 0 Then
     Set glbSpooler = Me                      'save legal instance
     spool_counter = spool_counter + 1     'count it
  End If
End Sub
'-----
Public Function GetSpooler() As PrintSpooler
     Set GetSpooler = glbSpooler      'return legal instance
End Function
```

We also have two global variables stored in module-level code where the one legal instance is stored.

```
'Singleton PrintSpooler static constants
Public spool_counter As Integer
Public glbSpooler As PrintSpooler
```

One major advantage to this approach is that you don't have to worry about error handling if the singleton already exists—you always get the same instance of the spooler. If, however, you create an instance of the PrintSpooler class and choose not to use the error handling, you need to put a flag in the spooler to indicate that only one instance is legal. Here we use the legalInstance variable to make sure that printing can only occur from the legal instance.

```
Option Explicit
Private legalInstance As Boolean       'true for only one
'Class PrintSpooler
'-----
Private Sub Class_Initialize()
   If spool_counter = 0 Then                 'create and save one instance
      legalInstance = True                   'flag it
      Set glbSpooler = Me                    'save it
      spool_counter = spool_counter + 1   'count it
   Else
      legalInstance = False                  'not the legal one
      Err.Description = "Illegal spooler instance"
      Err.Raise vbObjectError + 1     'could raise an error
```

```
      End If
   End Sub
   '-----
   Public Function GetSpooler() As PrintSpooler
         Set GetSpooler = glbSpooler   'return the legal one
   End Function
   '-----
   Public Sub Printit(str As String)
      If legalInstance Then
        'test to make sure this isn't called directly
        MsgBox str
      End If
   End Sub
   '-----
   Private Sub Class_Terminate()
    'terminate legal class
    If legalInstance Then
      Set glbSpooler = Nothing
      spooler_cnt = 0
    End If
   End Sub
```

Finally, if you need to change the program to allow two or three instances, this class is easily modified to allow this by keeping an array of instances in your module level code.

Catching the Error

User errors are always those you define and are constants added to the vbObjectError constant. You can only catch errors that are raised within class modules—if you select the option "Break on unhandled errors" from Tools | Options—on the General tab. Otherwise, the error will be raised within the class instead of being passed out for processing by the calling program.

```
'PrintSpooler Driver form
Dim prSp As PrintSpooler
'-----
Private Sub GetSpooler_Click()
On Local Error GoTo nospool
  'create a spooler
    Set prSp = New PrintSpooler 'create class
    Set prSp = prSp.GetSpooler  'get legal instance
    errText.Text = "Spooler created"
spexit:
    Exit Sub
'if the spooler causes an error we will get this message
nospool:
  errText.Text = "Spooler already exists"
  Resume spexit
End Sub
```

Providing a Global Point of Access to a Singleton

Since each Singleton is used to provide a single point of global access to a class, your program design must provide for a way to reference the Singletons throughout the program.

One solution is to create a collection of such Singletons at the beginning of the program and pass them as arguments to the major classes that might need to use them.

```
Dim Singletons as New Collection
Singletons.add prSpl, "PrintSpooler"
```

The disadvantage is that you might not need all the Singletons that you create for a given program execution, and this could have performance implications.

A more elaborate solution could be to create a registry of all the Singleton classes in the program and make the registry generally available. Each time a Singleton is instantiated, it notes that in the Registry. Then any part of the program can ask for the instance of any singleton using an identifying string and get back that instance variable.

Of course, the registry itself is probably a Singleton and must be passed to all parts of the program using the init method or various set functions or as a global variable.

The MSComm Control as a Singleton

The MSComm control provides you with convenient access to your PC's serial ports. You can set the port number, baud rate, parity, and the number of data bits and stop bits and can open the port and send or receive data. A PC's BIOS usually allows up to four serial ports, called COM1 through COM4, even though fewer may actually be installed, and this must be mirrored by the MSComm control. In addition, there can be only one instance of any of the ports at any given time, since two programs or devices cannot use the same port at the same time.

Serial ports are a good example of a resource that should be represented by a Singleton, since only one program at a time can have access to a serial port, and even within a program only one module or group of modules should be communicating over the port.

Two Singletons are possible here: one that manages the collection of ports and lets out only one instance of each port and the port objects themselves that must each refer to a single port.

In our example program, we'll create an array of MSComm controls in a small invisible form and then provide methods to query them. The design of our invisible form is shown in Figure 12-1.

Figure 12-1 The invisible form module

Then we can create public methods for this invisible form to list which ports are available and to try to open them.

```
Dim coms As New Collection
Dim loaded As Boolean
Dim validPorts As New Collection
Dim availablePorts As New Collection
'-----
Private Sub Form_Load()
 loaded = False
 loadComms     'load coms into collection
End Sub
'-----
Private Sub loadComms()
 'create array of 5 MSComm controls
 If Not loaded Then
    coms.Add comm(0)
    coms.Add comm(1)
    coms.Add comm(2)
    coms.Add comm(3)
    coms.Add comm(4)
    loaded = True     'collection is now loaded
 End If
End Sub
```

You might want to inquire which ports are available or which ports are valid. In either case, you need only move through the list of possible ports and try to open them. If they are open, you will get a "Port already open" error, and if they do not exist, you will get an "Invalid port number" error. The code for handling this looks like the following.

```
Public Function getValidPorts() As Collection
 Dim cm As MSComm, i As Integer
 Dim valid As Integer
 loadComms                'make sure ports list has been loaded
 On Local Error GoTo cmsb
 For i = 1 To 5
```

```
    Set cm = coms(1)        'get any MSComm control
    valid = True            'assume it is valid
    cm.CommPort = i         'set the port number
    cm.PortOpen = True      'try to open it
    cm.PortOpen = False     'if it opens, close it
    If valid Then           'if not negated by error
      validPorts.Add i      'then add to list
    End If
 Next i
 Set getValidPorts = validPorts   'return list
Exit Function

'error handling for opening ports
cmsb:
  Select Case Err.Number
    Case 8002    'invalid port
      valid = False
    Case 8005     'port already open
      valid = True
  End Select
  Resume Next
End Function
```

Available Ports

We can construct a similar method to return a list of ports still available. In that case the port is added to the list only if *neither* the "Port already open" nor the "Invalid port number" error occurs.

Figure 12-2 shows a program that allows you to open each port in succession and see what error occurs. It also shows the results of the getValidPorts and the getAvailablePorts methods.

The list of Com option buttons in Figure 12-2 consists of calls to the following comClick method, which just displays the error message (if any) or the port status in the list box.

```
Private Sub comClick(i As Integer)
Dim com As MSComm

On Error GoTo nocom
Set com = comFrm.getComm(i)            'Get a port from the array
com.CommPort = i
comFrm.getComm(i).PortOpen = True      'try to open it
'display status of port
List1.AddItem Str$(i) & " Port opened"
pexit:
Exit Sub

nocom:
'or display the error message
```

```
        List1.AddItem Str$(i) & Str$(Err.Number) & " " & _
                      Err.Description
      Resume pexit
End Sub
```

Which are the Singletons here? Well, each MSComm is an open book to be written on, but once it opens a particular port, it becomes a Singleton for that port. You cannot open another MSComm control using that port number. Similarly, we could regard the invisible commForm control as a Singleton. There could be more than one in a program, but it is unlikely that there would be any reason to have more than one. It manages and shows you the results of each port.

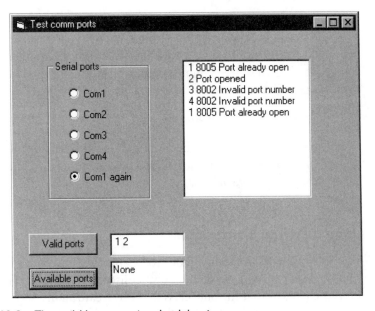

Figure 12-2   The available ports assigned and then in use

Writing a Singleton in VB.NET

VB7 provides an unusually powerful set of methods for creating and using Singletons, and it illustrates a number of the powerful features of this new language version. We want to be able to allocate one and only one spooler in our system and know whether one has been allocated. In VB7, we can create classes that have *shared methods*. These are methods that we can call using the class name rather than through an instance of the class. In other languages, these are called *static methods*. For example, the File class in VB7 can be used to get information about files without creating an instance of it.

```
If File.Exists("foo.txt")
```

And the MessageBox class has only shared methods.

```
MessageBox.Show("Error in program!")
```

Similarly, you can create your own class that has shared methods by simply declaring these methods to be Shared. Shared methods can be called using only the class name. They are also available from instances of the class.

In this Singleton example, you could create a method for getting a legal spooler instance.

```
Public Shared Function getSpooler() As Spooler
```

How would such a class decide whether a spooler has been allocated? You can keep a shared counter right inside the class and check whether a spooler has been allocated or not.

```
Private Shared Spool_counter as Integer
```

Shared variables like these are only accessible from Shared methods. Methods of the class that are not shared and are used by class instances cannot access these shared variables.

Using a Private Constructor

Since we don't want anyone to be able to create multiple instances of our Spooler class, we will make the New constructor private. The upshot of this simple change is that the only class that can create an instance of the Spooler class is the spooler class itself. While this seems at first as if it is a circular argument, we find that we can use a Shared method of the Spooler class to create an actual instance of the class. It might look like this.

```
Public Shared Function getSpooler() As Spooler
    getSpooler = New Spooler
End Function
```

Then we can call the nonshared methods, such as a Print method using the instance of the spooler that the shared method returns.

```
spl = Spooler.getSpooler
spl.Print("Hi there")
```

Error Handling in Our Singleton

Now we need to decide how to indicate errors when we have not allocated a spooler and when we try to allocate more than one. The ideal way to do this in VB7 is by using exceptions. We can create a simple SpoolerException class that has an appropriate error message for our Singleton as follows.

```
Public Class SpoolerException
    Inherits Exception
    Private mesg As String
    '-----
    Public Sub New()
        MyBase.New()
        mesg = "Only one spooler instance allowed"
    End Sub
    '-----
    Public Overrides ReadOnly Property Message() As String
        Get
            Message = mesg
        End Get
    End Property
End Class
```

Then all we have to do in the constructor of our Spooler class is verify if this is the first and only legal instance and, if it isn't, to create one. If it is, we throw this exception.

```
Public Class Spooler
    Private Shared Spool_counter As Integer
    Private Shared glbSpooler As Spooler
    Private legalInstance As Boolean
    '-----
    Private Sub New()
        MyBase.New()

        If spool_counter = 0 Then    'create one instance
            glbSpooler = Me          'save it
            spool_counter = spool_counter + 1   'count it
            legalInstance = True
        Else
            legalInstance = False
            Throw New SpoolerException()
        End If
    End Sub
```

In a similar fashion, we expand our getSpooler shared method to pass on that thrown exception to the calling program.

```
Public Shared Function getSpooler() As Spooler
        Try
            glbSpooler = New Spooler()
```

```
         Catch e As Exception
             Throw e                     'pass on to calling program
         Finally
             getSpooler = glbSpooler  'or return legal one
         End Try
     End Function
```

A VB.NET SpoolDemo Program

Now let's rewrite our simple spooler demo to display a message if we have a
spooler and if we don't. It really amounts to testing for and catching the exceptions in the two button click events.

```
Protected Sub Print_Click(ByVal sender As Object, _
                          ByVal e As System.EventArgs)
     Try
         spl.Print("Hi there")
     Catch ex As Exception
         ErrorBox("No spooler allocated")
     End Try
End Sub
'-----
Private Sub ErrorBox(ByVal mesg As String)
     MessageBox.Show(mesg, "Spooler Error", _
                MessageBoxButtons.OK, MessageBoxIcon.Error)
End Sub
'-----
   Private Sub btGetSpooler_Click( _
               ByVal sender As System.Object, _
               ByVal e As System.EventArgs) _
               Handles btGetSpooler.Click
     Try
         Spl = Spooler.getSpooler
         TextBox1.Text = "Got spooler"
     Catch ex As Exception
         ErrorBox("Spooler already allocated")
     End Try
End Sub
```

This creates the simple window shown in Figure 12-3, and it produces the
two error message boxes shown in Figure 12-4.

Figure 12-3   The VB7 spooler demo

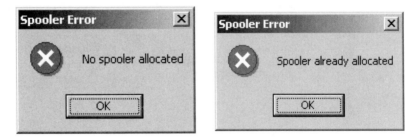

Figure 12-4   The error messages produced in the VB7 spooler demo

The Global Point of Access

In order to illustrate how we can use exceptions and pass them on to the calling program, we did not really provide a global point of access. Once we call the shared getSpooler function one time, additional calls to it throw an exception. It might actually be more appropriate to simply always return that instance once it is created.

```
Public Shared Function getSpooler() As Spooler
 If spooler_count = 0 then
   glbSpooler = New Spooler
 End If
GetSpooler = glbSpooler      'return instance

End Function
```

Other Consequences of the Singleton Pattern

You can easily change a Singleton so that it allows a small number of instances instead of a single instance where this makes sense as your system develops.

 THOUGHT QUESTION

Consider a system for processing ATM card transactions where a thief has obtained an ATM card number and is using it to steal funds concurrent with the legitimate user withdrawing funds. How could you design a Singleton to reduce this risk?

Programs on the CD-ROM

\Singleton\	VB6 spooler singleton
\Singleton\comms	VB6 com port singleton
\Singleton\VBNetSingleton	VB7 spooler singleton

CHAPTER 13

The Builder Pattern

In this chapter we'll consider how to use the Builder pattern to construct objects from components. We have already seen that the Factory pattern returns one of several different subclasses, depending on the data passed in arguments to the creation methods. But suppose we don't want just a computing algorithm but a whole different user interface because of the data we need to display. A typical example might be your e-mail address book. You probably have both individual people and groups of people in your address book, and you would expect the display for the address book to change so that the People screen has places for first and last name, company, e-mail address, and phone number.

On the other hand, if you were displaying a group address page, you'd like to see the name of the group, its purpose, and a list of members and their e-mail addresses. You click on a person and get one display and on a group and get the other display. Let's assume that all e-mail addresses are kept in an object called an Address and that people and groups are derived from this base class, as shown in Figure 13-1.

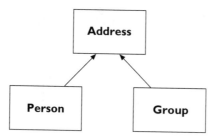

Figure 13-1   Both Person and Group are derived from Address.

Depending on which type of Address object we click on, we'd like to see a somewhat different display of that object's properties. This is a little more than just a Factory pattern because we aren't returning objects that are simple descendants of a base display object but totally different user interfaces made up of different combinations of display objects. The *Builder pattern* assembles a number of objects, such as display controls, in various ways, depending on the data. Furthermore, by using classes to represent the data and forms to represent the display, you can cleanly separate the data from the display methods into simple objects.

An Investment Tracker

Let's consider a somewhat simpler case where it would be useful to have a class build our UI for us. Suppose we are going to write a program to keep track of the performance of our investments. We might have stocks, bonds, and mutual funds, and we'd like to display a list of our holdings in each category so we can select one or more of the investments and plot their comparative performance.

Even though we can't predict in advance how many of each kind of investment we might own at any given time, we'd like to have a display that is easy to use for either a large number of funds (such as stocks) or a small number of funds (such as mutual funds). In each case, we want some sort of a multiple-choice display so that we can select one or more funds to plot. If there is a large number of funds, we'll use a multichoice list box, and if there are three or fewer funds, we'll use a set of check boxes. We want our Builder class to generate an interface that depends on the number of items to be displayed and yet have the same methods for returning the results.

Our displays are shown in Figure 13-2. The left display contains a large number of stocks, and the right contains a small number of bonds.

Figure 13-2   Stocks with the list interface and bonds with the check box interface

Now let's consider how we can build the interface to carry out this variable display. We'll start with a *multiChoice* interface that defines the methods we need to implement.

```
'Interface MultiChoice
'This is the interface for the multi-Select windows
'-----
'get collection of all selected stocks
Public Function getSelected() As Collection
End Function
'-----
'get window containing multichoice controls
Public Function getWindow() As Form
End Function
'-----
'store list of stocks
Public Sub init(stocks As Collection)
End Sub
```

The *getWindow* method returns a window with a multiple-choice display. The two displays we're using here, a check box panel or a list box panel, implement this interface.

```
'checkBox form
Implements MultiChoice
```

or

```
'Listbox form
Implements MultiChoice
```

Then we create a simple Factory class that decides which of these two classes to return.

```
'Class StockFactory
'gets correct window for number of stocks presented
Public Function getBuilder(stocks As Collection)
 Dim mult As MultiChoice
 If stocks.Count <= 3 Then
   Set mult = New checkForm   'get check box form
 Else
   Set mult = New listForm    'get list box form
 End If
 mult.init stocks             'initialize it
 Set getBuilder = mult
End Function
```

In the language of *Design Patterns*, this simple factory class is called the Director, and the actual classes derived from *multiChoice* are each Builders.

Calling the Builders

Visual Basic 6 doesn't make it easy to create and change forms dynamically during program execution, so we will instead create instances of the various types of multiChoice windows as components of an MDI form. Then we'll instantiate the one needed by the number of equities in a specific category.

Our user interface consists of an MDI form with the list of fund choices on the left and initially nothing on the right. Since windows grow to fill the available space, will fill the right space initially with a blank form, as shown in Figure 13-3.

Figure 13-3   The fund choice before any fund type is selected

We first define the interface Equities.

```
'Interface to Equities class
Public Function getFunds() As Collection
  'returns list of fund names
End Function
```

Then we'll keep our three lists of investments in three classes called Stocks, Bonds, and Mutuals, each of which implements Equities. We create an instance of each of them in the Funds class and fetch one or the other of them from that class.

```
'Class funds
Private fundList As New Collection
Private eq As Equities
```

```
Private Sub Class_Initialize()
 'Creates a collection of equities
 fundList.Add New stocks
 fundList.Add New Bonds
 fundList.Add New Mutuals
End Sub
'-----
Public Function getFund(i As Integer) As Equities
 'return selected equity from collection
 If i > 0 And i <= fundList.Count Then
   Set getFund = fundList(i)
 End If
End Function
```

We load them with arbitrary values as part of program initialization.

```
'Class stocks
Implements Equities
Private stockList As New Collection

Private Sub Class_Initialize()
 'add in arbitrary list of stocks
    stockList.Add "Cisco"
    stockList.Add "Coca Cola"
    stockList.Add "GE"
    stockList.Add "Harley Davidson"
    stockList.Add "IBM"
    stockList.Add "Microsoft"
End Sub
'-----
Private Function Equities_getFunds() As Collection
 'return collection of stocks
    Set Equities_getFunds = stockList
End Function
```

It is the same for Bonds and Mutuals. In a real system, we'd probably read them in from a file or database. Then, when the user clicks on one of the three investment types in the left list box, we get the correct Equity from the Funds class and use it to create the right display.

```
Private Sub fundList_Click()
 Dim i As Integer, selStocks As Collection, eq As Equities

 'catch list box click selecting fund type
 i = fundList.ListIndex + 1
 If (i > 0) Then
   'get one type of fund
   Set eq = fnds.getFund(i)       'get equit from funds class
   Set selStocks = eq.getFunds    'get list from equity
   'get a multiChoice form from the factory
   Set mchoice = sfact.getBuilder(selStocks)
   'tell the parent MDI to show it
   mParent.setShowForm mchoice
```

```
      End If
   End Sub
```

The List Box Builder

The simpler of the two Builders is the List Box Builder. It returns a form containing a list box showing the list of the investments in that equity type.

```
'Listbox form
Implements MultiChoice
Private sels As Collection
'-----
Private Sub MultiChoice_init(stocks As Collection)
 Private i As Integer
 For i = 1 To stocks.Count
   List1.AddItem stocks(i)
 Next i
End Sub
```

The other important method is the *getSelected* method that returns a collection of Strings of the investments the user selects.

```
Private Function MultiChoice_getSelected() As Collection
Dim i As Integer
Set sels = New Collection
For i = 0 To List1.ListCount - 1
  If List1.Selected(i) Then
    sels.Add List1.List(i)
  End If
Next i
Set MultiChoice_getSelected = sels
End Function
```

The Check Box Builder

The Check Box Builder is also quite simple. Here we need to find out how many elements are to be displayed and display them. The number can only be between 0 and 3, so we create them all in advance and display only those we need.

```
Private Sub MultiChoice_init(stocks As Collection)
 Dim i As Integer
 'set captions for the check boxes we are using
 For i = 1 To stocks.Count
   ckFunds(i - 1).Caption = stocks(i)
 Next i
 'make the rest invisible
 For i = stocks.Count + 1 To 3
   ckFunds(i).Visible = False
```

```
 Next i
End Sub
```

The *getSelected* method is analogous to the preceding one. It is shown here. We illustrate the final UML class diagram in Figure 13-4.

```
Implements MultiChoice
Private sels As Collection
'-----
Private Function MultiChoice_getSelected() As Collection
 Dim i As Integer
 'create collection of checked stock names
 Set sels = New Collection
 For i = 1 To 3
   If ckFunds(i - 1).Value = 1 Then
     sels.Add ckFunds(i - 1).Caption
  End If
 Next i
 'return collection to caller
 Set MultiChoice_getSelected = sels
End Function
```

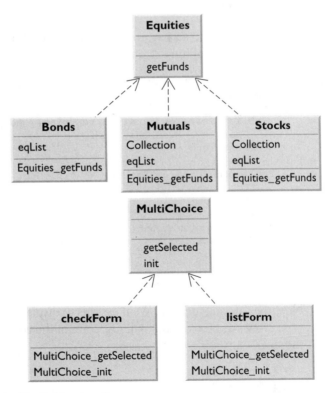

Figure 13-4 The Builder class diagram

Writing a Builder in VB.NET

VB7 gives us considerably more flexibility in designing Builder classes, since we have direct access to the methods that allow us to construct a window from basic components. For this example, we'll let each builder construct a Panel containing whatever components it needs. We can then add that Panel to the form and position it. When the display changes, you remove the old Panel and add a new one. VB6 does not have a Panel class, but in VB7, a Panel is just an unbordered container that can hold any number of Windows components. As we did previously, the two implementations of the Panel will satisfy the Multi-Choice interface.

```
Public Interface MultiChoice
    'an interface to any group of components
    'that can return zero or more selected items
    'the names are returned in an Arraylist
    Function getSelected() As ArrayList
    Sub clear()                'clear all selected
    Function getWindow() As Panel
End Interface
```

We will create a base abstract class called Equities and derive the stocks, bonds, and mutual funds from it.

```
Public MustInherit Class Equities
    Protected ar As Arraylist
    '-----
     Public Overrides Function toString() As String
        'must override this one
    End Function
    '-----
    Public Function getNames() As ArrayList
        Return ar
    End Function
    '-----
    Public Function count() As Integer
        Return ar.count
    End Function
    '-----
End Class
```

Note the toString method. We'll use this to display each kind of equity in the list box. Now our Stocks class will just contain the code to load the ArrayList with the stock names.

```
Public Class Stocks
    Inherits Equities
    '-----
```

```
      Public Sub New()
          MyBase.New()
          ar = New ArrayList()
          ar.Add("Cisco")
          ar.Add("Coca Cola")
          ar.Add("GE")
          ar.Add("Harley Davidson")
          ar.Add("IBM")
          ar.Add("Microsoft")
      End Sub
      '-----
      Public Overrides Function toString() As String
          Return "Stocks"
      End Function
End Class
```

All the remaining code (getNames and count) is implemented in the base Equities class. The Bonds and Mutuals classes are equally simple.

The Stock Factory

We need a little class to decide whether we want to return a check box panel or a list box panel. We'll call this class the StockFactory class. However, we will never need more than one instance of this class, so we'll create the class so its one method is Shared.

```
Public Class StockFactory
    'This class has only one shared method
    Public Shared Function getBuilder(ByVal _
            stocks As Equities) _
            As MultiChoice

        Dim mult As MultiChoice

        If stocks.Count <= 3 Then
            'get check boxes
            mult = New checkChoice(stocks)
        Else
            'get a list box
            mult = New listChoice(stocks)
        End If
        Return mult
    End Function
End Class
```

The CheckChoice Class

Our Check Box Builder constructs a panel containing 0 to 3 check boxes and returns that panel to the calling program.

```
Public Class CheckChoice
    Implements MultiChoice

    Private stocks As ArrayList
    Private pnl As Panel
    Private boxes As ArrayList
    '-----
    'create a Panel containing
    '0 to 3 check boxes
    Public Sub New(ByVal stks As Equities)
        MyBase.New()
        stocks = stks.getNames
        pnl = New Panel()
        boxes = New Arraylist() 'in an ArrayList
        Dim i As Integer
        For i = 0 To stocks.count - 1
            Dim Ck As New Checkbox()
            Ck.Location = _
                New System.Drawing.Point(8, 16 + i * 32)
            Ck.Text = stocks(i).toString
            Ck.Size = New Size(112, 24)
            Ck.TabIndex = 0
            Ck.TextAlign = _
                ContentAlignment.MiddleLeft
            boxes.add(ck)                'internal array
            pnl.Controls.add(ck)         'add into panel
        Next i

    End Sub

End Class
```

The methods for returning the window and the list of selected names are shown here. Note that we use the Ctype function to convert between the Object type returned by an ArrayList and the Checkbox type the method actually requires.

```
    'clear all selected check boxes
    Public Sub clear() Implements MultiChoice.clear
        Dim i As Integer
        Dim ck As Checkbox
        For i = 0 To boxes.count - 1
            ck = CType(boxes(i), Checkbox)
            ck.Checked = False
        Next i
    End Sub
'--------
```

```
'gets list of selected names
Public Function getSelected() As ArrayList _
        Implements MultiChoice.getSelected
    Dim ar As New ArrayList()
    Dim i As Integer
    Dim ck As Checkbox

    For i = 0 To Boxes.count - 1
        ck = CType(boxes(i), Checkbox)
        If ck.Checked Then
            ar.add(ck.Text)
        End If
    Next i
    Return ar
End Function
'--------
'gets the Panel containing the check boxes
Public Function getWindow() As Panel _
        Implements MultiChoice.getWindow
    Return pnl
End Function
```

The ListboxChoice Class

This class creates a multiselect list box, inserts it into a Panel, and loads the names into the list.

```
Public Class ListChoice
    Implements MultiChoice

    Private stocks As ArrayList
    Private pnl As Panel
    Private lst As ListBox
    '--------
    'create a panel containing a
    'multiselectable list box
    Public Sub New(ByVal stks As Equities)
        MyBase.New()
        stocks = stks.getNames 'get the names
        pnl = New Panel()
        'create the list box
        lst = New ListBox()
        lst.Location = New Point(16, 0)
        lst.Size = New Size(120, 160)
        lst.SelectionMode = _
            SelectionMode.MultiExtended
        lst.TabIndex = 0
        'add it into the panel
        pnl.Controls.Add(lst)
        'add the names into the list
        Dim i As Integer
        For i = 0 To stks.count - 1
```

```
            lst.items.add(stocks(i))
        Next i
    End Sub
```

Since this is a multiselect list box, we can get all the selected items in a single SelectedIndices collection. This method, however, only works for a multiselect list box. It returns a –1 for a single-select list box. We use it to load the array list of selected names as follows.

```
Public Function getSelected() As ArrayList _
        Implements MultiChoice.getSelected
    Dim i As Integer
    Dim item As String
    Dim arl As New ArrayList()

    'get items and put in ArrayList
    For i = 0 To lst.SelectedIndices.count - 1
        item = lst.Items( _
            lst.SelectedIndices(i)).toString
        arl.add(item)
    Next i
    Return arl    'return the ArrayList
End Function
'-----
'clear all selected items
Public Sub clear() Implements MultiChoice.clear
    lst.Items.clear()
End Sub
'-----
'return the constructed panel
Public Function getWindow() As Panel _
        Implements MultiChoice.getWindow
    Return pnl
End Function
```

Using the Items Collection in the ListBox Control

You are not limited to populating a list box with strings in VB7. When you add data to the Items collection, it can be any kind of object that has a toString method. This takes the place of the much more limited Itemdata property of the listbox in VB6.

Since we created our three Equities classes to have a toString method, we can add them directly to the list box in our main program's constructor.

```
Public Class wBuilder
    Inherits System.Windows.Forms.Form
    Private Pnl As Panel
    Private mchoice As MultiChoice
```

```
Private eq As Equities
'-----
Private Sub init()
    lsEqTypes.Items.Add(New Stocks())
    lsEqTypes.Items.Add(New Bonds())
    lsEqTypes.Items.Add(New Mutuals())
End Sub
```

Whenever we click on a line of the list box, the click method obtains that instance of an Equities class and passes it to the MultiChoice factory, which in turn produces a Panel containing the items in that class. It then removes the old panel and adds the new one.

```
Private Sub lsEqTypes_SelectedIndexChanged( _
    ByVal sender As System.Object, _
    ByVal e As System.EventArgs) _
    Handles lsEqTypes.SelectedIndexChanged

    Dim i As Integer
    i = lsEqTypes.SelectedIndex

    'get the Equity from the list box
    eq = CType(lsEqTypes.Items(i), Equities)

    'get the right Builder
    mchoice = StockFactory.getBuilder(eq)

    'remove the old panel
    Me.Controls.Remove(Pnl)

    'get the new one and add it to the window
    Pnl = mchoice.getWindow
    setPanel()
End Sub
```

The Final Choice

Now that we have created all the needed classes, we can run the program. It starts with a blank panel on the right side, so there will always be some panel there to remove. Then each time we click on one of the names of the Equities, that panel is removed and a new one is added in its place. We see the three cases in Figure 13-5.

You can see the relationships between the classes in the UML diagram in Figure 13-6.

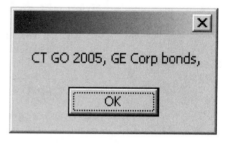

Figure 13-5   The VB7 WealthBuilder program

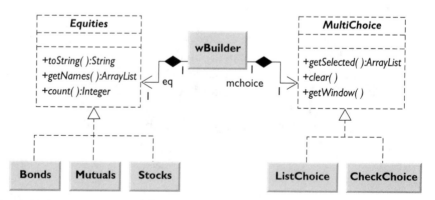

Figure 13-6   The inheritance relationships in the Builder pattern

Consequences of the Builder Pattern

1. A Builder lets you vary the internal representation of the product it builds. It also hides the details of how the product is assembled.

2. Each specific Builder is independent of the others and of the rest of the program. This improves modularity and makes the addition of other Builders relatively simple.

3. Because each Builder constructs the final product step by step, depending on the data, you have more control over each final product that a Builder constructs.

A Builder pattern is somewhat like an Abstract Factory pattern in that both return classes made up of a number of methods and objects. The main difference is that while the Abstract Factory returns a family of related classes, the Builder constructs a complex object step by step, depending on the data presented to it.

THOUGHT QUESTIONS

1. Some word-processing and graphics programs construct menus dynamically based on the context of the data being displayed. How could you use a Builder effectively here?

2. Not all Builders must construct visual objects. What might you construct with a Builder in the personal finance industry? Suppose you were scoring a track meet, made up of five or six different events. How can you use a Builder there?

Programs on the CD-ROM

\Builders\SimpleBuilder	VB6 basic equities Builder
\Builders\VBNetBuilder	VB7 equities Builder

CHAPTER 14

The Prototype Pattern

The Prototype pattern is another tool you can use when you can specify the general class needed in a program but need to defer the exact class until execution time. It is similar to the Builder in that some class decides what components or details make up the final class. However, it differs in that the target classes are constructed by cloning one or more prototype classes and then changing or filling in the details of the cloned class to behave as desired.

Prototypes can be used whenever you need classes that differ only in the type of processing they offer—for example, in parsing of strings representing numbers in different radixes. In this sense, the prototype is nearly the same as the Examplar pattern described by Coplien (1992).

Let's consider the case of an extensive database where you need to make a number of queries to construct an answer. Once you have this answer as a table or RecordSet, you might like to manipulate it to produce other answers without issuing additional queries.

In a case like the one we have been working on, we'll consider a database of a large number of swimmers in a league or statewide organization. Each swimmer swims several strokes and distances throughout a season. The "best times" for swimmers are tabulated by age group, and even within a single four-month season many swimmers will pass their birthdays and fall into new age groups. Thus, the query to determine which swimmers did the best in their age group that season is dependent on the date of each meet and on each swimmer's birthday. The computational cost of assembling this table of times is therefore fairly high.

Once we have a class containing this table sorted by sex, we could imagine wanting to examine this information sorted just by time or by actual age rather than by age group. It would not be sensible to recompute these data, and we don't want to destroy the original data order, so some sort of copy of the data object is desirable.

Cloning in Visual Basic 6

The idea of cloning a class (making an exact copy) is not a designed-in feature of Visual Basic, but nothing actually stops you from carrying out such a copy yourself. The only place the Clone method appears in VB is in database manipulation. You can create a Recordset as a result of a database query and move through it a row at a time. If for some reason you need to keep references to two places in this Recordset, you would need two "current rows." The simplest way to handle this in VB6 is to clone the Recordset.

```
Public Sub cloneRec(Query As String)
 Dim db As Database
 Dim rec As Recordset, crec As Recordset

 'open database recordset
 Set rec = db.OpenRecordset(Query, dbOpenDynaset)

 'clone a copy
 Set crec = rec.Clone
End Sub
```

Now this approach does not generate two *copies* of the Recordset. It just generates two sets of row pointers to use to move through the records independently of each other. Any change you make in one clone of the Recordset is immediately reflected in the other because there is in fact only one data table. We discuss a similar problem in the following example.

Using the Prototype

Now let's write a simple program that reads data from a database and then clones the resulting object. In our example program, we just read these data from a file, but the original data were derived from a large database, as we discussed previously. That file has the following form.

```
Kristen Frost, 9, CAT, 26.31, F
Kimberly Watcke, 10, CDEV,27.37, F
Jaclyn Carey, 10, ARAC, 27.53, F
Megan Crapster, 10, LEHY, 27.68, F
```

We'll use the vbFile class we developed earlier.

First, we create a class called Swimmer that holds one name, club name, sex, and time, and read them in using the File class.

```
Option Explicit
'Class Swimmer
```

```
Private ssex As String
Private sage As Integer
Private stime As Single
Private sclub As String
Private sfrname As String, slname As String
'-----
Public Sub init(Fl As vbFile)
 Dim i As Integer
 Dim nm As String

 nm = Fl.readToken     'read in name
 i = InStr(nm, " ")
 If i > 0 Then         'separate into first and last
   sfrname = Left(nm, i - 1)
   slname = Right$(nm, Len(nm) - i)
 Else
   sfrname = ""
   slname = nm          'or just use one
 End If

 sage = Val(Fl.readToken)     'get age
 sclub = Fl.readToken         'get club
 stime = Val(Fl.readToken)    'get time
 ssex = Fl.readToken          'get sex
End Sub
'-----
Public Function getTime() As Single
 getTime = stime
End Function
'-----
Public Function getSex() As String
 getSex = ssex
End Function
'-----
Public Function getName() As String
 getName = sfrname & " " & slname
End Function
'-----
Public Function getClub() As String
 getClub = sclub
End Function
'-----
Public Function getAge() As Integer
 getAge = sage
End Function
```

We also provide a *getSwimmer* method in SwimData and *getName*, *getAge*, and *getTime* methods in the Swimmer class. Once we've read the data into SwimInfo, we can display it in a list box.

Then we create an interface class called SwimData that maintains a Collection of the Swimmers we read in from the database.

```
'Interface SwimData
Public Sub init(Filename As String)
End Sub
'-----
Public Sub Clone(swd As SwimData)
End Sub
'-----
Public Sub setData(swcol As Collection)
End Sub
'-----
Public Sub sort()
End Sub
'-----
Public Sub MoveFirst()
End Sub
'-----
Public Function hasMoreElements() As Boolean
End Function
'-----
Public Function getNextSwimmer() As Swimmer
End Function
```

When the user clicks on the Clone button, we'll clone this class and sort the data differently in the new class. Again, we clone the data because creating a new class instance would be much slower, and we want to keep the data in both forms.

```
Private Sub SwimData_Clone(swd As SwimData)
    swd.setData swimmers      'copy data into new class
End Sub
```

In the original class, the names are sorted by sex and then by time, whereas in the cloned class they are sorted only by time. In Figure 14-1, we see the simple user interface that allows us to display the original data on the left and the sorted data in the cloned class on the right.

Now, let's click on the **Refresh** button to reload the left-hand list box from the original data. The somewhat disconcerting result is shown in Figure 14-2.

Why have the names in the left-hand list box also been re-sorted? This occurs because the clone method is a *shallow copy* of the original class. In other words, the references to the data objects are copies, but they refer to the same underlying data. Thus, any operation we perform on the copied data will also occur on the original data in the Prototype class.

In some cases, this shallow copy may be acceptable, but if you want to make a deep copy of the data, you must write a deep cloning routine of your own as part of the class you want to clone. In this simple class, you just create a new Collection and copy the elements of the old class's Collection into the new one.

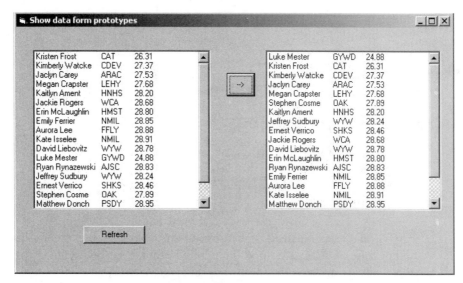

Figure 14-1 Prototype example. The left-hand list box is loaded when the program starts and the right-hand list box is loaded when you click on the **Clone** button.

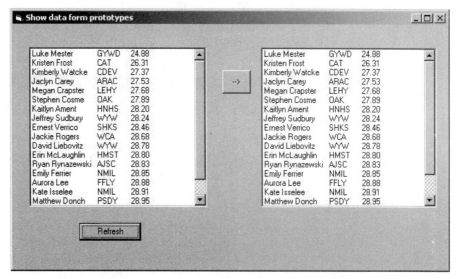

Figure 14-2 Prototype example after clicking on Clone and then on Refresh

```
Private Sub SwimData_Clone(swd As SwimData)
 Dim swmrs As New Collection
 Dim i As Integer
 'copy data from one collection
 ' to another
 For i = 1 To swimmers.Count
```

```
      swmrs.Add swimmers(i)
   Next i
   'and put into new class
   swd.setData swmrs
End Sub
```

Using the Prototype Pattern

You can use the Prototype pattern whenever any of a number of classes might be created or when the classes are modified after being created. As long as all the classes have the same interface, they can actually carry out rather different operations.

Let's consider a more elaborate example of the listing of swimmers we just discussed. Instead of just sorting the swimmers, let's create subclasses that operate on that data, modifying it and presenting the result for display in a list box. We start with the same abstract class SwimData.

Then it becomes possible to write different concrete SwimData classes, depending on the application's requirements. We always start with the SexSwimData class and then clone it for various other displays. For example, the OneSexSwimData class resorts the data by sex and displays only one sex. This is shown in Figure 14-3.

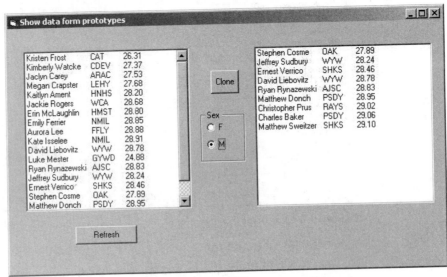

Figure 14-3   The OneSexSwimData class displays only one sex on the right.

In the OneSexSwimData class, we sort the data by time but return them for display based on whether girls or boys are supposed to be displayed. This class has this additional method.

```
Public Sub setSex(sx As String)
  Sex = sx 'copy current sex preference
End Sub
```

Each time you click on one of the sex option buttons, the class is given the current state of these buttons.

Additional Methods in Subclasses

The OneSexSwimData class implements the SwimData interface, but we want it to have an additional method as well, which allows us to tell it which sex we want to display. The setSex method is not part of the SwimData interface, and thus if we just create a SwimData object and assign it the value of a new OneSexSwimData class instance, we won't have access to the setSex method.

```
Private swd As SwimData
Private tsd As SwimData
'-----
Private Sub Clone_Click()
    Set tsd = New OneSexSwimData
    swd.Clone tsd    'clone into any type
    tsd.sort          'call interface method
```

On the other hand, if we create an instance of the OneSexSwimData class, we won't have access to the methods of the SwimData interface.

```
Private swd As SwimData
Private osd As OneSexSwimData
'-----
Private Sub Clone_Click()
Set osd = tsd    'copy to specific type
```

We can solve this problem by creating a variable of each type and referring to the same class using both the SwimData and the OneSexSwimData variables.

```
Private swd As SwimData
Private tsd As SwimData
Private osd As OneSexSwimData
'-----
Private Sub Clone_Click()
    Set tsd = New OneSexSwimData
    swd.Clone tsd    'clone into any type
    tsd.sort          'call interface method

    Set osd = tsd    'copy to specific type
    osd.setSex "F"   'call derived class method
    SexFrame.Enabled = True 'enable sex selection
    loadRightList
End Sub
```

Note that we enable the SexFrame containing the F and M sex selection option buttons only when a clone has been performed. This prevents performing the setSex method on a class that has not yet been initialized.

```
Private Sub Sex_Click(Index As Integer)
'sets the sex of the class to either F or M
  osd.setSex Sex(Index).Caption
  loadRightList
End Sub
```

Dissimilar Classes with the Same Interface

Classes, however, do not have to be even that similar. The AgeSwimData class takes the cloned input data array and creates a simple histogram by age. If you click on "F," you see the girls' age distribution and if you click on "M," you see the boys' age distribution, as shown in Figure 14-4.

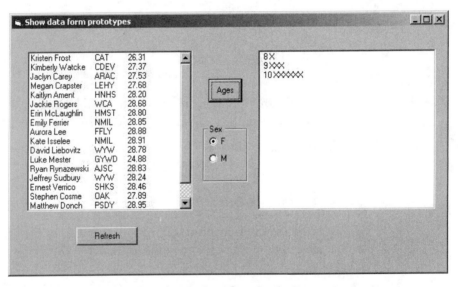

Figure 14-4   The AgeSwimData class displays an age distribution.

This is an interesting case where the AgeSwimData class uses all the interface methods of the base SwimData class and also uses the setSex method of the OneSexSwimData class we showed previously. We could just make the setSex method a new public method in our AgeSwimData class, or we could declare that AgeSwimData implements *both* interfaces.

```
'Class AgeSwimData
Implements OneSexSwimData
Implements SwimData
```

There is little to choose between them in this case, since there is only one extra method, setSex, in the OneSexSwimData class. However, the data are manipulated differently to create the histogram.

```
Private Sub SwimData_sort()
 Dim i As Integer, j As Integer
 Dim sw As Swimmer, age As Integer
 Dim ageString As String
 'Sort the data inbto increasing age order
 max = swimmers.Count
 ReDim sws(max) As Swimmer
 'copy the data into an array
 For i = 1 To max
    Set sws(i) = swimmers(i)
 Next i
 'sort by increasing age
 For i = 1 To max
    For j = i To max
      If sws(i).getAge > sws(j).getAge Then
        Set sw = sws(i)
        Set sws(i) = sws(j)
        Set sws(j) = sw
      End If
    Next j
 Next i
 'empty the collection
 For i = max To 1 Step -1
    swimmers.Remove i
 Next i
 'fill it with the sorted data
 For i = 1 To max
    swimmers.Add sws(i)
 Next i
 'create the histogram
 countAgeSex
End Sub
'----
Private Sub countAgeSex()
 Dim i As Integer, j As Integer
 Dim sw As Swimmer, age As Integer
 Dim ageString As String

 'now count number in each age
 Set ageList = New Collection
 age = swimmers(1).getAge
 ageString = ""
 i = 1
 While i <= max
    'add to histogram if in age and sex
    If age = swimmers(i).getAge And Sex = swimmers(i).getSex Then
      ageString = ageString & "X"
    End If
    If age <> swimmers(i).getAge And Sex = swimmers(i).getSex Then
      'create new swimmer if age changes
```

```
      Set sw = New Swimmer
      sw.setFirst Str$(age)  'put string of age in 1st name
      sw.setLast ageString   'put histogram in last name
      ageList.Add sw         'add to collection
      age = swimmers(i).getAge
      ageString = "X"         'start new age histogram
   End If
   i = i + 1
Wend
'copy last one in
 Set sw = New Swimmer
 sw.setFirst Str$(age)
 sw.setLast ageString
 ageList.Add sw
 amax = ageList.Count

End Sub
```

Now, since our original classes display first and last names of selected swimmers, note that we achieve this same display, returning Swimmer objects with the first name set to the age string and the last name set to the histogram.

The UML diagram in Figure 14-5 illustrates this system fairly clearly. The SwimInfo class is the main GUI class. It keeps two instances of SwimData but does not specify which ones. The TimeSwimData and SexSwimData classes are concrete classes derived from the abstract SwimData class, and the AgeSwimData class, which creates the histograms, is derived from the SexSwimData class.

You should also note that you are not limited to the few subclasses we demonstrated here. It would be quite simple to create additional concrete classes and register them with whatever code selects the appropriate concrete class. In our example program, the user is the deciding point or factory because he or she simply clicks on one of several buttons. In a more elaborate case, each concrete class could have an array of characteristics, and the decision point could be a class registry or *prototype manager* that examines this characteristic and selects the most suitable class. You could also combine the Factory Method pattern with the Prototype, where each of several concrete classes uses a different concrete class from those available.

Prototype Managers

A prototype manager class can be used to decide which of several concrete classes to return to the client. It can also manage several sets of prototypes at once. For example, in addition to returning one of several classes of swimmers, it could return different groups of swimmers who swam different strokes and distances. It could also manage which of several types of list boxes are returned

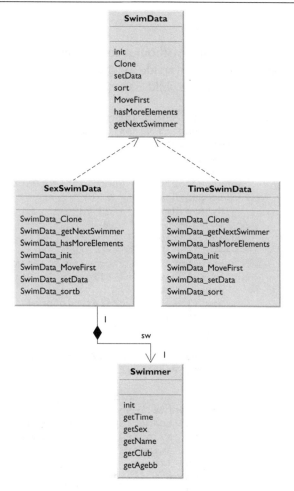

Figure 14-5   The UML diagram for the various SwimData classes

in which to display them, including tables, multicolumn lists, and graphical displays. It is best that whichever subclass is returned, it does not require conversion to a new class type to be used in the program. In other words, the methods of the parent abstract or base class should be sufficient, and the client should never need to know which actual subclass it is dealing with.

Writing a Prototype in VB7

In VB7, we can write more or less the same code. The major changes are that we will use ArrayLists and zero-based arrays and we can write a base SwimData class from which we can inherit a number of useful methods. We create the base

SwimData class without a sort method and specify using MustInherit for the class and MustOverride for the method that you must provide an implementation of sort in the child classes.

```
'Base class for SwimData
Public MustInherit Class SwimData
    Protected Swimmers As ArrayList
    Private index As Integer
    '-------
    'constructor to be used with setData
    Public Sub New()
        MyBase.New()
        index = 0
    End Sub
    '-----
    'Constructor to be used with filename
    Public Sub New(ByVal Filename As String)
        MyBase.New()
        Dim fl As New vbFile(Filename)
        Dim sw As Swimmer
        Dim sname As String

        swimmers = New ArrayList()
        Fl.OpenForRead(Filename)

        sname = fl.readLine
        While sname.length > 0
            If (sname.length > 0) Then
                sw = New Swimmer(sname)
                swimmers.Add(sw)
            End If
            sname = fl.readLine
        End While
        sort()
        index = 0
    End Sub
    '-------
    Public Sub setData(ByVal swcol As ArrayList)
        swimmers = swcol
        movefirst()
    End Sub
    '-------
    'Clone dataset from other swimdata object
    Public Sub Clone(ByVal swd As SwimData)
        Dim swmrs As New ArrayList()
        Dim i As Integer
        'copy data from one collection
        ' to another
        For i = 0 To swimmers.Count - 1
            swmrs.Add(swimmers(i))
        Next i
        'and put into new class
        swd.setData(swmrs)
```

```
End Sub
'-----
'sorting method must be specified
'in the child classes
Public MustOverride Sub sort()
'-----
Public Sub MoveFirst()
    index = -1
End Sub
'-----
Public Function hasMoreElements() As Boolean
    Return (index < (Swimmers.count - 1))
End Function
'-----
Public Function getNextSwimmer() As Swimmer
    index = index + 1
    Return CType(swimmers(index), Swimmer)
End Function

End Class
```

Note that we use the vbFile class we wrote earlier to read lines from the file. However, once we read the data, we parse each data line in the Swimmer class. Data conversions have a different form in VB7. Instead of using the Val function, we use the CInt function to convert integers.

```
sage = CInt(tok.nextToken)  'get age
```

We use the toSingle method to convert the time value.

```
stime = CSng(tok.nextToken)     'get time
```

This is the complete constructor for the Swimmer Class.

```
Public Class Swimmer
    Private ssex As String
    Private sage As Integer
    Private stime As Single
    Private sclub As String
    Private sfrname, slname As String
    '-----
    Public Sub New(ByVal nm As String)
        MyBase.New()
        Dim i As Integer
        Dim s As String
        Dim t As Single
        Dim tok As StringTokenizer

        tok = New StringTokenizer(nm, ",")
        nm = tok.nextToken
        i = nm.indexOf(" ")
        If i > 0 Then       'separate into first and last
```

```
            sfrname = nm.substring(0, i)
            slname = nm.substring(i + 1)
    Else
            sfrname = ""
            slname = nm          'or just use one
    End If
    sage = CInt(tok.nextToken)        'get age
    sclub = tok.nextToken             'get club
    stime = CSng(tok.nextToken)       'get time
    ssex = tok.nextToken              'get sex
End Sub
```

The final running VB7 Prototype program is shown in Figure 14-6.

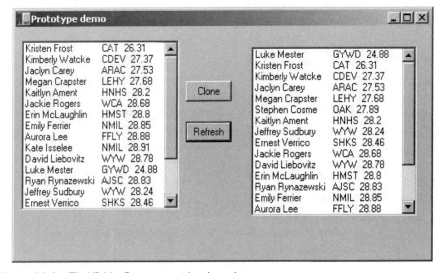

Figure 14-6   The VB.Net Prototype with a deep clone

Then our TimeSwimData class is very simple, consisting only of the New methods and the sort method.

```
Public Class TimeSwimData
    Inherits SwimData
    '---------
    Public Sub New(ByVal filename As String)
        MyBase.New(filename)
    End Sub
    '---------
    Public Sub New()
        MyBase.New()
    End Sub
    '---------
    'Required sort method
    Public Overrides Sub sort()
```

```
      Dim i, j, max As Integer
      Dim sw As Swimmer
      max = swimmers.Count
      'copy into array
      Dim sws(max) As Swimmer
      swimmers.CopyTo(sws)
      'sort by time
      For i = 0 To max - 1
         For j = i To max - 1
            If sws(i).getTime > sws(j).getTime Then
               sw = sws(i)
               sws(i) = sws(j)
               sws(j) = sw
            End If
         Next j
      Next i
      'copy back into new ArrayList
      swimmers = New Arraylist()
      For i = 0 To max - 1
         swimmers.Add(sws(i))
      Next i
   End Sub

End Class
```

Consequences of the Prototype Pattern

Using the Prototype pattern, you can add and remove classes at run time by cloning them as needed. You can revise the internal data representation of a class at run time, based on program conditions. You can also specify new objects at run time without creating a proliferation of classes.

One difficulty in implementing the Prototype pattern in VB is that if the classes already exist, you may not be able to change them to add the required clone methods. In addition, classes that have circular references to other classes cannot really be cloned.

Like the registry of Singletons discussed before, you can also create a registry of Prototype classes that can be cloned and ask the registry object for a list of possible prototypes. You may be able to clone an existing class rather than writing one from scratch.

Note that every class that you might use as a prototype must itself be instantiated (perhaps at some expense) in order for you to use a Prototype Registry. This can be a performance drawback.

Finally, the idea of having prototype classes to copy implies that you have sufficient access to the data or methods in these classes to change them after cloning. This may require adding data access methods to these prototype classes so that you can modify the data once you have cloned the class.

THOUGHT QUESTION

An entertaining banner program shows a slogan starting at different places on the screen at different times and in different fonts and sizes. Design the program using a Prototype pattern.

Programs on the CD-ROM

\Prototype\Ageplot	VB6 age plot
\Prototype\DeepProto	VB6 deep prototype
\Prototype\OneSex	VB6 display by sex
\Prototype\SimpleProto	VB6 shallow copy
\Prototype\TwoclassAgePlot	VB6 age and sex display
\Prototype\VBNet\DeepProt	VB7 deep prototype

Summary of Creational Patterns

The **Factory pattern** is used to choose and return an instance of a class from a number of similar classes, based on data you provide to the factory.

The **Abstract Factory pattern** is used to return one of several groups of classes. In some cases, it actually returns a Factory for that group of classes.

The **Builder pattern** assembles a number of objects to make a new object, based on the data with which it is presented. Frequently, the choice of which way the objects are assembled is achieved using a Factory.

The **Prototype pattern** copies or clones an existing class, rather than creating a new instance, when creating new instances is more expensive.

The **Singleton pattern** is a pattern that ensures there is one and only one instance of an object and that it is possible to obtain global access to that one instance.

PART 3

Structural Patterns

Structural patterns describe how classes and objects can be combined to form larger structures. The difference between *class* patterns and *object* patterns is that class patterns describe how inheritance can be used to provide more useful program interfaces. Object patterns, on the other hand, describe how objects can be composed into larger structures using object composition or the inclusion of objects within other objects.

For example, we'll see that the **Adapter pattern** can be used to make one class interface match another to make programming easier. We'll also look at a number of other structural patterns where we combine objects to provide new functionality. The **Composite**, for instance, is exactly that—a composition of objects, each of which may be either simple or itself a composite object. The **Proxy pattern** is frequently a simple object that takes the place of a more complex object that may be invoked later—for example, when the program runs in a network environment.

The **Flyweight pattern** is a pattern for sharing objects, where each instance does not contain its own state but stores it externally. This allows efficient sharing of objects to save space when there are many instances but only a few different types.

The **Façade pattern** is used to make a single class represent an entire subsystem, and the **Bridge pattern** separates an object's interface from its implementation so you can vary them separately. Finally, we'll look at the **Decorator pattern**, which can be used to add responsibilities to objects dynamically.

You'll see that there is some overlap among these patterns and even some overlap with the behavioral patterns in the next chapter. We'll summarize these similarities after we describe the patterns.

CHAPTER 15

The Adapter Pattern

The Adapter pattern is used to convert the programming interface of one class into that of another. We use adapters whenever we want unrelated classes to work together in a single program. The concept of an adapter is thus pretty simple: We write a class that has the desired interface and then make it communicate with the class that has a different interface.

There are two ways to do this: by inheritance and by object composition. In the first case, we derive a new class from the nonconforming one and add the methods we need to make the new derived class match the desired interface. The other way is to include the original class inside the new one and create the methods to translate calls within the new class. These two approaches, called class adapters and object adapters, are both fairly easy to implement in other languages, but before VB7 you were forced to use object composition preferentially, since inheritance was not available.

Moving Data between Lists

Let's consider a simple program that allows you to select some names from a list to be transferred to another list for a more detailed display of the data associated with them. Our initial list consists of a team roster, and the second list the names plus their times or scores.

In this simple program, shown in Figure 15-1, the program reads in the names from a roster file during initialization. To move names to the right-hand list box, you click on them and then click on the right arrow button. To remove a name from the right-hand list box, click on it and then on the left arrow button. This moves the name back to the left-hand list.

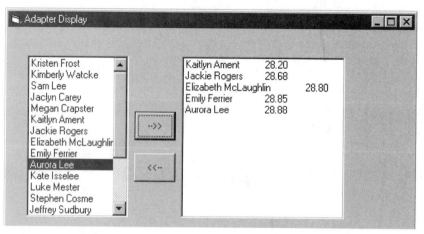

Figure 15-1   A simple program to choose names for display

This is a very simple program to write in VB. It consists of the visual layout and action routines for each of the button clicks. When we read in the file of team roster data, we store each child's name and score in a Swimmer object and then store all of these objects in a collection. When you select one of the names to display in expanded form, you simply obtain the list index of the selected child from the left-hand list and get that child's data to display in the right-hand list.

```
Private Sub Moveit_Click()
Dim i As Integer
i = lsKids.ListIndex + 1
  If i > 0 And i <= swmrs.Count Then
     Set sw = swmrs(i)
     lsTimes.AddItem sw.getName & vbTab & str$(sw.getTime)
  End If
End Sub
```

In a similar fashion, if we want to remove a name from the right-hand list, we just obtain the selected index and remove the name.

```
Private Sub putback_Click()
  Dim i As Integer
  i = lsTimes.ListIndex
  If i >= 0 Then
    lsTimes.RemoveItem i
  End If
End Sub
```

Note that we obtain the column spacing between the two rows using the tab character. This works fine as long as the names are more or less the same length.

However, if one name is much longer or shorter than the others, the list may end up using a different tab column, which is what happened for the third name in the list.

Using the MSFlexGrid

To circumvent this problem with the tab columns in the simple list box, we might turn to a grid display. One simple grid that comes with VB is called the MSFlexGrid. It is a subset of a more elaborate control available from a third-party vendor. The MSFlexGrid has Rows and Col properties that you can use to find out its current size. Then you can set the Row and Col properties to the row and column you want to change and use the Text property to change the text in the selected cell of the grid.

```
Private Sub Movetogrid_Click()
Dim i As Integer, row As Integer

i = lsKids.ListIndex + 1
  If i > 0 And i <= swmrs.Count Then
     Set sw = swmrs(i)
     grdTimes.AddItem ""
     row = grdTimes.Rows
     grdTimes.row = row - 1
     grdTimes.Col = 0
     grdTimes.Text = sw.getName
     grdTimes.Col = 1
     grdTimes.Text = Str$(sw.getTime)
  End If
End Sub
```

However, we would like to be able to use the grid without changing our code at all from what we used for the simple list box. It turns out that you can do that because the AddItem method of the MSFlexGrid interprets tab characters in an analogous fashion to the way the list box does.

The following statement

```
grdTimes.AddItem sw.getName & vbTab & Str$(sw.getTime)
```

works the same as the seven lines of code do that we showed in the previous example, and the resulting display will put the names in one column and the scores in the other, as shown in Figure 15-2.

In other words, the MSFlexGrid control provides the same programming interface as a convenience and is in fact its own Adapter between the list box and the MSFlexGrid control.

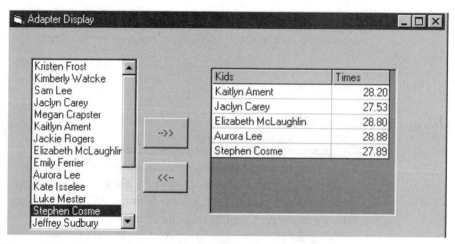

Figure 15-2   Selecting names for display in an MSFlexGrid control

In fact, since the list and grid have the same programming interface, it is quite easy to write a private subroutine to add the data to either of them.

```
Private Sub addText(ctl As Control, sw As Swimmer)
    ctl.AddItem sw.getName & vbTab & str$(sw.getTime)
End Sub
```

Then we could write the button click routines so they each call this method using a different list as an argument.

```
Private Sub Moveit_Click()
 Dim i As Integer
 i = lsKids.ListIndex + 1
 If i > 0 And i <= swmrs.Count Then
    Set sw = swmrs(i)
    addText lsTimes, sw
 End If
End Sub
'------
Private Sub Movetogrid_Click()
 Dim i As Integer, row As Integer
 i = lsKids.ListIndex + 1
 If i > 0 And i <= swmrs.Count Then
    Set sw = swmrs(i)
    addText grdTimes, sw
 End If
End Sub
```

However, this is clearly not very object oriented. The addText method really should be part of the class we are using. We shouldn't have to pass an instance of the list or grid into a method in the same class. Now in VB6 and before, there is no way to add methods to a control. Instead, we can create a simple Control-Adapter class that will handle both the grid and the list and contain the addText method we wrote as a simple subroutine above. This class is the following.

```
'Class ControlAdapter
Private ctrl As Control

Public Sub init(ctl As Control)
  Set ctrl = ctl   'copy control into class
End Sub
'-----
Public Sub addText(sw As Swimmer)
'add new line to list or grid
  ctrl.AddItem sw.getName & vbTab & str$(sw.getTime)
End Sub
```

We initialize this class with an instance of a list or grid in the Form_Load event.

```
Private grdAdapt As New ControlAdapter

'pass grid into Control Adapter
grdAdapt.init grdTimes
```

Then we can simply call the class's addText method when we click on the right arrow button, regardless of which display control we are using.

```
Private Sub Moveit_Click()
  Dim i As Integer
  i = lsKids.ListIndex + 1
  If i > 0 And i <= swmrs.Count Then
     Set sw = swmrs(i)
     grdAdapt.addText sw
  End If
End Sub
```

Using a TreeView

If, however, you choose to use a TreeView control to display the data you select, you will find that there is no conveniently adapted interface that you can use to keep your code from changing. Thus, our convenient ControlAdapter class can not be used for the TreeView. Instead, we need to write a new TreeAdapter class that has the same interface but carries out the adding of a line to the tree correctly.

The TreeView class contains a Nodes collection to which you add data by adding a node, setting its text, and defining whether it is a child node. Child nodes are related to the index of the parent node. The following code adds a parent node and then adds a child node to it.

```
'Class TreeAdapter
Private Tree As TreeView
Public Sub init(tr As TreeView)
  Set Tree = tr
End Sub
Public Sub addText(sw As Swimmer)
Dim scnt As String, nod As Node
    scnt = Str$(Tree.Nodes.Count)
    Set nod = Tree.Nodes.Add(, tvwNext, "r" & _
        sw.getName, sw.getName)
    Tree.Nodes.Add "r" & sw.getName, tvwChild, , Str$(sw.getTime)
    nod.Expanded = True
End Sub
```

We illustrate our TreeView program in Figure 15-3.

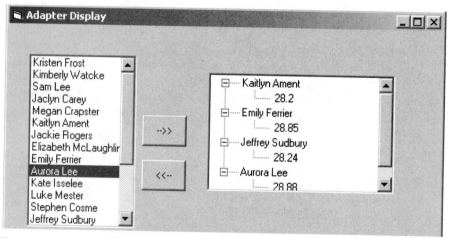

Figure 15-3   The TreeView adapter program

The Object Adapter

In the object adapter approach, (Figure 15-4), we create a class that *contains* a List Box class but that implements the methods of the ControlAdapter interface. This is the approach we took in the preceding example.

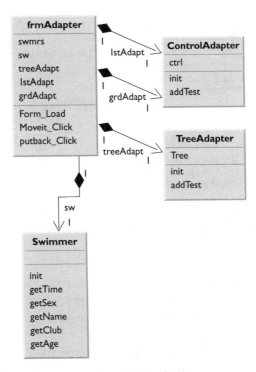

Figure 15-4 An object adapter approach to the list adapter

Using Adapters in VB7

Adapters can be even more powerful in VB7. Let's first consider the VB7 List-Box itself. This control has rather different methods from the VB6 list box, and we might very well want to hide this difference by using an adapter so that the methods that are brought to the surface appear to be the same.

In VB7, you add a line to a list box by adding a String to the listbox's Items collection.

```
list.Items.Add(s)
```

The ListIndex property is replaced by the SelectedIndex property. So we could easily write a simple wrapper class that translates these methods into the ListBox methods for VB7. The beginning of a ListAdapter class has a ListBox instance in its constructor and saves that instance within the class, thus using encapsulation or object composition.

```
Public Class ListAdapter
     'Adapter for ListBox emulating some of
     'the methods of the VB6 list box.
```

```
    Private List As ListBox              'instance of list box
    '--------
    Public Sub New(ByVal ls As ListBox)
        List = ls
    End Sub
    '--------
    Public Sub addItem(ByVal s As String)
        list.Items.Add(s)    'add into list box
    End Sub
    '--------
    Public Function ListIndex() As Integer
        Return list.SelectedIndex      'get list index
    End Function
    '--------
    Public Sub addText(ByVal sw As Swimmer)
        List.Items.Add(sw.getName & vbTab & sw.getTime.ToString)
    End Sub
End Class
```

However, in the program we have been discussing, we want to display the name of the swimmer and the swimmer's time. Thus, it is convenient to add a method that takes a Swimmer object as an argument and puts the name and time in the list box.

The code that reads the swimmers in from the file and loads their names into the left-hand list box also uses an instance of the ListAdapter. Here are declarations and initialization.

```
Private lsAdapter, ksAdapter As ListAdapter

        lsAdapter = New ListAdapter(lsNames)
        ksAdapter = New ListAdapter(lsKids)
```

This simple routine reads in the lines of data.

```
Private Sub ReadFile()
        Dim s As String
        Dim sw As Swimmer
        Dim fl As New vbFile("swimmers.txt")
        fl.openForRead()
        s = fl.readLine
        While Not fl.fEof
            sw = New Swimmer(s)
            swimmers.add(sw)
            ksAdapter.addItem(sw.getName)
            s = fl.readLine
        End While
    End Sub
```

The running program is shown in Figure 15-5.

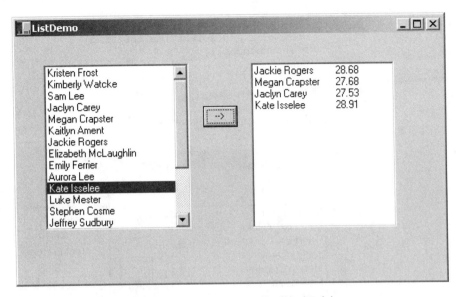

Figure 15-5   Two list boxes loaded using two instances of the ListAdapter

TreeView Adapters for VB.NET

The TreeView class in VB7 is only slightly different from that in VB6. For each node you want to create, you create an instance of the TreeNode class and add the root TreeNode collection to another node. In our example version using the TreeView, we'll add the swimmer's name to the root node collection and the swimmer's time as a subsidiary node. Here is the entire TreeAdapter class. Note that we only need implement the addText method.

```
Public Class TreeAdapter
    'An adapter to use TreeView
    'instead of list boxes
    Private Tree As TreeView      'instance of tree

    Public Sub New(ByVal tr As TreeView)
        Tree = tr
    End Sub
    '-------------
    Public Sub addText(ByVal sw As Swimmer)
        Dim scnt As String
        Dim nod As TreeNode
        'add a root node
        nod = Tree.Nodes.add(sw.getName)
```

```
            'add a child node to it
            nod.Nodes.add(sw.getTime.toString)
            Tree.expandAll()
        End Sub

    End Class
```

The TreeDemo program is shown in Figure 15-6.

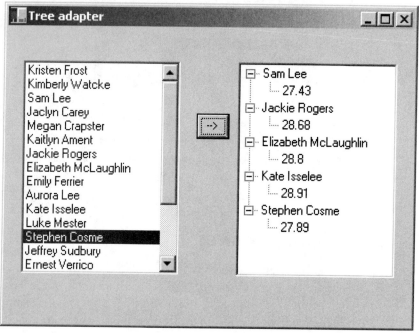

Figure 15-6   The same swimmer selection program using a TreeView adapter

Adapting a DataGrid

The VB7 DataGrid control is considerably more elaborate than the MSFlexGrid control in VB6. It can be bound to a database or to an in-memory data array. To use the DataGrid without a database, you create an instance of the DataTable class and add DataColumns to it. DataColumns are by default of String type, but you can define them to be of any type when you create them. Here is the general outline of how you create a DataGrid using a DataTable.

```
dTable = New DataTable("Kids")
dTable.MinimumCapacity = 100
dTable.CaseSensitive = False
```

```
Dim column As DataColumn
column = New DataColumn("Frname", _
    System.Type.GetType("System.String"))

dTable.Columns.Add(column)
column = New DataColumn("Lname", _
    System.Type.GetType("System.String"))

dTable.Columns.Add(column)
column = New DataColumn("Age", _
    System.Type.GetType("System.Int16"))

dTable.Columns.Add(column)

DGrid.DataSource = dTable
DGrid.CaptionVisible = False     'no caption
DGrid.RowHeadersVisible = False 'no row headers
DGrid.EndInit()
```

To add text to the DataTable, you ask the table for a row object and then set
the elements of the row object to the data for that row. If the types are all String,
then you copy the strings, but if one of the columns is of a different type, such as
the integer age column here, you must be sure to use that type in setting that column's data.

The complete GridAdapter class fills in each row in this fashion.

```
Public Class GridAdapter
    Private dtable As DataTable
    Private Dgrid As DataGrid
    '-----
    Public Sub New(ByVal grid As DataGrid)
        dtable = CType(grid.DataSource, DataTable)
        dgrid = grid
    End Sub
    '-----
    Public Sub addText(ByVal sw As Swimmer)
        Dim scnt As String
        Dim row As DataRow

        row = dtable.NewRow
        row("Frname") = sw.getFirstName
        row(1) = sw.getLastName
        row(2) = sw.getAge  'This one is an integer
        dtable.Rows.Add(row)
        dtable.AcceptChanges()
    End Sub
End Class
```

Note that you can refer to each column either by numeric position or by name.
The running program is shown in Figure 15-7.

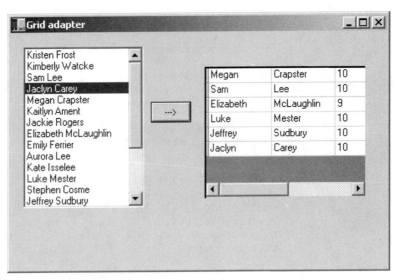

Figure 15-7   The GridAdapter program

The Class Adapter

In the class adapter approach, we derive a new class from Listbox (or the grid or tree control) and add the desired methods to it. This is possible in VB7 but not in earlier versions of Visual Basic. In the class adapter example on the CD-ROM, we create a new class called OurList which is derived from the Listbox class and which implements the following interface:

```
Public Interface ListAdapter
    'Interface Adapter for ListBox emulating some of
    'the methods of the VB6 list box.
    Sub addItem(ByVal s As String)
    Function ListIndex() As Integer
    Sub addText(ByVal sw As Swimmer)
End Interface
```

The class diagram is shown in Figure 15-8. The remaining code is much the same as in the object adapter version.

There are also some differences between the class and the object adapter approaches, although they are less significant than in C++.

The class adapter

- Won't work when we want to adapt a class and all of its subclasses, since you define the class it derives from when you create it.
- Lets the adapter change some of the adapted class's methods but still allows the others to be used unchanged.

An object adapter

- Could allow subclasses to be adapted by simply passing them in as part of a constructor.
- Requires that you specifically bring any of the adapted object's methods to the surface that you wish to make available.

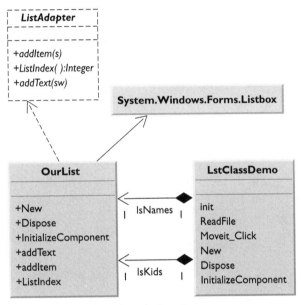

Figure 15-8   The class adapter approach to the list adapter

Two-Way Adapters

The two-way adapter is a clever concept that allows an object to be viewed by different classes as being either of type ListBox or type MSFlexGrid. This is most easily carried out using a class adapter, since all of the methods of the base class are automatically available to the derived class. However, this can only work if you do not override any of the base class's methods with any that behave differently.

Object versus Class Adapters in VB.NET

The VB.Net List, Tree, and Grid adapters we previously illustrated are all object adapters. That is, they are all classes that *contain* the visual component we are adapting. However, it is equally easy to write a List or Tree Class adapter that is derived from the base class and contains the new addText method.

In the case of the DataGrid, this is probably not a good idea because we would have to create instances of DataTables and Columns inside the DataGrid class, which makes one large complex class with too much knowledge of how other classes work.

Pluggable Adapters

A pluggable adapter is one that adapts dynamically to one of several classes. Of course, the adapter can only adapt to classes it can recognize, and usually the adapter decides which class it is adapting based on differing constructors or setParameter methods.

Adapters in VB

In a broad sense, there are already a number of adapters built into the VB7 language to allow for compatibility with VB6. These wrap new functions in the API of the older ones in much the same way we did for the Listbox previously.

THOUGHT QUESTION

How would you go about writing a class adapter to make the Grid look like a two-column list box?

Programs on the CD-ROM

`\Adapter\TreeAdapter`	The VB6 Tree adapter
`\Adapter\VBNet\LstAdapter`	VB7 List adapter
`\Adapter\VBNet\GrdAdapter`	VB7 Grid adapter
`\Adapter\VBNet\TreAdapter`	VB7 Treeview adapter
`\Adapter\VBNet\ClassAdapter`	VB7 Class-based list adapter

CHAPTER 16

The Bridge Pattern

At first sight, the Bridge pattern looks much like the Adapter pattern in that a class is used to convert one kind of interface to another. However, the intent of the Adapter pattern is to make one or more classes' interfaces look the same as that of a particular class. The Bridge pattern is designed to separate a class's interface from its implementation so you can vary or replace the implementation without changing the client code.

In the language of *Design Patterns,* the participants in the Bridge pattern are the Abstraction, which defines the class's interface; the Refined Abstraction, which extends and implements that interface; the Implementor, which defines the interface for the implementation classes; and the ConcreteImplementors, which are the implementation classes.

Suppose we have a program that displays a list of products in a window. The simplest interface for that display is a simple Listbox. But once a significant number of products have been sold, we may want to display the products in a table along with their sales figures.

Since we have just discussed the adapter pattern, you might think immediately of the class-based adapter, where we adapt the interface of the Listbox to our simpler needs in this display. In simple programs, this will work fine, but as we'll see, there are limits to that approach.

Let's further suppose that we need to produce two kinds of displays from our product data: a customer view that is just the list of products we've mentioned and an executive view that also shows the number of units shipped. We'll display the product list in an ordinary Listbox and the executive view in an MSFlexGrid table display. These two displays are the implementations of the display classes, as shown in Figure 16-1.

Now we want to define a single interface that remains the same regardless of the type and complexity of the actual implementation classes. We'll start by defining an abstract Bridger class.

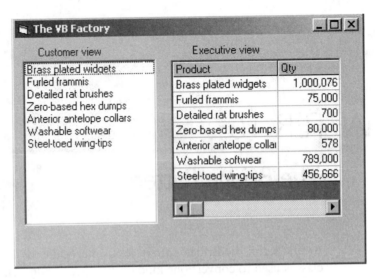

Figure 16-1   Two displays of the same information using a Bridge pattern

```
'Bridge interface to display classes
'add data to display
Public Sub addData(col As Collection)
End Sub
'-------------------
'initialize with list class
Public Sub init(visL As visList)
End Sub
```

This class just receives a Collection of data and passes it on to the display classes.

We also define a Product class that holds the names and quantities and parses the input string from the data file.

```
'Product class - reads in data
'and provides accessor methods
Private prodName As String
Private qty As String
'-----
Public Sub init(prodString As String)
 Dim i As Integer
 i = InStr(prodString, "--")
 If i > 0 Then
   prodName = Trim(Left$(prodString, i - 1))
   qty = Trim(Right(prodString, Len(prodString) - i - 1))
 Else
   prodName = prodString
   qty = ""
 End If
```

```
End Sub
'------------
Public Function getName() As String
 getName = prodName
End Function
'------------
Public Function getQty() As String
 getQty = qty
End Function
```

On the other side of the bridge are the implementation classes, which usually have a more elaborate and somewhat lower-level interface. Here we'll have them add the data lines to the display one at a time.

```
'add a line to the display
Public Sub addLine(p As Product)
End Sub
'------------
'remove a line from the display
Public Sub removeLine(ByVal num As Integer)
End Sub
'------------
'initialize the class with
'the appropriate visual control
Public Sub init(c As Control)
End Sub
```

The bridge between the interface on the left and the implementation on the right is the listBridge class, which instantiates one or the other of the list display classes. Note that it implements the Bridger class for use of the application program.

```
Implements Bridger
'A bridge between lists and display
Private visL As visList
'-----
Private Sub Bridger_addData(col As Collection)
 Dim i As Integer, p As Product
 'add data to list from product collection
 For i = 1 To col.Count
  Set p = col(i)
  visL.addLine p
 Next i
End Sub
'-----
'Initialize with visible list class
Private Sub Bridger_init(vis As visList)
 Set visL = vis
End Sub
```

At the top programming level, we just create instances of a table and a list using the listBridge class.

```
'create visList class for list box
Set prodList = New ProductList
prodList.init pList

'create a bridge to the list
Set br = New ListBridge

'pass in the list box
br.init prodList
br.addData products 'display data

'create visList for the grid
Set execList = New ProductTable
execList.init pGrid

'create a bridge to the grid
Set gbr = New ListBridge

'pass in the grid
gbr.init execList
gbr.addData products 'display data
```

The visList Classes

The two visList classes are really quite similar. The customer version operates on a ListBox and adds the names to it.

```
'Class ProductList
Implements visList
'class wrapper for the list box
'to give it a common interface
Private lst As ListBox
'-----
Private Sub visList_addLine(p As Product)
 lst.AddItem p.getName
End Sub
'-----
Private Sub visList_init(c As Control)
 Set lst = c
End Sub
'-----
Private Sub visList_removeLine(ByVal num As Integer)
 lst.RemoveItem num
End Sub
```

The ProductTable version of the visList is also similar except that it adds both the product name and quantity to the two columns of the grid.

```
Private Sub visList_addLine(p As Product)
 gridList.AddItem p.getName & vbTab & p.getQty
End Sub
```

The Class Diagram

The UML diagram in Figure 16-2 for the Bridge class shows the separation of the interface and the implementation quite clearly. The *Bridger* class on the left is the Abstraction, and the *listBridge* class is the implementation of that abstraction. The *visList* interface describes the public interface to the list classes *productList* and *productTable*. The *visList* interface defines the interface of the Implementor, and the Concrete Implementors are the *productList* and *productTable* classes.

Note that these two concrete implementors are quite different in their specifics even though they both support the *visList* interface.

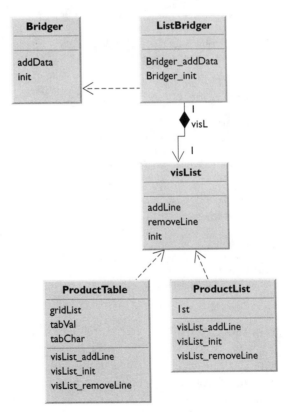

Figure 16-2 The UML diagram for the Bridge pattern used in the two displays of product information

Extending the Bridge

Now suppose we need to make some changes in the way these lists display the data. For example, maybe you want to have the products displayed in alphabetical order. You might think you'd need to either modify or subclass *both* the list and table classes. This can quickly get to be a maintenance nightmare, especially if more than two such displays are needed eventually. Instead, we simply make the changes in the extended interface class, creating a new *sortBridge* class similar to the *listBridge* class.

```
'Class SortBridge
'sorts the data before passing it
'to the visList class
Implements Bridger
Private brdg As Bridger
Private prods() As Product
'----------
Private Sub Bridger_addData(col As Collection)
 Dim max As Integer, tprod As Product
 max = col.Count
 ReDim prods(max) As Product
 Dim i As Integer, j As Integer

 'copy into array
  'details on CDROM

 'sort array
  'details on CDROM

 'put back into collection
  'details on CDROM

 'pass on to basic bridge class
 brdg.addData col
End Sub
'----------
Private Sub Bridger_init(visL As visList)
 Set brdg = New ListBridge
 brdg.init visL
End Sub
```

You can see the sorted result in Figure 16-3.

This clearly shows that you can vary the interface without changing the implementation. The converse is also true. For example, you could create another type of list display and replace one of the current list displays without any other program changes as long as the new list also implements the *visList* interface.

In Figure 16-4, we have created a tree list component that implements the *visList* interface and replaced the ordinary list without any change in the public interface to the classes.

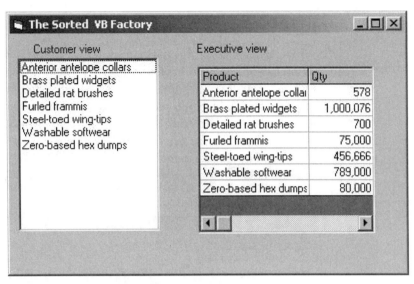

Figure 16-3   The sorted list generated using SortBridge class

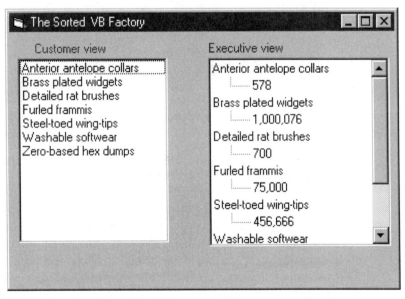

Figure 16-4   Another display using a Bridge to a tree list

ActiveX Controls as Bridges

The visual ActiveX control is itself an ideal example of a Bridge pattern implementation. An ActiveX control is a reusable software component that can be manipulated visually in a builder tool. All of the VB6 controls are written as ActiveX controls, which means they support a query interface that enables builder programs to enumerate their properties and display them for easy modification. Figure 16-5 is a screen from VB displaying a panel with a text field and a check box. The builder panel to the right shows how you can modify the properties of either of those components using a simple visual interface.

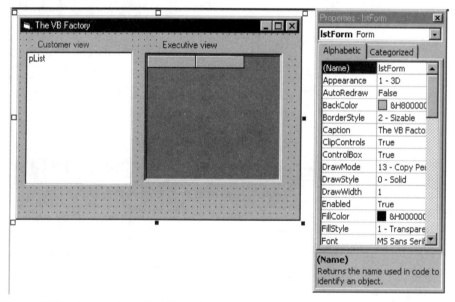

Figure 16-5   A screen from Visual Basic showing a properties interface. The property lists are effectively implemented using a Bridge pattern.

In other words, all ActiveX controls have the same interface used by the Builder program, and you can substitute any control for any other and still manipulate its properties using the same convenient interface. The actual program you construct uses these classes in a conventional way, each having its own rather different methods, but from the builder's point of view, they all appear to be the same.

The Bridge Pattern in VB.NET

In VB7, you can write the same program in much the same fashion. The important thrust of the Bridge pattern remains unchanged: to separate the management of the data from the management of the display methods. So we communicate between the underlying data and the Bridge, using the simple Bridger interface.

```
'Bridge interface to data
Public Interface Bridger
    Sub addData(ByVal col As ArrayList)
End Interface
```

We communicate between the Bridge and the visual display classes, using the VisList interface, which is now just this.

```
Public Interface VisList
    'add a line to the display
    Sub addLine(ByVal p As Product)
    'remove a line from the display
    Sub removeLine(ByVal num As Integer)
End Interface
```

As before, the Listbridge class is the bridge between the data and the display. When you create an instance of this class, you pass in the visList class you want to use to display the data, and the Bridge loads that data into the display without having to know what sort of display control it actually uses.

```
Public Class ListBridge
    Implements Bridger
    Private visL As visList
    '-----
    Public Sub New(ByVal vis As visList)
        MyBase.New()
        visL = vis     'copy in display class
    End Sub
    '-----
    'Adds array of product data
    Public Sub addData(ByVal col As ArrayList) Implements _
            Bridger.addData
        Dim i As Integer
        Dim p As Product

        'add data to list from product array
        For i = 0 To col.Count - 1
            p = CType(col(i), Product)
            visL.addLine(p)
        Next i
    End Sub
End Class
```

The ListBox VisList Class

The ProductList class is the class wrapper that converts a ListBox into a VisList object by implementing the VisList interface. In essence, it is an Adapter between the ListBox class and the VisList interface we need for the Bridge. It is, however, quite simple.

```
Public Class ProductList
    Implements visList
    'class wrapper for the list box
    'to give it a common interface
    Private lst As ListBox
    '----------
    Private Sub addLine(ByVal p As Product) _
     Implements visList.addLine
        lst.Items.Add(p.getName)
    End Sub
    '----------
    Public Sub New(ByVal c As ListBox)
        lst = c           'copy in list box
    End Sub
    '----------
    Public Sub removeLine(ByVal num As Integer) _
        Implements visList.removeLine
        lst.Items.remove(num)
    End Sub
End Class
```

The Grid VisList Class

The ProductTable class puts a VisList interface around the DataGrid control. However, since the DataGrid is a fairly complex control, we use the Grid-Adapter class we developed in Chapter 15. This makes this class quite a bit easier to write as well.

```
Public Class ProductTable
    Implements visList
    Private gridList As GridAdapter
    '-----
    Public Sub addLine(ByVal p As Product) _
        Implements visList.addLine
        gridList.AddLine(p)
    End Sub
    '-----
    Public Sub New(ByVal c As DataGrid)
        gridList = New GridADapter(c)
    End Sub
    '-----
```

```
      Public Sub removeLine(ByVal num As Integer) _
          Implements visList.removeLine
          gridList.removeLine(num)
      End Sub
End Class
```

Loading the Data

The main BasicBridge program just creates these objects, reads in the data, and passes it to the two Bridges to pass on to the two VisList classes. The init method called by New is shown below.

```
Private Sub init()
    Dim dtable As DataTable
    dtable = New DataTable("Products")
    Dim column As DataColumn
    column = New DataColumn("ProdName")

    dtable.Columns.Add(column)
    column = New DataColumn("Qty")

    dtable.Columns.Add(column)
    lsExecList.DataSource = dtable

    products = New ArrayList()    'array list
    'create visList classes
    execList = New ProductTable(lsExecList)
    prodList = New ProductList(lsProdList)

    'read in the data
    readData(products)
    'create the two bridges
    'and populate the displays
    Dim prodBridge As New ListBridge(prodList)
    Dim tableBridge As New ListBridge(execList)
    prodBridge.addData(products)
    tableBridge.addData(products)

End Sub
```

The resulting display is shown in Figure 16-6.

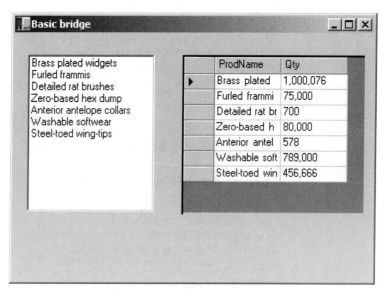

Figure 16-6   The BasicBridge program implemented in VB7

Changing the Data Side of the Bridge

Just as in the VB6 version, you can vary the interface and implementation separately. In the preceding display we see two interface displays of the data. The data implementation just reads the data into an ArrayList and passes it on into the Bridge for display. However, the Bridge could sort the data before displaying it, as we show here.

```
'A sorted version of the Data to Vislist
'Bridge class
Public Class ListBridge
    Implements Bridger
    'A bridge between lists and display
    Private visL As visList
    '-----
    Public Sub New(ByVal vis As visList)
        MyBase.New()
        visL = vis
    End Sub
    '-----
    Public Sub addData(ByVal col As ArrayList) _
            Implements Bridger.addData
        Dim i, j, max As Integer
        Dim p As Product
        max = col.count
```

```
      Dim products(max) As Product
      For i = 0 To max - 1
          products(i) = CType(col(i), Product)
      Next i
      'sort array into alphabetical order
      For i = 0 To max - 1
          For j = i To max - 1
              If products(i).getName > _
                      products(j).getName Then
                  p = products(i)
                  products(i) = products(j)
                  products(j) = p
              End If
          Next j
      Next i
      'add data to list from product collection
      For i = 0 To max - 1
          visL.addLine(products(i))
      Next i
    End Sub
End Class
```

This produces the sorted display in Figure 16-7.

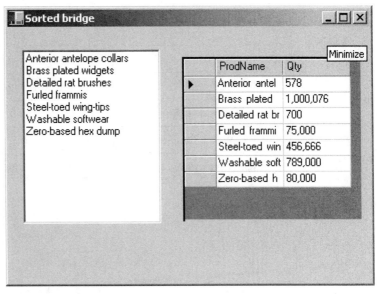

Figure 16-7   The sorted bridge display in VB7

Consequences of the Bridge Pattern

1. The Bridge pattern is intended to keep the interface to your client program constant while allowing you to change the actual kind of class you display or use. This can prevent you from recompiling a complicated set of user interface modules and only require that you recompile the bridge itself and the actual end display class.

2. You can extend the implementation class and the bridge class separately, and usually without much interaction with each other.

3. You can hide implementation details from the client program much more easily.

THOUGHT QUESTION

In plotting a stock's performance, you usually display the price and price-earnings ratio over time, whereas in plotting a mutual fund, you usually show the price and the earnings per quarter. Suggest how you can use a Bridge to do both.

Programs on the CD-ROM

\Bridge\BasicBridge	VB6 bridge from list to grid
\Bridge\SortBridge	VB6 sorted bridge
\Bridge\TreeBridge	VB6 list to tree bridge
\Bridge\VBNet\BasicBridge	VB7 bridge from list to grid
\Bridge\VBNet\SortBridge	VB7 sorted bridge from list to grid

CHAPTER 17

The Composite Pattern

Frequently programmers develop systems in which a component may be either an individual object or a collection of objects. The Composite pattern is designed to accommodate both cases. You can use the Composite to build part-whole hierarchies or to construct data representations of trees. In summary, a composite is a collection of objects, any one of which may be either a composite or just a primitive object. In tree nomenclature, some objects may be nodes with additional branches and some may be leaves.

The problem that develops is the dichotomy between having a single, simple interface to access all the objects in a composite and the ability to distinguish between nodes and leaves. Nodes have children and can have children added to them, whereas leaves do not at the moment have children, and in some implementations they may be prevented from having children added to them.

Some authors have suggested creating a separate interface for nodes and leaves where a leaf could have the methods, such as the following:

```
public Function getName() As String
public Function getValue() As String
```

and a node could have the additional methods:

```
public Function elements() As Collection
public Function getChild(nodeName As String) As Node
public Sub add(obj As Object)
public Sub remove(obj As Object);
```

This then leaves us with the programming problem of deciding which elements will be which when we construct the composite. However, *Design Patterns* suggests that each element should have the *same* interface, whether it is a composite or a primitive element. This is easier to accomplish, but we are left with the question of what the *getChild* operation should accomplish when the object is actually a leaf.

VB can make this quite easy for us, since every node or leaf can return a Collection of the child nodes. If there are no children, the count property returns zero. Thus, if we simply obtain the Collection of child nodes from each element, we can quickly determine whether it has any children by checking the *count* property.

Just as difficult is the issue of adding or removing leaves from elements of the composite. A nonleaf node can have child leaves added to it, but a leaf node cannot. However, we would like all of the components in the composite to have the same interface. We must prevent attempts to add children to a leaf node, and we can design the leaf node class to raise an error if the program attempts to add to such a node.

An Implementation of a Composite

Let's consider a small company. It may have started with a single person who got the business going. He was, of course, the CEO, although he may have been too busy to think about it at first. Then he hired a couple of people to handle the marketing and manufacturing. Soon each of them hired some additional assistants to help with advertising, shipping, and so forth, and they became the company's first two vice-presidents. As the company's success continued, the firm continued to grow until it has the organizational chart in Figure 17-1.

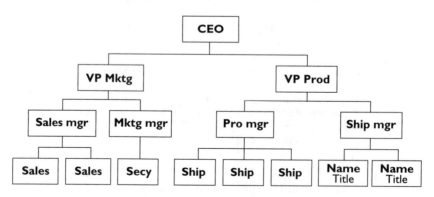

Figure 17-1   A typical organizational chart

Computing Salaries

If the company is successful, each of these company members receives a salary, and we could at any time ask for the cost of the control span of any employee to the company. We define this control cost as the salary of that person and those of all subordinates. Here is an ideal example for a composite.

- The cost of an individual employee is simply his or her salary (and benefits).
- The cost of an employee who heads a department is his or her salary plus those of subordinates.

We would like a single interface that will produce the salary totals correctly whether the employee has subordinates or not.

```
public Function getSalaries() As Single
```

At this point, we realize that the idea of all Composites having the same standard method names in their interface is probably naïve. We'd prefer that the public methods be related to the kind of class we are actually developing. So rather than have generic methods like *getValue,* we'll use *getSalaries.*

The Employee Classes

We could now imagine representing the company as a Composite made up of nodes: managers and employees. It would be possible to use a single class to represent all employees, but since each level may have different properties, it might be more useful to define at least two classes: Employees and Bosses. Employees are leaf nodes and cannot have employees under them. Bosses are nodes that may have employee nodes under them.

We'll start with the AbstractEmployee class and derive our concrete employee classes from it.

```
'Class AbstractEmployee
'Interface for all Employee classes
'---------
Public Function getSalary() As Single
End Function
'---------
Public Function getName() As String
End Function
'---------
Public Function isLeaf() As Boolean
End Function
```

```
'---------
Public Sub add(nm As String, salary As Single)
End Sub
'---------
Public Sub addEmp(emp As AbstractEmployee)
End Sub
'---------
Public Function getSubordinates() As Subords
End Function
'---------
Public Sub remove(emp As AbstractEmployee)
End Sub
'----------
Public Function getChild(nm As String) As AbstractEmployee
End Function
'---------
Public Function getSalaries() As Single
End Function
'---------
Public Sub init(name As String, salary As Single)
End Sub
```

Our concrete Employee class will store the name and salary of each employee and allow us to fetch them as needed.

```
'Class Employee
'implementation of AbstractEmployee interface
Implements AbstractEmployee
Private nm As String
Private salary As String
Private subordinates As Subords
'--------
Private Function AbstractEmployee_getChild(nm As String) _
  As AbstractEmployee
  Set AbstractEmployee_getChild = Null
End Function
'--------
Private Function AbstractEmployee_getName() As String
  AbstractEmployee_getName = nm
End Function
'--------
Private Function AbstractEmployee_getSalaries() As Single
  AbstractEmployee_getSalaries = salary
End Function
'--------
Private Function AbstractEmployee_getSalary() As Single
  AbstractEmployee_getSalary = salary
End Function
'--------
Private Sub AbstractEmployee_init(name As String, _
  money As Single)
  nm = name
  salary = money
```

```
    Set subordinates = New Subords
End Sub
'--------
Private Function AbstractEmployee_isLeaf() As Boolean
  AbstractEmployee_isLeaf = True
End Function
'--------
Private Sub AbstractEmployee_remove(emp As AbstractEmployee)
  Err.Raise vbObjectError + 513, , & _
  "No subordinates in base employee class"
End Sub
'--------
Private Sub Class_Initialize()
  nm = ""
  salary = 0
End Sub
```

The Employee class must have concrete implementations of the *add, remove, getChild,* and *subordinates* classes. Since an Employee is a leaf, all of these will return some sort of error indication. For example, *subordinates* could return *null,* but programming will be more consistent if it returns an empty enumeration.

```
Private Function AbstractEmployee_getSubordinates() _
                                        As Subords
Set AbstractEmployee_getSubordinates = subordinates
End Function
```

The *add* and *remove* methods must generate errors, since members of the basic Employee class cannot have subordinates.

```
Private Sub AbstractEmployee_add(nm As String, _
    salary As Single)
Err.Raise vbObjectError + 513, , & _
            "No subordinates in base employee class"
End Sub
'--------
Private Sub AbstractEmployee_addEmp(emp As _
                               AbstractEmployee)
Err.Raise vbObjectError + 513, , & _
                "No subordinates in base employee class"
End Sub
```

The Subords Class

VB does not provide an enumeration class that contains its own internal pointer to move through a list. So we create a simple class that contains a collection and an index to move through that collection. The advantage of using this class, here called Subords, is that you can search down through the composite tree without having to maintain indexes outside of each instance of the Collection that you search through.

```
'Class Subords
'A simple enumeration of a collection
Private subNames As Collection   'the collection
Private index As Integer         'the internal index
'-----
Public Sub moveFirst()
   index = 1
End Sub
'-----
Public Function hasMoreElements()
   hasMoreElements = index <= subNames.count
End Function
'-----
Public Function nextElement() As Object
   Set nextElement = subNames(index)
   index = index + 1
End Function
'-----
Private Sub Class_Initialize()
   Set subNames = New Collection
   index = 1
End Sub
'-----
Public Sub add(obj As Object)
   subNames.add obj
End Sub
'-----
Public Function element(i As Integer) As Object
   Set element = subNames(i)
End Function
'-----
Public Function count() As Integer
   count = subNames.count
End Function
```

Using the Subords class, we can simply call the hasMoreElements method and the nextElement method to move through a collection without having to use and maintain an index ourselves.

The Boss Class

Our Boss class is a subclass of Employee and allows us to store subordinate employees as well. We'll store them in a Collection called *subordinates* and return them through an enumeration. Thus, if a particular Boss has temporarily run out of Employees, the enumeration will just be empty. We'll make this Boss class *contain* an instance of Employee, which will then return the name and salary information. The Boss class itself will handle the subordinate list.

```
'Class Boss
'A Boss implementation of AbstractEmployee
'which allows subordinates
Implements AbstractEmployee
Private emp As AbstractEmployee 'keeps employee data
Private subordinates As Subords 'list of subordinates
'--------
Private Sub AbstractEmployee_add(nm As String, _
          salary As Single)
Dim newEmp As AbstractEmployee
 Set newEmp = New Employee
 newEmp.init nm, salary
 subordinates.add newEmp
End Sub
'--------
Private Sub AbstractEmployee_addEmp(emp As _
          AbstractEmployee)
 subordinates.add emp
End Sub
'--------
Private Function AbstractEmployee_getName() As String
 AbstractEmployee_getName = emp.getName
End Function
'--------
Private Function AbstractEmployee_getSalary() As Single
 AbstractEmployee_getSalary = emp.getSalary
End Function
'--------
Private Function AbstractEmployee_getSubordinates() _
     As Subords
 Set AbstractEmployee_getSubordinates = subordinates
End Function
'--------
Private Sub AbstractEmployee_init(name As String, _
          salary As Single)
 Set emp = New Employee
 emp.init name, salary
 Set subordinates = New Subords
End Sub
'--------
Private Function AbstractEmployee_isLeaf() As Boolean
 AbstractEmployee_isLeaf = False
End Function
```

If you want to get a list of employees of a given supervisor, you can obtain an Enumeration of them directly from the Subords collection. Similarly, you can use this same Collection to returns a sum of salaries for any employee and his subordinates.

```
Private Function AbstractEmployee_getSalaries() As Single
Dim sum As Single, esub As AbstractEmployee
'get the salaries of the boss and subordinates
  sum = emp.getSalary
  subordinates.moveFirst
  While subordinates.hasMoreElements
    Set esub = subordinates.nextElement
    sum = sum + esub.getSalaries
  Wend
  AbstractEmployee_getSalaries = sum
End Function
```

Note that this method starts with the salary of the current Employee and then calls the *getSalaries()* method on each subordinate. This is, of course, recursive, and any employees who have subordinates will be included. A diagram of these classes is shown in Figure 17-2.

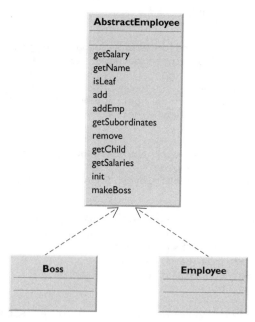

Figure 17-2   The AbstractEmployee class and how Employee and Boss are derived from it

Building the Employee Tree

We start by creating a CEO Employee and then add his or her subordinates and their subordinates, as follows.

```
Private Sub buildEmployeeList()

Dim i As Integer
Dim marketVP As AbstractEmployee
Dim salesMgr As AbstractEmployee
Dim advMgr As AbstractEmployee, emp As AbstractEmployee
Dim prodVP As AbstractEmployee, prodMgr As AbstractEmployee
Dim shipMgr As AbstractEmployee

  Set prez = New Boss
  prez.init "CEO", 200000

  Set marketVP = New Boss
  marketVP.init "Marketing VP", 100000
  prez.addEmp marketVP

  Set salesMgr = New Boss
  salesMgr.init "Sales Mgr", 50000

  Set advMgr = New Boss
  advMgr.init "Advt Mgr", 50000

  marketVP.addEmp salesMgr
  marketVP.addEmp advMgr
  Set prodVP = New Boss
  prodVP.init "Production VP", 100000

  prez.addEmp prodVP
  advMgr.add "Secy", 20000

'add salesmen reporting to sales manager
  For i = 1 To 5
    salesMgr.add "Sales" & Str$(i), rand_sal(30000)
  Next i

  Set prodMgr = New Boss
  prodMgr.init "Prod Mgr", 40000
  Set shipMgr = New Boss
  shipMgr.init "Ship Mgr", 35000
  prodVP.addEmp prodMgr
  prodVP.addEmp shipMgr

  For i = 1 To 3
    shipMgr.add "Ship" & Str$(i), rand_sal(25000)
  Next i
  For i = 1 To 4
```

```
        prodMgr.add "Manuf" & Str$(i), rand_sal(20000)
    Next i
End Sub
```

Once we have constructed this Composite structure, we can load a visual TreeView list by starting at the top node and calling the *addNode()* method recursively until all the leaves in each node are accessed.

```
Private Sub addNodes(nod As Node, ByVal emp As AbstractEmployee)
Dim col As Subords, i As Integer, newNode As Node
Dim newEmp As AbstractEmployee, cnt As Integer
Dim index As Integer

Set col = emp.getSubordinates
index = nod.index      'get node's index
col.moveFirst
While col.hasMoreElements
  Set newEmp = col.nextElement
  Set newNode = empTree.Nodes.add(index, tvwChild)
  newNode.Text = newEmp.getName
  newNode.Expanded = True
  addNodes newNode, newEmp
Wend
End Sub
```

The final program display is shown in Figure 17-3.

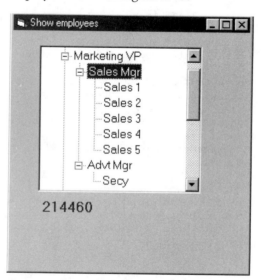

Figure 17-3   The corporate organization shown in a TreeView control

In this implementation, the cost (sum of salaries) is shown in the bottom bar for any employee you click on. This simple computation calls the *getChild()* method recursively to obtain all the subordinates of that employee.

```
Private Sub empTree_Click()
 Dim newEmp As AbstractEmployee
 'finds the salary of the selected employee and
 'all the subordinates

 Set newEmp = prez.getChild(empTree.SelectedItem)
 lblSalary.Caption = Str$(newEmp.getSalaries)

End Sub
```

Self-Promotion

We can imagine cases where a simple Employee would stay in his current job but have new subordinates. For example, a Salesman might be asked to supervise sales trainees. For such a case, it is convenient to provide a method in the Boss class that creates a Boss from an Employee.

```
Private Sub AbstractEmployee_makeBoss(newBoss As _
                                      AbstractEmployee)
 Set emp = newBoss
End Sub
```

In this implementation, we have all the classes (Employee *and* Boss) implement the AbstractEmployee interface. However, so we can treat each object as one having the methods of an AbstractEmployee, we have to include the make-Boss methods in the AbstractEmployee interface. Then we have to add this method to the Employee class as well, raising an error if it is called inadvertently.

```
Private Sub AbstractEmployee_makeBoss( _
     emp As AbstractEmployee)
Err.Raise vbObjectError + 514, , "Employee is not a boss"
End Sub
```

Doubly Linked Lists

In the preceding implementation, we keep a reference to each subordinate in the Collection in each Boss class. This means that you can move down the chain from the president to any employee, but there is no way to move back up to find out who an employee's supervisor is. This is easily remedied by providing a constructor for each AbstractEmployee subclass that includes a reference to the parent node.

```
Private Sub AbstractEmployee_init(parnt As AbstractEmployee, _
 name As String, money As Single)
   Set parent = parnt
   hasParent = True
   nm = name
```

```
    salary = money
    Set subordinates = New Subords
End Sub
```

Then you can quickly walk up the tree to produce a reporting chain.

```
Public Sub setBoss(empl As AbstractEmployee)
Dim nm As String
Set emp = empl
Do
  nm = emp.getName
  empList.AddItem nm
  Set emp = emp.getBoss
Loop Until emp.getName = nm
End Sub
```

See Figure 17-4.

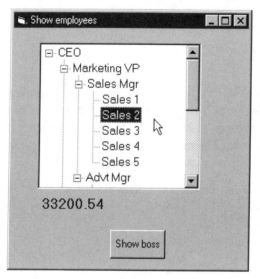

Figure 17-4   The tree list display of the composite with a display of the parent nodes on the right

Consequences of the Composite Pattern

The Composite pattern allows you to define a class hierarchy of simple objects and more complex composite objects so they appear to be the same to the client program. Because of this simplicity, the client can be that much simpler, since nodes and leaves are handled in the same way.

The Composite pattern also makes it easy for you to add new kinds of components to your collection, as long as they support a similar programming interface. On the other hand, this has the disadvantage of making your system overly general. You might find it harder to restrict certain classes where this would normally be desirable.

A Simple Composite

The intent of the Composite pattern is to allow you to construct a tree of various related classes, even though some have different properties than others and some are leaves that do not have children. However, for very simple cases, you can sometimes use just a single class that exhibits both parent and leaf behavior. In the SimpleComposite example, we create an Employee class that always contains the Collection *employees*. This Collection of employees will either be empty or populated, and this determines the nature of the values that you return from the *getChild* and *remove* methods. In this simple case, we do not raise errors and always allow leaf nodes to be promoted to have child nodes. In other words, we always allow execution of the *add* method.

While you may not regard this automatic promotion as a disadvantage, in systems where there are a very large number of leaves, it is wasteful to keep a Collection initialized and unused in each leaf node. In cases where there are relatively few leaf nodes, this is not a serious problem.

Composites in VB

In VB, you will note that the *Node* object class we use to populate the TreeView is in fact just such a simple composite pattern. You will also find that the Composite describes the hierarchy of Form, Frame, and Controls in any user interface program. Similarly, toolbars are containers, and each may contain any number of other containers.

Any container may then contain components such as Buttons, Checkboxes, and TextBoxes, each of which is a leaf node that cannot have further children. They may also contain ListBoxes and grids that may be treated as leaf nodes or that may contain further graphical components. You can walk down the Composite tree using the *Controls* collection.

The Composite in VB.NET

In VB7 we do not need to use the Subords class because we have a built-in enumeration interface called IEnumerator. This interface consists of these methods.

```
Function MoveNext() as Boolean     'False if no more left
Function Current() as Object       'get current object
Sub Reset()                        'move to first
```

So we can create an AbstractEmployee interface that returns an Enumerator. You move through an enumeration, allowing for the fact that it might be empty, using the following approach.

```
e.Reset
While e.MoveNext
  Emp = Ctype(e.Current, Employee)
  '...do computation..
End While
```

This Enumerator may, of course, be empty and can thus be used for both nodes and leaves of the composite. Here is our AbstractEmployee interface.

```
Public Interface AbstractEmployee
    Inherits IEnumerable
    'Interface for all Employee classes
    Function getSalary() As Single
    Function getName() As String
    Function isLeaf() As Boolean
    Overloads Sub add(ByVal nm As String, _
            ByVal salary As Single)
    Overloads Sub add(ByVal emp As AbstractEmployee)
    Function getSubordinates() As IEnumerator
    Sub remove(ByVal emp As AbstractEmployee)
    Function getChild(ByVal nm As String) _
                As AbstractEmployee
    Function getSalaries() As Single
End Interface
```

Since VB7 allows polymorphism, we have two polymorphic versions of the add method. Note that VB7 syntax requires that we specifically declare them using the Overloads keyword.

The other major change we make for VB7 is that we can throw an exception if a program tries to add or remove an Employee from an Employee class when that employee is not a Boss and has no subordinates.

```
Public Overridable Overloads Sub add( _
        ByVal nm As String,_
        ByVal salary As Single) _
        Implements AbstractEmployee.add
    Throw New Exception("No subordinates")
End Sub
'------
Public Overridable Overloads Sub add( _
        ByVal emp As AbstractEmployee) _
        Implements AbstractEmployee.add
    Throw New Exception("No subordinates")
End Sub
```

In our VB6 version of the composite, we had to completely implement every method of the AbstractEmployee interface in both the Employee and the Boss class. In VB7 we can derive the Boss from the Employee class and only implement the methods that differ. VB7's syntax does require that we specifically declare the fact that we are overriding these methods, as shown below.

```
Public Overloads Overrides Sub add( _
        ByVal nm As String, ByVal salary As Single)
    Dim newEmp As AbstractEmployee
    newEmp = New Employee(nm, salary)
    subordinates.add(newEmp)
End Sub
'--------
Public Overloads Overrides Sub add( _
        ByVal emp As AbstractEmployee)
    subordinates.add(emp)
End Sub
```

The Enumerator

The Enumerator we use in our Boss and Employee classes to enumerate employees is a member of the ArrayList class. Classes that can return an IEnumerator are said to implement the IEnumerable interface. However, the advantage here is that we can create an empty ArrayList in the Employee class and never allow additions to the array. However, we need not handle requests for an enumeration of subordinates separately because the enumeration will always be empty.

For this reason, we do not have to create separate versions of the getSalaries method for Employees and Bosses because if the enumeration of subordinates is empty, the method will simply return the salary of the current employee.

```
Public Function getSalaries() As Single _
        Implements AbstractEmployee.getSalaries
    Dim sum As Single
    Dim esub As AbstractEmployee
    Dim enumSub As IEnumerator
    'get the salaries of the boss and subordinates
    sum = getSalary
    enumSub = subordinates.getEnumerator
    While enumSub.moveNext
        esub = CType(enumSub.current, AbstractEmployee)
        sum = sum + esub.getSalaries
    End While
    Return sum
End Function
```

Multiple Boss Constructors

In our VB6 version of the composite, we had a specific makeBoss method to create a Boss from an employee. We can do that in VB7 with a second, overloaded version of the constructor.

```
Public Sub New(ByVal name As String, _
        ByVal salary As Single)
    MyBase.New(name, salary)
    subordinates = New ArrayList()
End Sub
'-----
Public Sub New(ByVal emp As Employee)
    MyBase.New(emp.getName, emp.getSalary)
End Sub
```

When you click on an element of the tree view, you can catch the afterSelect event.

```
Protected Sub EmpTree_AfterSelect( _
        ByVal sender As Object, _
        ByVal e As System.WinForms.TreeViewEventArgs)
    Dim node As EmpNode
    node = CType(EmpTree.SelectedNode, EmpNode)
    getNodeSum(node)
End Sub
```

Then you can compute the salary recursively.

```
Private Function getNodeSum(ByVal node As EmpNode)_
 As Single
    Dim emp As AbstractEmployee
    Dim sum As Single

    emp = node.getEmployee
    sum = emp.getSalaries

    lbSalary.Text = sum.Format("n", Nothing)
End Function
```

Note that the label text is generated using the Single variable object's Format method.

The final Composite program for VB7 is shown in Figure 17-5.

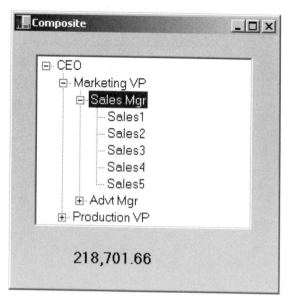

Figure 17-5   The VB7 Composite

Other Implementation Issues

Ordering components. In some programs, the order of the components may be important. If that order is somehow different from the order in which they were added to the parent, then the parent must do additional work to return them in the correct order. For example, you might sort the original collection alphabetically and return a new sorted collection.

Caching results. If you frequently ask for data that must be computed from a series of child components, as we did here with salaries, it may be advantageous to cache these computed results in the parent. However, unless the computation is relatively intensive and you are quite certain that the underlying data have not changed, this may not be worth the effort.

THOUGHT QUESTIONS

1. A baseball team can be considered an aggregate of its individual players. How could you use a composite to represent individual and team performance?

2. The produce department of a supermarket needs to track its sales performance by food item. Suggest how a composite might be helpful.

Programs on the CD-ROM

\Composite\SimpleComposite	VB6 composite shows tree
\Composite\ParentChild	VB6 composite that uses both child links and parent links
\Composite\VBNetComposite	VB7 composite of same employee tree

CHAPTER 18

The Decorator Pattern

The Decorator pattern provides us with a way to modify the behavior of individual objects without having to create a new derived class. Suppose we have a program that uses eight objects, but three of them need an additional feature. You could create a derived class for each of these objects, and in many cases this would be a perfectly acceptable solution. However, if each of these three objects requires *different* features, this would mean creating three derived classes. Further, if one of the classes has features of *both* of the other classes, you begin to create complexity that is both confusing and unnecessary.

For example, suppose we wanted to draw a special border around some of the buttons in a toolbar. If we created a new derived button class, this means that all of the buttons in this new class would always have this same new border when this might not be our intent.

Instead, we create a Decorator class that *decorates* the buttons. Then we derive any number of specific Decorators from the main Decorator class, each of which performs a specific kind of decoration. In order to decorate a button, the Decorator has to be an object derived from the visual environment so it can receive paint method calls and forward calls to other useful graphic methods to the object that it is decorating. This is another case where object containment is favored over object inheritance. The decorator is a graphical object, but it contains the object it is decorating. It may intercept some graphical method calls, perform some additional computation, and pass them on to the underlying object it is decorating.

Decorating a CoolButton

Recent Windows applications such as Internet Explorer and Netscape Navigator have a row of flat, unbordered buttons that highlight themselves with outline borders when you move your mouse over them. Some Windows programmers call this toolbar a CoolBar and the buttons CoolButtons. There is no analogous button behavior in VB controls, but we can obtain that behavior by *decorating* a PictureBox and using it as a button. In this case, we decorate it by drawing black and white border lines to highlight the button, or gray lines to remove the button borders.

Let's consider how to create this Decorator. *Design Patterns* suggests that Decorators should be derived from some general Visual Component class and then every message for the actual button should be forwarded from the decorator. In VB6, this is impractical because it is not possible to create a new visual control that contains an existing one. Further, even if we derived a control from an existing one, it would not have the line drawing methods we need to carry out decoration.

Design Patterns suggests that classes such as Decorator should be abstract classes and that you should derive all of your actual working (or concrete) decorators from the Abstract class. Here we show an Abstract class for a decorator that we can use to decorate picture boxes or other decorators.

```
'Class AbstractDecorator
'Used to decorate pictureBoxes
'and other Decorators
'--------
Public Sub init(c As Control, title As String)
'initializes decorator with control
End Sub
'--------
Public Sub initContents(d As AbstractDecorator)
'initializes decorator with another decorator
End Sub
'--------
Public Sub mouseUp()
End Sub
'--------
Public Sub mouseDown()
End Sub
'--------
Public Sub mouseMove(ByVal x As Single, ByVal y As Single)
End Sub
'--------
Public Sub refresh()
End Sub
'--------
Public Sub paint()
```

```
End Sub
'--------
Public Function getControl() As Control
End Function
```

Now, let's look at how we could implement a CoolButton. All we really need to do is to draw the white and black lines around the button area when it is highlighted and draw gray lines when it is not. When a MouseMove is detected over the button, it should draw the highlighted lines, and when the mouse leaves the button area, the lines should be drawn in gray.

However, VB does not have a MouseLeft event, so you cannot know for certain when the mouse is no longer over the button. As a first approximation, we detect the mouse crossing the outer 8 twips of the button area and treat that as an exit. To make sure that the button eventually un-highlights even if the mouse moves too quickly to trigger the exit criteria, we also use a timer to turn off the highlighting after 1 second if the mouse is no longer over the button.

```
Public Sub mouseMove(x As Single, y As Single)
Dim h As Integer, w As Integer, col As Long
h = pic.Height
w = pic.Width

If x < 8 Or y < 8 Or x > w - 16 Or y > h - 16 Then
    col = pic.BackColor
    drawLines True, col, False
    isOver = False
Else
    cTime = Time
    col = vbBlack
    drawLines False, col, False
    'isOver = True
End If

End Sub
'--------
Public Sub mouseDown()
  drawLines False, vbBlack, True
  isOver = True
End Sub
'--------
Public Sub mouseUp()
  isOver = False
  drawLines False, vbBlack, False
End Sub
'--------
Public Sub paint()
Dim x As Integer, y As Integer, h As Integer
  x = 10
  h = pic.Height
```

```
      y = 0.33 * h
      pic.PSet (x, y), pic.BackColor
      pic.Print btText;
End Sub
'--------
Private Sub drawLines(hide As Boolean, col As Long, _
      down As Boolean)
Dim h As Integer, w As Integer
h = pic.Height
w = pic.Width
If down Then
    col = vbBlack
      pic.Line (0, 0)-(w - 8, 0), col
      pic.Line -(w - 8, h - 8), col
      pic.Line -(0, h - 8), col
      pic.Line -(1, 1), col
Else
  If hide Then
      pic.Line (0, 0)-(w - 8, 0), col
      pic.Line -(w - 8, h - 8), col
      pic.Line -(0, h - 8), col
      pic.Line -(1, 1), col
  Else
      pic.Line (0, 0)-(w - 8, 0), vbWhite
      pic.Line -(w - 8, h - 8), col
      pic.Line -(0, h - 8), col
      pic.Line -(1, 1), vbWhite
  End If
End If

End Sub
```

We use a timer to see if it is time to repaint the button without highlights.

```
Public Sub tick()
Dim thisTime As Variant, diff As Variant
  thisTime = Time
  diff = DateDiff("s", cTime, thisTime)
  If diff >= 1 And Not isOver Then
    drawLines True, pic.BackColor, False
    isOver = False
  End If
End Sub
```

Using a Decorator

Now that we've written a CoolDecorator class, how do we use it? We simply put
PictureBoxes on the VB Form, create an instance of the Decorator, and pass it the
PictureBox it is to decorate. Let's consider a simple program with two Cool-

Buttons and one ordinary Button. We create the buttons in the Form_Load event as follows.

```
Private Sub Form_Load()
cTime = Time     'get the time
Set deco = New Decorator
deco.init Picture1, "A Button"
deco.paint

Set deco2 = New Decorator
deco2.init picture2, "B Button"
deco2.paint
```

This program is shown in Figure 18-1, with the mouse hovering over one of the buttons.

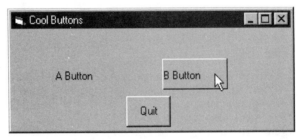

Figure 18-1 The A button and B button are CoolButtons, which are outlined when a mouse hovers over them. Here the B button is outlined.

Now that we see how a single decorator works, what about multiple decorators? It could be that we'd like to decorate our CoolButtons with another decoration—say, a diagonal red line. Since we have provided an alternate initializer with a Decorator as an argument, we can encapsulate one decorator inside another and paint additional decorations without ever having to change the original code. In fact, it is this containment and passing on of events that is the real crux of the Decorator pattern.

Let's consider the ReDecorator, which draws that diagonal red line. It draws the line and then passes control to the enclosed decorator to draw suitable Cool Button lines. Since Redecorator implants the AbstractDecorator interface, we can use it wherever we would have used the original decorator.

```
'Class Redecorator
'contains a Decorator which it further decorates
Implements AbstractDecorator
Private deco As AbstractDecorator
Private pic As PictureBox
'--------
```

```
Public Sub init(d As Decorator)
  Set deco = d
  Set pic = deco.getControl
End Sub
'--------
Private Function AbstractDecorator_getControl() As Control
  Set AbstractDecorator_getControl = pic
End Function
'--------
Private Sub AbstractDecorator_init(c As Control, title As String)
  'never called- included for completeness
End Sub
'--------
Private Sub AbstractDecorator_initContents(d As AbstractDecorator)
  init d
End Sub
'--------
Private Sub AbstractDecorator_mouseDown()
 deco.mouseDown
 AbstractDecorator_paint
End Sub
'--------
Private Sub AbstractDecorator_mouseMove(ByVal x As Single,_
                              ByVal y As Single)
 deco.mouseMove x, y
 AbstractDecorator_paint
End Sub
'-----
Private Sub AbstractDecorator_mouseUp()
 deco.mouseUp
End Sub
'--------
Private Sub AbstractDecorator_paint()
Dim w As Integer, h As Integer
 w = pic.Width
 h = pic.Height
 'draw diagonal red line
 pic.Line (0, 0)-(w, h), vbRed
 deco.paint 'and repaint contained decorator
End Sub
'--------
Private Sub AbstractDecorator_refresh()
 deco.refresh
 AbstractDecorator_paint
End Sub
```

You can create the CoolButton with these two decorators by just calling one and then the other during the Form_Load event.

```
Private Sub Form_Load()
  cTime = Time    'get the time
  'create first cool button
```

```
    Set deco = New Decorator
    deco.init Picture1, "A Button"
    deco.paint
    'create cool button
    Set deco2 = New Decorator
    deco2.init picture2, "B Button"
    'put it inside new decorator
    Set redec = New Redecorator
    redec.initContents deco2
    redec.paint
End Sub
```

This gives us a final program that displays the two buttons, as shown in Figure 18-2. The class diagram is shown in Figure 18-3.

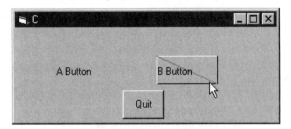

Figure 18-2   The B button is also decorated with a SlashDecorator.

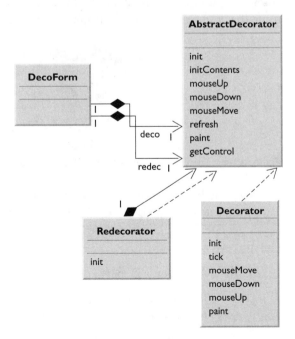

Figure 18-3   The UML class diagram for Decorators and two specific Decorator implementations

Using ActiveX Controls as Decorators

The HiText control we created in Chapter 5 is an example of a control containing another control and operating on it. This is in fact a kind of decorator, too, and it is ideal for creating new derived controls. However, for simple things like borders, it is probably overkill.

A Decorator in VB.NET

We make a CoolButton in VB7 by deriving a container from the Panel class and putting the button inside it. Then, rather than subclassing the button (or any other control), we simply add handlers for the mouse and paint events of the button and carry out the operations in the panel class.

To create our panel decorator class, we create our form and then, using the VB7 designer IDE, use the menu items Project | Add User Control to create a new user control. Then, as before, we change the class from which the control inherits from UserControl to Panel.

```
Public Class DecoPanel
    Inherits System.WinForms.Panel
```

After compiling this simple and so-far empty class we can add it to the form, using the designer, and put a button inside it (see Figure 18-4).

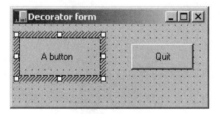

Figure 18-4   The Design window for the Decorator panel

Now the button is there, and we need to know its size and position so we can repaint it as needed. We could do this in the constructor, but this would break the IDE builder. Instead, we'll simply ask for the control the first time the OnPaint event occurs.

```
Protected Overrides Sub OnPaint _
                ByVal e As System.Windows.Forms.PaintEventArgs)
        'This is where we find out about the control
        If Not gotControl Then   'once only
            'get the control
            c = CType(Me.Controls(0), Control)
```

```
'set the panel size  1 pixel bigger all around
Dim sz As Size
sz.Width = c.Size.Width + 2
sz.Height = c.Size.Height + 2
Me.Size = sz
'Me.Size.Width = c.Size.Width + 2
'Me.Size.Height = c.Size.Height + 2
x1 = c.Location.X - 1
y1 = c.Location.Y - 1
x2 = c.Size.Width
y2 = c.Size.Height
'create the overwrite pen
gpen = New Pen(c.BackColor, 2)
gotControl = True          'only once
```

Next we need to intercept the mouse events so we can tell if the mouse is over the button.

```
Dim evh As EventHandler = _
        New EventHandler(AddressOf ctMouseEnter)
  AddHandler c.MouseHover, evh
  AddHandler c.MouseEnter, evh
  AddHandler c.MouseMove, _
        New MouseEventHandler(AddressOf ctMouseMove)
  AddHandler c.MouseLeave, _
        New EventHandler(AddressOf ctMouseLeave)
```

The events these point to simply set a mouse_over flag to true or false and then repaint the control.

```
Public Sub ctMouseEnter(ByVal sender As Object, _
              ByVal e As EventArgs)
     mouse_over = True
     Refresh()
  End Sub
  '-----
  Public Sub ctMouseLeave(ByVal sender As Object, _
                    ByVal e As EventArgs)
     mouse_over = False
     Refresh()
  End Sub
  '-----
  Public Sub ctMouseMove(ByVal sender As Object, _
                    ByVal e As MouseEventArgs)
     mouse_over = True
  End Sub
```

However, we don't want to just repaint the panel but to paint right over the button itself so we can change the style of its borders. We can do this by handling the paint event of the button itself. Note that we are adding an event handler and the button gets painted, and then this additional handler gets called.

```
'paint handler catches button's paint
 AddHandler c.Paint, _
            New PaintEventHandler(AddressOf ctPaint)
```

Our paint method draws the background (usually gray) color over the button's border and then draws the new border on top.

```
Public Sub ctPaint(ByVal sender As Object, _
 ByVal e As PaintEventArgs)
          'draw over button to change its outline
          Dim g As Graphics = e.Graphics
          'draw over everything in gray first
          g.DrawRectangle(gpen, 0, 0, x2, y2)
          'draw black and white boundaries
          'if the mouse is over
          If mouse_over Then
              g.DrawLine(bpen, 0, 0, x2 - 1, 0)
              g.DrawLine(bpen, 0, 0, 0, y2 - 1)
              g.DrawLine(wpen, 0, y2 - 1, x2 - 1, y2 - 1)
              g.DrawLine(wpen, x2 - 1, 0, x2 - 1, y2 - 1)
          End If
      End Sub
```

The resulting CoolButton is shown in Figure 18-5.

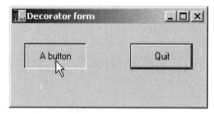

Figure 18-5   The CoolButton in VB.NET

Using the general method of overriding panels and inserting controls in them, we can decorate any control to any length and can even redraw the face of the button if we want to. This sort of approach makes sense when you can't subclass the button itself because your program requires that it be of a particular class.

Nonvisual Decorators

Decorators, of course, are not limited to objects that enhance visual classes. You can add or modify the methods of any object in a similar fashion. In fact, non-visual objects can be easier to decorate because there may be fewer methods to intercept and forward. Whenever you put an instance of a class inside another class and have the outer class operate on it, you are essentially "decorating" that inner class. This is one of the most common tools for programming available in Visual Basic.

Decorators, Adapters, and Composites

As noted in *Design Patterns,* there is an essential similarity among these classes that you may have recognized. Adapters also seem to "decorate" an existing class. However, their function is to change the interface of one or more classes to one that is more convenient for a particular program. Decorators add methods to particular instances of classes rather than to all of them. You could also imagine that a composite consisting of a single item is essentially a decorator. Once again, however, the intent is different.

Consequences of the Decorator Pattern

The Decorator pattern provides a more flexible way to add responsibilities to a class than by using inheritance, since it can add these responsibilities to selected instances of the class. It also allows you to customize a class without creating subclasses high in the inheritance hierarchy. *Design Patterns* points out two disadvantages of the Decorator pattern. One is that a Decorator and its enclosed component are not identical. Thus, tests for object types will fail. The second is that Decorators can lead to a system with "lots of little objects" that all look alike to the programmer trying to maintain the code. This can be a maintenance headache.

Decorator and Façade evoke similar images in building architecture, but in design pattern terminology, the Façade is a way of hiding a complex system inside a simpler interface, whereas Decorator adds function by wrapping a class. We'll take up the Façade next.

THOUGHT QUESTIONS

1. When someone enters an incorrect value in a cell of a grid, you might want to change the color of the row to indicate the problem. Suggest how you could use a Decorator.

2. A mutual fund is a collection of stocks. Each one consists of an array or Collection of prices over time. Can you see how a Decorator can be used to produce a report of stock performance for each stock and for the whole fund?

Programs on the CD-ROM

\Decorator\Cooldecorator	VB6 cool button decorator
\Decorator\Redecorator	VB6 cool button and slash decorator
\Decorator\DecoVBNet	VB7 cool button decorator

CHAPTER 19

The Façade Pattern

The Façade pattern is used to wrap a set of complex classes into a simpler enclosing interface. As your programs evolve and develop, they grow in complexity. In fact, for all the excitement about using design patterns, these patterns sometimes generate so many classes that it is difficult to understand the program's flow. Furthermore, there may be a number of complicated subsystems, each of which has its own complex interface.

The Façade pattern allows you to simplify this complexity by providing a simplified interface to these subsystems. This simplification may in some cases reduce the flexibility of the underlying classes, but it usually provides all the function needed for all but the most sophisticated users. These users can still, of course, access the underlying classes and methods.

Fortunately, we don't have to write a complex system to provide an example of where a Façade can be useful. VB provides a set of classes that connect to databases, using either an interface called ODBC or direct connection to Microsoft databases, using the ADO or MSJet engines. You can connect to any database for which the manufacturer has provided an ODBC connection class—almost every database on the market. Let's take a minute and review how databases are used and a little about how they work.

What Is a Database?

A *database* is a series of tables of information in some sort of file structure that allows you to access these tables, select columns from them, sort them, and select rows based on various criteria. Databases usually have *indexes* associated with many of the columns in these tables, so we can access them as rapidly as possible.

Databases are used more than any other kind of structure in computing. You'll find databases as central elements of employee records and payroll systems, in travel scheduling systems, and all through product manufacturing and marketing.

In the case of employee records, you could imagine a table of employee names and addresses and of salaries, tax withholding, and benefits. Let's consider how these might be organized. You can imagine one table of employee names, addresses, and phone numbers. Other information that you might want to store would include salary, salary range, last raise, next raise, employee performance ranking, and so forth.

Should this all be in one table? Almost certainly not. Salary ranges for various employee types are probably invariant between employees, and thus you would store only the employee type in the employee table and the salary ranges in another table that is pointed to by the type number. Consider the data in Table 19-1.

Table 19-1   Employee Names and Salary Type Tables

Key	Lastname	Salary Type
1	Adams	2
2	Johnson	1
3	Smyth	3
4	Tully	1
5	Wolff	2

Salary Type	Min	Max
1	30000	45000
2	45000	60000
3	60000	75000

The data in the `salaryType` column refers to the second table. We could imagine many such tables for things like state of residence and tax values for each state, health plan withholding, and so forth. Each table will have a primary key column like the ones at the left of each table and several more columns of data. Building tables in a database has evolved to both an art and a science. The structure of these tables is referred to by their *normal form*. Tables are said to be in first, second, or third normal form, abbreviated as 1NF, 2NF, or 3NF.

- *First.* Each cell in a table should have only one value (never an array of values). (1NF)
- *Second.* 1NF and every nonkey column is fully dependent on the key column. This means there is a one-to-one relationship between the primary key and the remaining cells in that row. (2NF)

- *Third.* 2NF and all nonkey columns are mutually independent. This means that there are no data columns containing values that can be calculated from other columns' data. (3NF)

Today, nearly all databases are constructed so that all tables are in third normal form (3NF). This means that there are usually a fairly large number of tables, each with relatively few columns of information.

Getting Data Out of Databases

Suppose we wanted to produce a table of employees and their salary ranges for some planning exercise. This table doesn't exist directly in the database, but it can be constructed by issuing a query to the database. We'd like to have a table that looked like the data in Table 19-2.

Table 19-2 Employee Salaries Sorted by Name

Name	Min	Max
Adams	$45,000.00	$60,000.00
Johnson	$30,000.00	$45,000.00
Smyth	$60,000.00	$75,000.00
Tully	$30,000.00	$45,000.00
Wolff	$45,000.00	$60,000.00

Maybe we want data sorted by increasing salary, as shown in Table 19-3.

Table 19-3 Employee Salaries Sorted by Magnitude

Name	Min	Max
Tully	$30,000.00	$45,000.00
Johnson	$30,000.00	$45,000.00
Wolff	$45,000.00	$60,000.00
Adams	$45,000.00	$60,000.00
Smyth	$60,000.00	$75,000.00

We find that the query we issue to obtain these tables has this form.

```
SELECT DISTINCTROW Employees.Name, SalaryRanges.Min,
SalaryRanges.Max FROM Employees INNER JOIN SalaryRanges ON
Employees.SalaryKey = SalaryRanges.SalaryKey
ORDER BY SalaryRanges.Min;
```

This language is called Structured Query Language or SQL (often pronounced "sequel"), and it is the language of virtually all databases currently available. There have been several standards issued for SQL over the years, and most PC databases support much of these ANSI standards. The SQL-92 standard is considered the floor standard, and there have been several updates since. However, not all of these databases support the later SQL versions perfectly, and most offer various kinds of SQL extensions to exploit various features unique to their database.

Kinds of Databases

Since the PC became a major office tool, there have been a number of popular databases developed that are intended to run by themselves on PCs. These include elementary databases like Microsoft Works and more sophisticated ones like Approach, dBase, Borland Paradox, Microsoft Access, and FoxBase.

Another category of PC databases includes that databases intended to be accessed from a server by a number of PC clients. These include IBM DB/2, Microsoft SQL Server, Oracle, and Sybase. All of these database products support various relatively similar dialects of SQL, and thus all of them would appear at first to be relatively interchangeable. The reason they are *not* interchangeable, of course, is that each was designed with different performance characteristics involved and each with a different user interface and programming interface. While you might think that since they all support SQL, programming them would be similar, quite the opposite is true. Each database has its own way of receiving the SQL queries and its own way of returning the results. This is where the next proposed level of standardization came about: ODBC.

ODBC

It would be nice if we could somehow write code that was independent of the particular vendor's database that would allow us to get the same results from any of these databases without changing our calling program. If we could only write some wrappers for all of these databases so that they all appeared to have similar programming interfaces, this would be quite easy to accomplish.

Microsoft first attempted this feat in 1992 when they released a specification called Object Database Connectivity. It was supposed to be the answer for connection to all databases under Windows. Like all first software versions, this suffered some growing pains, and another version was released in 1994 that was somewhat faster as well as more stable. It also was the first 32-bit version. In addition, ODBC began to move to platforms other than Windows and has by now become quite pervasive in the PC and Workstation world. Nearly every major database vendor provides ODBC drivers.

Microsoft Database Connection Strategies

The original database connection methods in Visual Basic were based on ODBC and wrapped in a layer now called RDO for Remote Data Objects. The libraries supporting RDO have shipped with every version of Visual Basic since version 4.0. However, in the past year or so, Microsoft has adopted a new approach, termed ADO for ActiveX Data Objects, that supplants RDO and has a number of advantages. Up through Visual Basic 6, ADO was only lightly supported and somewhat incomplete. However, Microsoft has provided a set of downloads to support ADO called MDAC for Microsoft Data Access Components. As of this writing, you can download MDAC 2.6 from Microsoft and use it with VB6 to gain the advantages of ADO. We'll provide examples in both RDO and ADO for VB6 and for ADO in VB7, all using more or less the same façade.

Database Structure

At the lowest level, then, a database consists of a series of tables, each having several named columns, and some relationships between these tables. This can get pretty complicated to keep track of, and we would like to see some simplification of this in the code we use to manipulate databases. To some degree, Microsoft has provided this simplification in the following objects built into VB.

- Database—an object representing the connection to a database
- Tabledef—a database table
- Field—a column in a database
- Recordset—the result of a database query

In addition, you can use the AddNew, Edit, and Update methods of the Recordset object to add rows to a database table. So to a large degree, VB provides a simple Façade around the complexities of connecting to and using a database.

The DBase Class

However, once you set about building a database from data you have accumulated, you discover that there might perhaps be some advantages to building some classes and hiding the implementation details inside these classes. For example, suppose we wanted to connect to different types of databases. The connection details are clearly different in each case and could well be buried in instances of a Dbase class. In addition, the details of how one creates tables for a database and adds indexes to these tables can be simplified by putting it inside a Dbase class.

Our Dbase class hides the connection details and allows us to create new databases and connect to existing ones.

```
'Class DBase
'hides details of connection to specific database
'contains factory for creating indexe for adding tables and 'indexes
to tables
Private db As Database    'actual database connection
Private ws As Workspace 'used to connect to database
Private fl As File       'used to check for file existence
Private tb As TableDef   'used to create tables
'--------
Public Sub createDatabase(dbname As String)
 Set fl = New File
 Set ws = Workspaces(0)

 fl.setFilename dbname
 If fl.exists() Then
   fl.delete
 End If
 Set db = ws.createDatabase(dbname, dbLangGeneral)
End Sub
'--------
Public Sub openDatabase(dbname As String)
 Set ws = Workspaces(0)
 Set db = ws.openDatabase(dbname, dbLangGeneral)
End Sub
'--------
Public Function makeTable(nm As String) As Indexer
 Dim inx As New Indexer
 inx.makeTable db, nm
 Set makeTable = inx
End Function
'--------
Public Function openTable(tbName As String) As Recordset
 Set openTable = db.OpenRecordset(tbName, dbOpenTable)
End Function
'-----
Public Function openQuery(qry As String) As Recordset
```

```
Set openQuery = db.OpenRecordset(qry, dbOpenDynaset)
End Function
```

It also contains a factory that produces an instance of the Indexer class. This class allows you to create new tables, add fields to them, and create indexes. You can create table columns of type Text, Integer, Single, and Boolean. Here is part of the indexer class for Text fields.

```
'Class Indexer
'Used to create tables
'add fields to them
'and create indexes of these fields
Private tb As TableDef
Private db As Database
'--------
Public Sub makeTable(datab, nm As String)
  Set db = datab
  Set tb = db.CreateTableDef(nm)
End Sub
'--------
Public Sub openTable(datab As Database, nm As String)
  Set db = datab
  Set tb = db.TableDefs(nm)
End Sub
'--------
Public Sub addTable()
  db.TableDefs.Append tb
End Sub
'--------
Public Sub createKey(nm As String)
Dim key As Field
  Set key = tb.CreateField(nm, dbLong)
  key.Attributes = dbAutoIncrField
  tb.Fields.Append key
End Sub
'--------
Public Sub createText(nm$, length As Integer)
Dim tx As Field
  Set tx = tb.CreateField(nm$, dbText)
  tx.Size = length
  tx.AllowZeroLength = True
  tx.DefaultValue = ""
  tb.Fields.Append tx
End Sub
'--------
Public Sub createDateField(nm As String)
  Dim dt As Field
  Set dt = tb.CreateField(nm$, dbDate)
  tb.Fields.Append dt
End Sub
'--------
Public Sub createCurrency(nm As String)
```

```
    Dim c As Field
    Set c = tb.CreateField(nm$, dbCurrency)
    tb.Fields.Append c
End Sub
'--------
Public Sub makeIndex(nm$, primary As Boolean)
Dim pindex As Index, pf As Field
    Set pindex = tb.CreateIndex(nm)
    If primary Then
      pindex.primary = True
      pindex.Unique = True
    Else
      pindex.primary = False
      pindex.Unique = False
    End If
    Set pf = pindex.CreateField(nm)
    pindex.Fields.Append pf
    tb.Indexes.Append pindex
End Sub
'--------
Public Sub createLong(nm As String)
    Dim dt As Field
    Set dt = tb.CreateField(nm$, dbLong)
    dt.DefaultValue = 0
    tb.Fields.Append dt
End Sub
'--------
Public Sub createInteger(nm As String)
    Dim dt As Field
    Set dt = tb.CreateField(nm$, dbInteger)
    dt.DefaultValue = 0
    tb.Fields.Append dt
End Sub
'--------
Public Sub createSingle(nm As String)
    Dim dt As Field
    On Local Error Resume Next
    Set dt = tb.CreateField(nm$, dbSingle)
    dt.DefaultValue = 0
    tb.Fields.Append dt
End Sub
'--------
Public Sub createBoolean(nm As String)
    Dim dt As Field
    Set dt = tb.CreateField(nm$, dbBoolean)
    tb.Fields.Append dt
End Sub
'--------
Public Sub createBooleanTrue(nm As String)
    Dim dt As Field
    Set dt = tb.CreateField(nm$, dbBoolean)
    dt.DefaultValue = "-1"
    tb.Fields.Append dt
End Sub
```

Building the Façade Classes

This description is the beginning of the new Façade we are developing to handle creating, connecting to, and using databases. In order to carry out the rest, let's consider Table 19-4, grocery prices at three local stores.

Table 19-4   Grocery Pricing Data

Stop and Shop,	Apples,	0.27
Stop and Shop,	Oranges,	0.36
Stop and Shop,	Hamburger,	1.98
Stop and Shop,	Butter,	2.39
Stop and Shop,	Milk,	1.98
Stop and Shop,	Cola,	2.65
Stop and Shop,	Green beans,	2.29
Village Market,	Apples,	0.29
Village Market,	Oranges,	0.29
Village Market,	Hamburger,	2.45
Village Market,	Butter,	2.99
Village Market,	Milk,	1.79
Village Market,	Cola,	3.79
Village Market,	Green beans,	2.19
Waldbaum's,	Apples,	0.33
Waldbaum's,	Oranges,	0.47
Waldbaum's,	Hamburger,	2.29
Waldbaum's,	Butter,	3.29
Waldbaum's,	Milk,	1.89
Waldbaum's,	Cola,	2.99
Waldbaum's,	Green beans,	1.99

It would be nice if we had this information in a database so we could easily answer the question "Which store has the lowest prices for oranges?" Such a database should contain three tables: the supermarkets, the foods, and the prices. We also need to keep the relations among the three tables. One simple way to handle this is to create a Stores table with StoreName and StoreKey, a Foods table with a FoodName and a FoodKey, and a Price table with a PriceKey, a Price, and references to the StoreKey and Foodkey.

In our Façade, we will make each of these three tables its own class and have it take care of creating the actual tables. Since these three tables are so similar, we'll have them all implement a DBTable interface:

```
'Class DBTable
'An interface for creating tables
Public Sub createTable(datab As DBase)
End Sub
'--------
Public Sub openTable()
End Sub
'--------
Public Sub setDB(datab As Database)
End Sub
'--------
Public Sub addTableValue(nm As String)
End Sub
'--------
Public Sub makeTable()
End Sub
'--------
Public Function getKey(nm As String) As Integer
End Function
'--------
Public Function hasMoreElements() As Boolean
End Function
'--------
Public Sub moveFirst()
End Sub
'--------
Public Function getValue() As String
End Function
```

The Stores Class

The Stores class creates the Stores table with a column for the StoreKey and a column for the StoreName.

```
Implements DBTable
'Class Stores
'creates the Stores table
'and allows you to query it for the list of names
Private db As DBase
Private tNames As Collection
```

```
Private rec As Recordset
Private opened As Boolean
'--------
Private Sub DBTable_createTable(datab As DBase)
Dim inx As Indexer
'creates the table in the database
  Set tNames = New Collection
  Set db = datab
  Set inx = db.makeTable("Stores")
  inx.createKey "StoreKey"
  inx.createText "StoreName", 50
  inx.makeIndex "Storekey", True
  inx.makeIndex "StoreName", False
  inx.addTable
End Sub
'--------
Private Function DBTable_getKey(nm As String) As Integer
'returns the key for any store name
  DBTable_openTable
  rec.Index = "StoreName"
  rec.Seek "=", nm
  If Not rec.NoMatch Then
    DBTable_getKey = rec![storekey]
  Else
    DBTable_getKey = 0
  End If
End Function
'--------
Private Function DBTable_getValue() As String
'returns the next name in the table
  DBTable_getValue = rec![storename]
  rec.MoveNext
End Function
'--------
Private Function DBTable_hasMoreElements() As Boolean
'returns whether there are more names in the list
  DBTable_hasMoreElements = Not rec.EOF
End Function
'--------
Private Sub DBTable_moveFirst()
 rec.moveFirst
End Sub
'--------
Private Sub DBTable_openTable()
  If Not opened Then
    Set rec = db.openTable("Stores")
    Opened = True
  End If
End Sub
'--------
```

```
Private Sub DBTable_setDB(datab As Database)
  Set db = datab
  Set tNames = New Collection
End Sub
```

Now when we start to create the Stores table, we don't know how many stores there will be. So we write code to keep adding store names to a collection, testing for duplicates until we have gone all through the file. Then we can create the actual entries in the table. This is done in the following two methods.

```
Private Sub DBTable_addTableValue(nm As String)
Dim tbn As String

  On Local Error GoTo noname
  tbn = tNames(nm)     'see if the name is already there

sbexit:              'yes it is
  Exit Sub

noname:              'no it isn't
  tNames.Add nm, nm 'add it to the collection
  Resume sbexit
End Sub
'--------
Private Sub DBTable_makeTable()
Dim i As Integer, nm As String
'Adds the names from the collection
'into the database table
  DBTable_openTable
  For i = 1 To tNames.Count
    nm = tNames(i)
    rec.AddNew
    rec![storename] = nm
    rec.Update
  Next i
End Sub
```

The Foods class is almost identical.

Building the Stores and Foods Tables

Now that we have built these wrapping classes, it is very easy to read the file, parse it into tokens, and add the stores and food names into the tables.

```
Set db = New DBase
dbname = App.Path & "\Groceries.mdb"
db.createDatabase dbname
```

```
Set fl = New vbFile
fname = App.Path & "\" & "Groceries.txt"
fl.setFilename fname
If fl.exists() Then
    fl.OpenForRead fname  'open the file
    'create the tables
    Set stors = New Stores
    stors.createTable db  'Stores table
    Set fods = New Foods
    fods.createTable db   'Foods table
    Set price = New Prices
    price.createTable db  'Price table
    'read the file and create
    'internal collections of names
    While Not fl.fEof
      nstore = fl.readToken
      nfood = fl.readToken
      nprice = fl.readToken
      stors.addTableValue nstore 'store name
      fods.addTableValue nfood    'food name
    Wend
    fl.closeFile
    'make tables from the collections
    stors.makeTable
    fods.makeTable
```

Building the Price Table

The Price table is a little more complicated because it contains keys from the other two tables. When it is completed, it will look like Table 19-5.

To create it, we have to reread the file, finding the store and food names, looking up their keys, and adding them to the Price table. The DBTable interface doesn't include this final method, but we can add additional specific methods to the Price class that are not part of that interface.

```
Public Sub addRow(storekey As Integer, foodkey As Integer, _
                  price As Single)
    DBTable_openTable
    rec.AddNew
    rec![storekey] = storekey
    rec![foodkey] = foodkey
    rec![price] = price
    rec.Update
End Sub
```

Table 19-5   The Price Table in the Grocery Database

Pricekey	Foodkey	StoreKey	Price
1	1	1	0.27
2	2	1	0.36
3	3	1	1.98
4	4	1	2.39
5	5	1	1.98
6	6	1	2.65
7	7	1	2.29
8	1	2	0.29
9	2	2	0.29
10	3	2	2.45
11	4	2	2.99
12	5	2	1.79
13	6	2	3.79
14	7	2	2.19
15	1	3	0.33
16	2	3	0.47
17	3	3	2.29
18	4	3	3.29
19	5	3	1.89
20	6	3	2.99
21	7	3	1.99

This just means that we have to treat the Price class instance both as a DBTable and as a Price object. Here is the code that adds the final table.

```
Set tbPrice = price  'treat as price table class
'reread datafile and create price table with keys
'to the two other tables
fl.OpenForRead fname
While Not fl.fEof
   nstore = fl.readToken
   nfood = fl.readToken
   sPrice = Val(fl.readToken)
   storekey = stors.getKey(nstore)
   foodkey = fods.getKey(nfood)
   tbPrice.addRow storekey, foodkey, sPrice
Wend
fl.closeFile
```

Building the Price Query

For every food name, we'd like to get a report of which stores have the cheapest prices. This means writing a simple SQL query against the database. We can do this within the Price class and have it return a recordset with the store names and prices.

```
Public Sub getPrices(nm As String)
Dim qry As String

If precOpened Then
   prec.Close
End If

qry = "SELECT Foods.Foodname, Stores.StoreName, Prices.Price " & _
"FROM Stores INNER JOIN (Foods INNER JOIN Prices ON " & _
"Foods.Foodkey = Prices.Foodkey) ON " & _
"Stores.StoreKey = Prices.StoreKey " & _
"Where (((Foods.Foodname) = '" & nm & "')) " & _
"ORDER BY Prices.Price;"

Set prec = db.openQuery(qry)
precOpened = True
End Sub
```

The final application simply fills one list box with the food names and files the other list box with prices when you click on a food name, as shown in Figure 19-1.

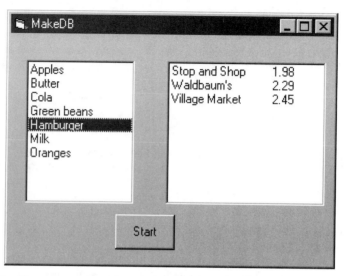

Figure 19-1   The grocery program using a Façade pattern

Summary of the Façade Pattern

There is no specific set of classes that constitutes a Façade pattern. Rather, you use the Façade pattern to simplify a complex series of operations into a more tractable set of operations. For example, the File object we developed earlier in Chapter 3 and use in the preceding examples is just a Façade around the somewhat awkward VB file manipulation statements.

In this example, we started with VB's database objects, as shown in Figure 19-2. We then further simplify these objects with our own new Façade, as shown in Figure 19-3.

ADO Database Access in VB6

The ADO libraries provide much the same function but with some differences in details. We'll see in this section that we can use the same Dbase, DBTable, and Indexer classes and simply change their internals. So in a sense, this façade is very nearly the whole house, and we simply open the garage door and drive out with the whole heating plant and drive in with a new one. The functions of the house don't change at all.

ADO functions in VB6 are divided into two groups: ADO, which provides data access to an existing database, and ADOX, the ADO extensions, that provide ways to create databases and add tables, columns, and indexes.

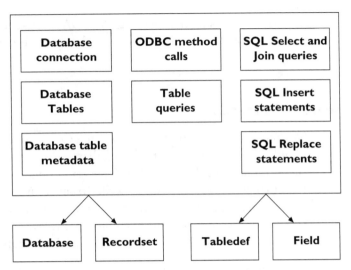

Figure 19-2   The Façade around database operations created by VB

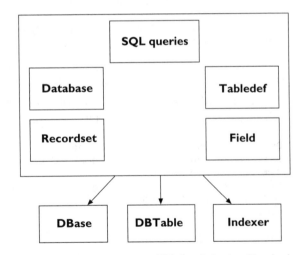

Figure 19-3   The new Façade we impose over VB's façade for handling database access

In order to use ADO in VB6, you need to download and install Microsoft's MDAC package. Then you need to (1) open your database project, (2) select Project | References in the VB5 environment, and (3) select the check boxes for Microsoft ActiveX Data Objects and Microsoft ADO Extensions for DDL and Security.

Also, make sure that the Microsoft DAO reference is *not* checked, since it is not advisable to have both kinds of database connections active in the same project.

The ADO Connection

The most important part of ADO is the Connection object, which defines and establishes the connection to the database. The connection strings are defined in the ADO help for Access and SQL Server databases, but you can connect to all the other popular databases as well. To open an Access database that already exists, you simply define the database path and the database driver and open the connection. Note that in the examples that follow, we are using the variable *db* to represent a connection, rather than the RDO Database object.

```
Dim db as Connection

Set db = New Connection
'Engine Type 5 is Access 2000 and Type 4 is Access 97
'construct the connection string
con = "Provider=Microsoft.Jet.OLEDB.4.0;Data source=" & _
     dbname &  "; Jet OLEDB:Engine Type=5;"
db.ConnectionString = con
db.Open
```

Then, to execute queries, you use a Command object to carry out the query. This returns a Recordset object, which has pretty much the same properties as the one we used in the previous RDO example.

```
'Open a recordset from an SQL query
Dim cmd As New Command       'command object
Dim rec As Recordset
cmd.ActiveConnection = db  'get the connection
cmd.CommandType = adCmdText
cmd.CommandText = qry
'execute the SQL
Set rec = cmd.Execute
```

To connect to a table for the purpose of seeking rows or adding rows, you can use the Recordset object directly.

```
'open a table
Dim rec As New Recordset
rec.LockType = adLockOptimistic
rec.CursorType = adOpenKeyset
'open the database connection if not open
If db.State = adStateClosed Then
   db.ConnectionString = con
```

```
   db.Open
  End If
   'open the table recordset
  rec.Open tbName, db, , , adCmdTableDirect
```

Adding and Seeking Rows Table Rows

Adding rows to an existing table is exactly the same in ADO. You use a Recordset as before and use the AddNew and Update methods.

```
For i = 1 To tbNames.Count
  nm = tbNames(i)
  rec.AddNew
  rec![Foodname] = nm
  rec.Update
Next i
```

To find a row that matches some criteria, the syntax is only very slightly different.

```
rec.Index = "FoodName"
 rec.Seek "Apples", adSeekFirstEQ
 If Not rec.EOF Then
     getKey = rec![foodkey]
 Else
     getKey = 0
 End If
```

Using the ADO Extensions

The ADO Extensions allow you to create databases and tables as well as add columns to tables. All of these extensions use a Catalog object to operate on the database. The catalog connects to the database, using exactly the same connection string, so it is quite reasonable to create and initialize both at the same time. Setting the connection string in the Catalog object effectively opens the Catalog connection to the database.

```
  Set db = New Connection
  Set cat = New Catalog
 'construct the connection string
  con = "Provider=Microsoft.Jet.OLEDB.4.0;Data source=" & _
      dbname & "; Jet OLEDB:Engine Type=5;"
  db.ConnectionString = con
  db.Open
  cat.ActiveConnection = con 'open the catalog
```

You can create a table in ADO by creating a new instance of a Table object and setting its name.

```
Dim tb = New Table
tb.Name = nm
```

Then, after you have set all the columns and indexes, you just add the table to the Tables collection.

```
cat.Tables.Append tb
```

To add columns to the table, you create a Column object and set its properties. This code create a text column.

```
Dim tx As New Column
  tx.Name = nm
  tx.DefinedSize = length
  tx.Type = adWChar
  tb.Columns.Append tx, adWChar, length
```

To create a primary key, you actually make an entry in the Indexes collection and add it to the Connection. Note that the Autoincrement property is set as one of the Properties.

```
Dim indx As New Index
Dim colm As New Column
  colm.Name = nm
  colm.Type = adInteger
  'you must set this before setting autoincrement
  Set colm.ParentCatalog = cat
  colm.Properties("AutoIncrement") = True
  tb.Columns.Append colm
  indx.Name = nm + "_" + "Index"
  indx.PrimaryKey = True
  indx.Columns.Append nm, adInteger, 20
  indx.Unique = True
  tb.Indexes.Append indx
```

The ADO DBase Class

With this simple outline, we can write a new version of our DBase class with exactly the same methods as we used for the RDO example.

```
'Class DBase
'hides details of connection to specific database
'contains factory for creating indexes
'for adding tables and indexes to tables
'This version uses ADO and ADOX connections
Private db As ADODB.Connection   'actual database connection
Private cat As Catalog
Private fl As File        'used to check for file existence
```

```
Private con As String
'--------
Public Sub createDatabase(dbname As String)
 Set fl = New File
 Set cat = New Catalog
 fl.setFilename dbname
 If fl.exists() Then
   fl.delete
 End If
 Set db = New Connection
 'Engine Type 5 is Access 2000 and Engine Type 4 is Access 97
 'construct the connection string
 con = "Provider=Microsoft.Jet.OLEDB.4.0;Data source=" & _
 dbname &   "; Jet OLEDB:Engine Type=5;"
   cat.Create con
End Sub
'--------
Public Sub openDatabase(dbname As String)

 Set db = New Connection
 Set cat = New Catalog
 'construct the connection string
  con = "Provider=Microsoft.Jet.OLEDB.4.0;Data source=" & _
  dbname &   "; Jet OLEDB:Engine Type=5;"
  db.ConnectionString = con
  db.Open
  cat.ActiveConnection = con
End Sub
'--------
Public Function makeTable(nm As String) As Indexer
 Dim inx As New Indexer
 inx.makeTable cat, nm
 Set makeTable = inx
End Function
'--------
Public Function openTable(tbName As String) As Recordset
  'open a table
 Dim rec As New Recordset
 rec.LockType = adLockOptimistic
 rec.CursorType = adOpenKeyset
 'open the database connection if not open
 If db.State = adStateClosed Then
   db.ConnectionString = con
   db.Open
  End If
  'open the table recordset
 rec.Open tbName, db, , , adCmdTableDirect
  Set openTable = rec
End Function
'--------
Public Function openQuery(qry As String) As Recordset
'Open a recordset from an SQL query
 Dim cmd As New Command       'command object
```

```
Dim rec As Recordset
cmd.ActiveConnection = db   'get the connection
cmd.CommandType = adCmdText
cmd.CommandText = qry
 'execute the SQL
Set rec = cmd.Execute
Set openQuery = rec            'return the recordset
End Function
```

All of the functions we need to create tables and add them into the database are in the same Indexer class we wrote before. Here is the salient section of that class.

```
'Class Indexer
'Used to create tables using ADO Extensions
'add fields to them
'and create indexes of these fields
Private tb As Table
Private db As Connection
Private cat As Catalog
'--------
Public Sub makeTable(ctg As Catalog, nm As String)
   Set cat = ctg          'get the catalog
   Set tb = New Table     'create a table object
   tb.Name = nm
End Sub
'--------
Public Sub openTable(ctg As Catalog, nm As String)
   Set cat = ctg
   Set tb = cat.Tables.Item(nm)
End Sub
'--------
Public Sub addTable()
   cat.Tables.Append tb
End Sub
'--------
Public Sub createKey(nm As String)
Dim indx As New Index
Dim colm As New Column
 colm.Name = nm
 colm.Type = adInteger
 'you must set this before setting autoincrement
 Set colm.ParentCatalog = cat
 colm.Properties("AutoIncrement") = True
 tb.Columns.Append colm
 indx.Name = nm & "_" & "Index"
 indx.PrimaryKey = True
 indx.Columns.Append nm, adInteger, 20
 indx.Unique = True
 tb.Indexes.Append indx
End Sub
'--------
```

```
Public Sub createText(nm As String, length As Integer)
Dim tx As New Column
  tx.Name = nm
  tx.DefinedSize = length
  tx.Type = adWChar
  tb.Columns.Append tx, adWChar, length
End Sub
'--------
Public Sub createDateField(nm As String)
Dim dt As New Column
 dt.Type = adDate
 dt.Name = nm
 tb.Columns.Append dt
End Sub
'--------
Public Sub createCurrency(nm As String)
 Dim c As New Column
 c.Type = adCurrency
 c.Name = nm
 tb.Columns.Append c
End Sub
'--------
Public Sub makeIndex(nm As String, primary As Boolean)
 Dim ind As New Index
 ind.Name = nm
 ind.PrimaryKey = primary
 ind.Columns.Append nm
 tb.Indexes.Append ind
End Sub
'--------
Public Sub createLong(nm As String)
 Dim dt As New Column
 dt.Name = nm
 dt.Type = adLongVarBinary
 tb.Columns.Append dt
End Sub
'--------
Public Sub createInteger(nm As String)
 Dim dt As New Column
 dt.Name = nm
 dt.Type = adInteger
 tb.Columns.Append dt
End Sub
'--------
Public Sub createSingle(nm As String)
 Dim dt As New Column
 dt.Name = nm
 dt.Type = adSingle
 tb.Columns.Append dt, adSingle, 4
End Sub
'--------
Public Sub createBoolean(nm As String)
 Dim dt As Column
```

```
dt.Name = nm
dt.Type = adBoolean
tb.Columns.Append dt, adBoolean
End Sub
```

With these straightforward changes, our main program for creating the Groceries database is unchanged. It reads in the data file and creates the same database using ADO, and it executes the same queries. This shows the great power of the Façade pattern. We have not changed any main program code or interfaces to the Façade, and the program executes in this new environment just as it did in the old one.

Database Access in VB.NET

VB7 and all of VisualStudio.Net use a different database access model, called ADO.NET, for ActiveX Data Objects. The design philosophy of ADO.NET is one in which you define a connection between your program and a database and use that connection sporadically, with much of the computation actually taking place in disconnected objects on your local machine. Further, ADO.NET uses XML for definition of the objects that are transmitted between the database and the program, primarily under the covers, although it is possible to access this data description using some of the built-in ADO.NET classes.

Using ADO.NET

ADO.NET as implemented in VB7 consists of a fairly large variety of interrelated objects. Since the operations we want to perform are still the same relatively simple ones, the Façade pattern will be an ideal way to manage them.

- **OleDbConnection**—This object represents the actual connection to the database. You can keep an instance of this class available but open and close the connection as needed. You must specifically close it when you are done, before it is garbage collected.
- **OleDbCommand**—This class represents a SQL command you send to the database, which may or may not return results.
- **OleDbDataAdapter**—Provides a bridge for moving data between a database and a local DataSet. You can specify an OleDbCommand, a Dataset, and a connection.
- **DataSet**—A representation of one or more database tables or results from a query on your local machine.
- **DataTable**—A single data table from a database or query.
- **DataRow**—A single row in a DataTable.

Connecting to a Database

To connect to a database, you specify a connection string in the constructor for the database you want to use. For example, for an Access database, your connection string would be the following.

```
connectionString = "Provider=Microsoft.Jet.OLEDB.4.0;" & _
        "Data Source=" & dbName
```

And the following makes the actual connection.

```
Private conn As OleDbConnection
conn = New OleDbConnection(connectionString)
```

Reading Data from a Database Table

To read data in from a database table, you create an ADOCommand with the appropriate Select statement and connection.

```
Public Function openTable(ByVal tbName As String) As DataTable
        Dim adapter As New OleDbDataAdapter()
        Dim query As String
        query = "Select * From " & tbName
        adapter.SelectCommand = New OleDbCommand(query, conn)
```

Then, you create a dataset object into which to put the results.

```
    'create the desintination dataset
      Dim dset As New DataSet() ()
```

Then, you simply tell the command object to use the connection to fill the dataset. You must specify the name of the table to fill in the FillDataSet method, as we show here.

```
    'open the connection and fill the table
        Try
            openConnection()
            adapter.Fill(dset)
        Catch e As Exception
            MsgBox(e.Message)
        End Try
```

The dataset then contains at least one table, and you can obtain it by index or by name and examine its contents.

```
        'get the table from the dataset
        Dim dtable As DataTable = dset.Tables(0)
        Return dtable    'return the table we read
End Function
```

Executing a Query

Executing a Select query is exactly identical to the preceding code, except the query can be an SQL Select statement of any complexity. Here we show the steps wrapped in a Try block in case there are SQL or other database errors.

```
Public Function openQuery(ByVal query As String) As DataTable
      Dim dsCmd As New OleDbDataAdapter()
      Try
            dsCmd.SelectCommand = New OleDbCommand(query, conn)
            Dim dset As New DataSet()
            openConnection()
            'fill the dataset
            dsCmd.Fill(dset, "mine")
            'get the table
            Dim dtable As DataTable = dset.Tables(0)
            closeConnection()
            Return dtable     'and return it
      Catch e As Exception
            MessageBox.Show(e.Message)
      End Try
  End Function
```

Deleting the Contents of a Table

You can delete the contents of a table using the "Delete * from Table" SQL statement. However, since this is not a Select command, and there is no local table to bridge to, you can simply use the ExecuteNonQuery method of the OleDbCommand object.

```
Public Sub delete()
      'deletes entire table
      conn = db.getConnection
      openConn()
      Dim adcmd As New OleDbCommand( _
                  "Delete * from " & tableName, conn)
      Try
          adcmd.ExecuteNonQuery()
          closeConn()
      Catch e As Exception
          MessageBox.Show(e.Message)
      End Try
  End Sub
```

Adding Rows to Database Tables Using ADO.NET

The process of adding data to a table is closely related. You generally start by getting the current version of the table from the database. If it is very large, you can get only the empty table by getting just its schema. We follow these steps.

1. Create a DataTable with the name of the table in the database.

2. Add it to a dataset.

3. Fill the dataset from the database.

4. Get a new row object from the DataTable.

5. Fill in its columns.

6. Add the row to the table.

7. When you have added all the rows, update the database from the modified DataTable object.

The process looks like this.

```
dset = New DataSet(tableName)                'create the data set
      columnName = colName
      Dim name As String
      dtable = New DataTable(tableName)      'and a datatable
      dset.Tables.Add(dtable)                'add to collection
      conn = db.getConnection
      openConn()                             'open the connection
      Dim adcmd As New OleDbDataAdapter()

      'open the table
      adcmd.SelectCommand = _
          New OleDbCommand("Select * from " & tableName, conn)
      Dim olecb As New OleDbCommandBuilder(adcmd)
      adcmd.TableMappings.Add("Table", tableName)

      'load current data into the local table copy
      adcmd.Fill(dset, tableName)
      'create a new row
       row = dtable.NewRow       'get new rows
       row(colName) = name
       dtable.Rows.Add(row)      'add into table

      'Now update the database with this table
      Try
          adcmd.Update(dset)
          closeConn()
          filled = True
      Catch e As Exception
          MessageBox.Show(e.Message)
      End Try
```

It is this table editing and update process that is central to the ADO style of programming. You get the table, modify the table, and update the changes back to the database. You use this same process to edit or delete rows, and updating the database makes these changes as well.

Making the VB.NET ADO Façade

The Façade we will make for our VB7-style grocery database is similar to the VB6 version, but it makes a little more use of inheritance. We start with a DBase class that represents a connection to a database. This encapsulates making the connection and opening a table and an SQL query.

```
Public Class DBase
    Private conn As OleDbConnection
    '-----
    Public Sub New(ByVal dbName As String, _
                ByVal connectionType As String)
        Dim connectionString As String
        connectionType = connectionType.ToLower
        Select Case connectionType
            Case "access"
                connectionString=
                "Provider=Microsoft.Jet.OLEDB.4.0; " & _
                "Data Source=" & dbName
            Case "sqlserver"
                connectionString = & _
                "Persist Security Info = False;" & _
                "Initial Catalog =" & dbName & ";" & _
                "Data Source = myDataServer;User ID = myName;" & _
                "password="

            Case Else
                connectionString = dbName
        End Select
        conn = New OleDbConnection(connectionString)
    End Sub

    '-----
    Public Sub New(ByVal dbname As String, ByVal userid As String, _
        ByVal servername As String, ByVal password As String, _
        ByVal connectionType As String)
        Dim connection As String
        connectionType = connectionType.ToLower
        Select Case connectionType
            Case "sqlserver"
                connection = "Persist Security Info = False;" & _
                "Initial Catalog =" & dbname & ";" & _
                "Data Source =" & servername & ";" & _
                "User ID =" & userid & ";" & _
```

```
                              "password=" & password
                    Case Else
                         connection = dbname
              End Select
              conn = New OleDbConnection(connection)
         End Sub
'-------
Public Function openTable(ByVal tbName As String) _
                 As DataTable
   'shown above
   End Function
'-------
Public Function openQuery(ByVal query As String) _
                 As DataTable
   'shown above
   End Function
'-------
Public Function getConnection() As OleDbConnection
          Return conn
   End Function
   End Class
```

The DBTable Class

The other major class we will need is the DBTable class. It encapsulates opening, loading, and updating a single database table. We will also use this class in this example to add the single values. Then we can derive food and store classes that do this addition for each class.

```
Public Class DBTable
    Private names As Hashtable
    Protected db As DBase
    Protected tableName As String
    Private index As Integer
    Private dtable As DataTable
    Private filled As Boolean
    Private columnName As String
    Private rowIndex As Integer
    Private opened As Boolean
    Dim conn As OleDbConnection
    Dim cmd As OleDbCommand
    Dim dset As DataSet
    Dim row As DataRow
'-------
    Public Sub New(ByVal datab As DBase, ByVal tname As String)
        names = New Hashtable()
        db = datab
        tablename = tname
        index = 1
        filled = False
        opened = False
```

```
      End Sub
'-------
Public Sub openTable()
      dtable = db.openTable(tableName)
      rowIndex = 0
      opened = True
End Sub
'-------
Public Sub delete()
'deletes entire table
' shown above
End Class
```

Creating Classes for Each Table

We can derive the Store, Food, and Prices classes from DBTable and reuse much
of the code. When we parse the input file, both the Store and Food classes will
require that we create a table of unique names: store names in one class and
food names in the other.

VB7 provides a very convenient way to create these classes using the
Hashtable. A Hashtable is an unbounded array where each element is identified
with a unique key. One way people use Hashtables is to add long names to a
table and a short nickname as the key. Then you can fetch the longer name from
the table by using its nickname to access the table. The long names need not be
unique, but, of course, the keys must be unique.

The other place Hashtables are convenient is in making a list of unique
names. If we make the names the keys and some other number the contents,
then we can add names to the Hashtable and assure ourselves that each will be
unique. For them to be unique, the Hashtable must treat attempts to add a sup-
plicate key in a predictable way. For example, the Java Hashtable simply
replaces a previous entry having that key with the new one. The VB7 implementation of the Hashtable, on the other hand, throws an exception when we try to
add a non-unique key value.

Now bearing in mind that we want to accumulate the entire list of names
before adding them into the database, we can use the following method to add
names to a Hashtable and make sure they are unique.

```
Public Overridable Sub addTableValue(ByVal nm As String)
    'accumulates names in hash table
    Try
        names.Add(nm, index)
        index = index + 1
    Catch e As ArgumentException
        'do not allow duplicate names to be added
    End Try
End Sub
```

Then, once we have added all the names, we can add each of them to the database table. Here we use the Enumerator property of the Hashtable to iterate though all the names we have entered in the list.

```
Public Overridable Sub makeTable(ByVal colName As String)
        'stores current hash table values in data table
        dset = New DataSet(tableName)    'create the data set
        columnName = colName
        Dim name As String
        dtable = New DataTable(tableName)    'and a datatable
        dset.Tables.Add(dtable)              'add to collection
        conn = db.getConnection
        openConn()                          'open the connection
        Dim adcmd As New OleDbDataAdapter()
        'open the table
        adcmd.SelectCommand = _
            New OleDbCommand("Select * from " & tableName, conn)
        Dim olecb As New OleDbCommandBuilder(adcmd)
        adcmd.TableMappings.Add("Table", tableName)
        'load current data into the local table copy
        adcmd.Fill(dset, tableName)
        'get the Enumerator from the Hashtable
        Dim ienum As IEnumerator = names.Keys.GetEnumerator
        'move through the table, adding the names to new rows
        While ienum.MoveNext
            name = CType(ienum.Current, String)
            row = dtable.NewRow      'get new rows
            row(colName) = name
            dtable.Rows.Add(row)     'add into table
        End While
        'Now update the database with this table
        Try
            adcmd.Update(dset)
            closeConn()
            filled = True
        Catch e As Exception
            MessageBox.Show(e.Message)
        End Try
    End Sub
```

This simplifies our derived Stores table to just the following.

```
Public Class Stores
    Inherits DBTable
    '-----
    Public Sub New(ByVal datab As DBase)
        MyBase.New(datab, "Stores")
    End Sub
    '-----
    Public Overloads Sub makeTable()
        MyBase.makeTable("StoreName")
    End Sub
End Class
```

And it simplifies the Foods table to much the same thing.

```
Public Class Foods
    Inherits DBTable
    '-------
    Public Sub New(ByVal datab As DBase)
        MyBase.New(datab, "Foods")
    End Sub
    '-------
    Public Overloads Sub makeTable()
        MyBase.makeTable("FoodName")
    End Sub
    '-------
    Public Overloads Function getValue() As String
        Return MyBase.getValue("FoodName")
    End Function
End Class
```

The getValue method allows us to enumerate the list of names of Stores or Foods, and we can put it in the base DBTable class.

```
Public Function getValue(ByVal columnName As String) As String
        'returns the next name in the table
        'assumes that openTable has already been called
        If opened Then
            Dim row As DataRow
            row = dtable.Rows(rowIndex)
            rowIndex = rowIndex + 1
            Return row(columnName).ToString
        Else
            Return ""
        End If
    End Function
```

Storing the Prices

The Prices class stores a series of StoreFoodPrice objects in an ArrayList and then loads them all into the database at once. Note that we have overloaded the classes of DBTable to take arguments for the store and food key values as well as the price.

```
Public Class Prices
    Inherits DBTable
    Private priceList As ArrayList
    Public Sub new(ByVal datab As DBase)
        MyBase.New(datab, "Prices")
        pricelist = New ArrayList()
    End Sub
    '------
    Public Sub addRow(ByVal storekey As Long,    _
```

```vbnet
        ByVal foodkey As Long, ByVal price As Single)
            pricelist.Add(New StoreFoodPrice( _
            storekey, foodkey, price))
        End Sub
        '------
        Public Overloads Sub makeTable()
            'stores current array list values in data table
            Dim adc As oledbConnection
            Dim cmd As OleDbCommand
            Dim dset As New DataSet(tablename)
            Dim row As DataRow
            Dim fprice As StoreFoodPrice
            Dim dtable As New DataTable(tablename)

            dset.Tables.Add(dtable)
            adc = db.getConnection
            If adc.State = ConnectionState.Closed Then adc.Open()
            Dim adcmd As New OleDbDataAdapter()

            'fill in price table
            adcmd.SelectCommand = _
                New OleDbCommand("Select * from " & tablename, adc)
            Dim custCB As OleDbCommandBuilder = _
                New OleDbCommandBuilder(adcmd)
            adcmd.TableMappings.Add("Table", tablename)
            adcmd.Fill(dset, tablename)
            Dim ienum As IEnumerator = priceList.GetEnumerator
            'add new price entries
            While ienum.MoveNext
                fprice = CType(ienum.Current, StoreFoodPrice)
                row = dtable.NewRow
                row("foodkey") = fprice.getFood
                row("storekey") = fprice.getStore
                row("price") = fprice.getPrice
                dtable.Rows.Add(row)        'add to table
            End While
            adcmd.Update(dset)         'send back to database
            adc.Close()
        End Sub
        '------
        Public Function getPrices(ByVal food As String) As DataTable
         Dim query As String
         query = "SELECT Stores.StoreName, " & _
         "Foods.Foodname, Prices.Price " & _
         "FROM (Prices INNER JOIN Foods ON " & _
         "Prices.Foodkey = Foods.Foodkey) " & _
         "INNER JOIN Stores ON Prices.StoreKey = Stores.StoreKey " & _
         "WHERE(((Foods.Foodname) = """ & food & """)) " & _
         "ORDER BY Prices.Price;"
         Return db.openQuery(query)
        End Function

End Class
```

Loading the Database Tables

With all these classes derived, we can write a class to load the table from the data file. It reads the file once and builds the Store and Food database tables. Then it reads the file again and looks up the store and food keys and adds them to the array list in the Price class. Finally, it creates the Price table.

```
Public Class DataLoader
    Private vfile As vbFile
    Private stor As Stores
    Private fods As Foods
    Private price As Prices
    Private db As DBase
    '--------------
    Public Sub New(ByVal datab As DBase)
        db = datab
        stor = New Stores(db)     'create class instances
        fods = New Foods(db)
        price = New Prices(db)
    End Sub
    '--------------
    Public Sub load(ByVal datafile As String)
        Dim sline As String
        Dim storekey As Long, foodkey As Long
        Dim tok As StringTokenizer

        'delete current table contents
        stor.delete()
        fods.delete()
        price.delete()
        'now read in new ones
        vfile = New vbFile(datafile)
        vfile.OpenForRead()
        sline = vfile.readLine
        While (sline <> "")
            tok = New StringTokenizer(sline, ",")
            stor.addTableValue(tok.nextToken)    'store name
            fods.addTableValue(tok.nextToken)    'food name
            sline = vfile.readLine
        End While
        vfile.closeFile()
        'construct store and food tables
        stor.makeTable("StoreName")
        fods.makeTable("FoodName")
        vfile.OpenForRead()
        sline = vfile.readLine
        While (sline <> "")
            'get the gets and add to storefoodprice objects
            tok = New StringTokenizer(sline, ",")
            storekey = stor.getKey(tok.nextToken, "Storekey")
```

```
            foodkey = fods.getKey(tok.nextToken, "Foodkey")
            price.addRow(storekey, foodkey, CSng(tok.nextToken))
            sline = vfile.readLine
        End While
        'add all to price table
        price.makeTable()
        vfile.closeFile()
    End Sub
End Class
```

The Final Application

The program loads a list of food prices into a list box on startup.

```
Private Sub loadFoodTable()
    Dim fods As New Foods(db)
    fods.openTable()
    While fods.hasMoreElements
        lsFoods.Items.Add(fods.getValue)
    End While
End Sub
```

And it displays the prices of the selected food when you click on it.

```
Private Sub lsFoods_SelectedIndexChanged( _
    ByVal sender As System.Object, _
    ByVal e As System.EventArgs) _
    Handles lsFoods.SelectedIndexChanged

    Dim food As String = lsFoods.Text
    Dim dtable As DataTable = prc.getPrices(food)
    Dim rw As DataRow
    lsPrices.Items.Clear()
    For Each rw In dtable.Rows
        lsPrices.Items.Add(rw("StoreName").ToString.Trim & _
                    vbTab & rw("Price").ToString)
    Next
End Sub
```

The final program is shown in Figure 19-4.

If you click on the "load data" button, it clears the database and reloads it from the text file.

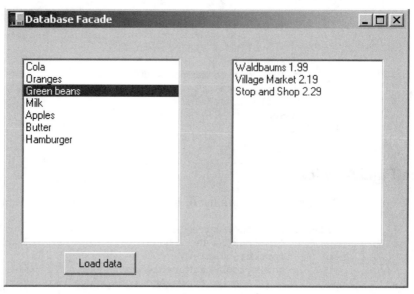

Figure 19-4   The VB7 grocery database program

What Constitutes the Façade?

The Facade in this case wraps the classes as follows.

- Dbase—Contains ADOConnection, Database, DataTable, ADOCommand, ADODatasetCommand
- DBTable—Contains ADOCommand, Dataset, Datarow, Datatable, ADODatasetCommand

You can quickly see the advantage of the Façade approach when dealing with such complicated data objects.

Consequences of the Façade

The Façade pattern shields clients from complex subsystem components and provides a simpler programming interface for the general user. However, it does not prevent the advanced user from going to the deeper, more complex classes when necessary.

In addition, the Façade allows you to make changes in the underlying subsystems without requiring changes in the client code and reduces compilation dependencies.

THOUGHT QUESTION

Suppose you had written a program with a File|Open menu, a text field, and some buttons controlling font (bold and italic). Now suppose that you need to have this program run from a line command with arguments. Suggest how to use a Façade pattern.

Programs on the CD-ROM

\Façade	VB6 database Façade classes using RDO
\Façade\VBNetFaçade	VB7 database Façade classes
\Façade\VB6ADO	VB6 database Façade using ADO

CHAPTER 20

The Flyweight Pattern

The Flyweight pattern is used to avoid the overhead of large numbers of very similar classes. There are cases in programming where it seems that you need to generate a very large number of small class instances to represent data. Sometimes you can greatly reduce the number of different classes that you need to instantiate if you can recognize that the instances are fundamentally the same except for a few parameters. If you can move those variables outside the class instance and pass them in as part of a method call, the number of separate instances can be greatly reduced by sharing them.

The Flyweight design pattern provides an approach for handling such classes. It refers to the instance's *intrinsic* data that makes the instance unique and the *extrinsic* data that is passed in as arguments. The Flyweight is appropriate for small, fine-grained classes like individual characters or icons on the screen. For example, you might be drawing a series of icons on the screen in a window, where each represents a person or data file as a folder, as shown in Figure 20-1.

In this case, it does not make sense to have an individual class instance for each folder that remembers the person's name and the icon's screen position. Typically, these icons are one of a few similar images, and the position where they are drawn is calculated dynamically based on the window's size in any case.

In another example in *Design Patterns*, each character in a Document is represented as a single instance of a character class, but the positions where the characters are drawn on the screen are kept as external data, so there only has to be one instance of each character, rather than one for each appearance of that character.

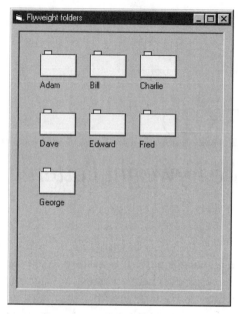

Figure 20-1   A set of folders representing information about various people. Since these are so similar, they are candidates for the Flyweight pattern.

Discussion

Flyweights are sharable instances of a class. It might at first seem that each class is a Singleton, but in fact there might be a small number of instances, such as one for every character or one for every icon type. The number of instances that are allocated must be decided as the class instances are needed, and this is usually accomplished with a FlyweightFactory class. This Factory class usually *is* a Singleton, since it needs to keep track of whether a particular instance has been generated yet. It then either returns a new instance or a reference to one it has already generated.

To decide if some part of your program is a candidate for using Flyweights, consider whether it is possible to remove some data from the class and make it extrinsic. If this makes it possible to greatly reduce the number of different class instances your program needs to maintain, this might be a case where Flyweights will help.

Example Code

Suppose we want to draw a small folder icon with a name under it for each person in an organization. If this is a large organization, there could be a large number of such icons, but they are actually all the same graphical image. Even if we have two icons—one for "is Selected" and one for "not Selected"—the number of different icons is small. In such a system, having an icon object for each person, with its own coordinates, name, and selected state, is a waste of resources. We show two such icons in Figure 20-2.

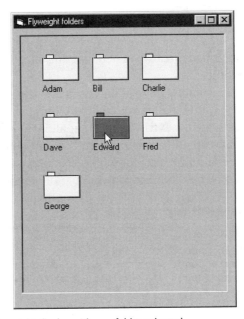

Figure 20-2   The Flyweight display with one folder selected

Instead, we'll create a FolderFactory that returns either the selected or the unselected folder drawing class but does not create additional instances once one of each has been created. Since this is such a simple case, we just create them both at the outset and then return one or the other.

```
'Class FolderFactory
'Returns selected or unselected folder
Private Selected As Folder, unSelected As Folder
Const selColor = vbActiveTitlebar
'---------
Public Sub init(Pic As PictureBox)

   'create one instance of each of 2 folders
   Set Selected = New Folder
   Selected.init Pic, selColor

   Set unSelected = New Folder
   unSelected.init Pic, vbYellow
End Sub
```

```
'---------
Public Function getFolder(isSelected As Boolean) As Folder
   If isSelected Then
      Set getFolder = Selected
   Else
      Set getFolder = unSelected
   End If
End Function
```

For cases where more instances could exist, the Factory could keep a table of those it had already created and only create new ones if they weren't already in the table.

The unique thing about using Flyweights, however, is that we pass the coordinates and the name to be drawn into the folder when we draw it. These coordinates are the extrinsic data that allow us to share the folder objects and, in this case, create only two instances. The complete folder class shown here simply creates a folder instance with one background color or the other and has a public Draw method that draws the folder at the point you specify.

```
'Class Folder
'draws a folder on the picture box panel
Private Pic As PictureBox
Private bColor As Long
Private Const w As Integer = 50, h As Integer = 30
Private Const Gray As Long = vbWindowBackground
'---------
Public Sub init(pc As PictureBox, bc As Long)
  Set Pic = pc
  bColor = bc
End Sub
'---------
Public Sub draw(X As Integer, Y As Integer, title As String)
   Pic.Line (X, Y)-(X + w, Y + h), bColor, BF
   Pic.Line (X, Y)-(X + w, Y + h), vbBlack, B
   Pic.Line (X + 1, Y + 1)-(X + w - 1, Y + 1), vbWhite
   Pic.Line (X + 1, Y)-(X + 1, Y + h), vbWhite
   Pic.Line (X + 5, Y)-(X + 15, Y - 5), bColor, BF
   Pic.Line (X + 5, Y)-(X + 15, Y - 5), vbBlack, B
   Pic.Line (X, Y + h - 1)-(X + w, Y + h - 1), Gray
   Pic.Line (X + w - 1, Y)-(X + w - 1, Y + h - 1), Gray
   Pic.PSet (X, Y + h + 5), Pic.BackColor
   Pic.Print title;
End Sub
```

To use a Flyweight class like this, your main program must calculate the position of each folder as part of its paint routine and then pass the coordinates to the folder instance. This is actually rather common, since you need a different layout, depending on the window's dimensions, and you would not want to have to keep telling each instance where its new location is going to be. Instead, we compute it dynamically during the paint routine.

Here we note that we could have generated an array or Collection of folders at the outset and simply scan through the array to draw each folder.

```
For i = 1 To names.Count
  Set fol = folders(i)     'get a folder
  fol.draw X, Y, names(i) 'and draw it
  cnt = cnt + 1
  If cnt > HCount Then
    cnt = 1
    X = pLeft
    Y = Y + VSpace
  Else
    X = X + HSpace
  End If
Next I
```

Such an array is not as wasteful as a series of different instances because it is actually an array of references to one of only two folder instances. However, since we want to display one folder as "selected," and we would like to be able to change which folder is selected dynamically, we just use the FolderFactory itself to give us the correct instance each time.

```
Private Sub Form_Paint()
'repaint entire pictureBox
Dim i As Integer
Dim X As Integer, Y As Integer
X = pLeft
Y = pTop
cnt = 1
'go through all names
For i = 1 To names.count
  'get one kind of folder or other
  Set fol = factory.getFolder(names(i) = selectedName)
  fol.draw X, Y, names(i)
  cnt = cnt + 1
  If cnt > HCount Then
    cnt = 1
    X = pLeft
    Y = Y + VSpace
  Else
    X = X + HSpace
  End If
Next i
End Sub
```

The Class Diagram

The diagram in Figure 20-3 shows how these classes interact.

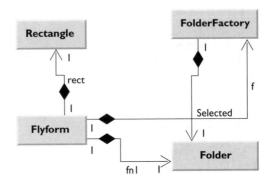

Figure 20-3   How Flyweights are generated

The FlyCanvas class is the main UI class, where the folders are arranged and drawn. It contains one instance of the FolderFactory and one instance of the Folder class. The FolderFactory class contains two instances of Folder: *selected* and *unselected*. One or the other of these is returned to the FlyCanvas by the FolderFactory.

Selecting a Folder

Since we have two folder instances, selected and unselected, we'd like to be able to select folders by moving the mouse over them. In the previous paint routine, we simply remember the name of the folder that was selected and ask the factory to return a "selected" folder for it. Since the folders are not individual instances, we can't listen for mouse motion within each folder instance. In fact, even if we did listen within a folder, we'd need a way to tell the other instances to deselect themselves.

Instead, we check for mouse motion at the Picturebox level, and if the mouse is found to be within a Rectangle, we make that corresponding name the selected name. We create a single instance of a Rectangle class where the testing can be done as to whether a folder contains the mouse at that instant.

```
'Class Rectangle
'used to find out if an x,y coordinate
'lies within a rectangle area
Private x1 As Integer
Private y1 As Integer
Private x2 As Integer
Private y2 As Integer
```

```
Private w As Integer
Private h As Integer
'--------
Public Function contains(X As Single, Y As Single) As Boolean
  If x1 <= X And X <= x2 And y1 <= Y And Y <= y2 Then
    contains = True
  Else
    contains = False
  End If
End Function
'--------
Public Sub init(x1_ As Integer, y1_ As Integer)
  x1 = x1_
  x2 = x1 + w
  y1 = y1_
  y2 = y1 + h
End Sub
'--------
Public Sub setSize(w_ As Integer, h_ As Integer)
  w = w_
  h = h_
End Sub
```

This allows us to just check each name when we redraw and create a selected folder instance where it is needed.

```
Private Sub Pic_MouseMove(Button As Integer, Shift As Integer, _
                          mX As Single, mY As Single)
Dim i As Integer, found As Boolean
Dim X As Integer, Y As Integer
'go through folder list
'looking to see if mouse posn
'is inside any of them
  X = pLeft
  Y = pTop
  cnt = 1
  i = 1
  found = False
  selectedName = ""
  While i <= names.count And Not found
    rect.init X, Y
    If rect.contains(mX, mY) Then
      selectedName = names(i) 'save that name
      found = True
    End If
    cnt = cnt + 1
    If cnt > HCount Then
      cnt = 1
      X = pLeft
      Y = Y + VSpace
    Else
      X = X + HSpace
```

```
        End If
        i = i + 1
    Wend
    Refresh
End Sub
```

Writing a Flyweight Folder in VB.NET

You can write very similar code in VB7 to handle this Flyweight pattern. Since we create only two instances of the Folder class and then select one or the other using a FolderFactory, we do not make any use of inheritance. Instead, our FolderFactory creates two instances in the constructor and returns one or the other.

```
Public Class FolderFactory
    Private selFolder, unselFolder As Folder
    '-----
    Public Sub New()
        'create the two folders
        selFolder = New Folder(Color.Brown)
        unselFolder = New Folder(color.Bisque)
    End Sub
    '-----
    Public Function getFolder(ByVal isSelected As Boolean) _
                              As Folder
        'return one or the other
        If isSelected Then
            Return selFolder
        Else
            Return unselFolder
        End If
    End Function
End Class
```

The folder class itself differs only in that we use the Graphics object to do the drawing. Note that the drawRectangle method uses a width and height as the last two arguments rather than the second pair of coordinates.

```
Public Class Folder
    'Draws a folder at the specified coordinates
    Private Const w As Integer = 50, h As Integer = 30
    Private blackPen As Pen, whitePen As Pen
    Private grayPen As Pen
    Private backBrush, blackBrush As SolidBrush
    Private fnt As Font
    '-----
    Public Sub New(ByVal col As Color)
        backBrush = New SolidBrush(Col)
        blackBrush = New SolidBrush(Color.Black)
```

```
        blackPen = New Pen(color.Black)
        whitePen = New Pen(color.White)
        grayPen = New Pen(color.Gray)
        fnt = New Font("Arial", 12)
    End Sub
    '-----
Public Sub draw(ByVal g As Graphics,_
        ByVal x As Integer, _
        ByVal y As Integer, ByVal title As String)
    g.FillRectangle(backBrush, x, y, w, h)
    g.DrawRectangle(blackPen, x, y, w, h)
    g.Drawline(whitePen, x + 1, y + 1, x + w - 1, y + 1)
    g.Drawline(whitePen, x + 1, y, x + 1, y + h)

    g.DrawRectangle(blackPen, x + 5, y - 5, 15, 5)
    g.FillRectangle(backBrush, x + 6, y - 4, 13, 6)

    g.DrawLine(graypen, x, y + h - 1, x + w, y + h - 1)
    g.DrawLine(graypen, x + w - 1, y, x + w - 1, y + h - 1)
    g.DrawString(title, fnt, blackBrush, x, y + h + 5)
  End Sub
End Class
```

The only real differences in the VB7 approach are the ways we intercept the paint and mouse events. In both cases, we add an event handler. To do the painting of the folders, we add a paint event handler to the picture box.

```
AddHandler Pic.Paint, _
New PaintEventHandler(AddressOf picPaint)
```

The paint handler we add draws the folders, much as we did in the VB6 version.

```
'paints the folders in the picture box
Private Sub picPaint(ByVal sender As Object, _
 ByVal e As PaintEventArgs)
Dim i, x , y , cnt As Integer
Dim g As Graphics = e.Graphics
  x = pleft
   y = ptop
   cnt = 0
   For i = 0 To names.Count - 1
       fol = folfact.getFolder(selectedname = _
         CType(names(i), String))
       fol.draw(g, x, y, CType(names(i), String))
       cnt = cnt + 1
       If cnt > 2 Then
           cnt = 0
           x = pleft
           y = y + vspace
       Else
```

```
            x = x + hspace
        End If
    Next
    End Sub
```

The mouse move event handler is very much analogous. We add a handler for mouse movement inside the picture box during the form's constructor.

```
AddHandler Pic.MouseMove, (AddressOf evMouse)
```

In order to detect whether a mouse position is inside a rectangle, we use a single instance of a Rectangle class. Since there already is a Rectangle class in the System.Drawing namespace, we put this rectangle in a VBPatterns namespace.

```
Namespace vbPatterns
    Public Class Rectangle
        Private x1, x2, y1, y2 As Integer
        Private w, h As Integer
        '-----
        Public Sub init(ByVal x_ As Integer,_
                ByVal y_ As Integer)
            x1 = x_
            y1 = y_
            x2 = x1 + w
            y2 = y1 + h
        End Sub
        '-----
        Public Sub setSize(ByVal w_ As Integer, _
            ByVal h_ As Integer)
            w = w_
            h = h_
        End Sub
        '-----
        Public Function contains(ByVal xp As Integer, _
            ByVal yp As Integer) As Boolean
            Return x1 <= xp And xp <= x2 And _
            y1 <= yp And yp <= y2
        End Function
    End Class
End Namespace
```

Then, using the contains method of the rectangle, we can check for whether the mouse is over a folder in the mouse move event handler.

```
'mouse move event handler
    Public Sub evMouse(ByVal sender As Object, _
            ByVal e As MouseEventArgs)
        Dim x, y, i, cnt As Integer
        Dim oldname As String
        Dim found As Boolean
        oldname = selectedname   'save old name
```

```
x = pleft    'move through coordinates
y = ptop
i = 0
cnt = 0
found = False
While i < names.Count And Not found
    rect.init(x, y)
    'see if a rectangle contains the mouse
    If rect.contains(e.X, e.Y) Then
        selectedname = CType(names(i), String)
        found = True
    End If
    i = i + 1
    cnt = cnt + 1
    'move on to next rectangle
    If cnt > 2 Then
        cnt = 0
        x = pleft
        y = y + vspace
    Else
        x = x + hspace
    End If

End While
'only refresh if mouse in new rectangle
If found And oldname <> selectedname Then
    pic.Refresh()
End If
End Sub
```

You can see the final VB.Net Flyweight example in Figure 20-4.

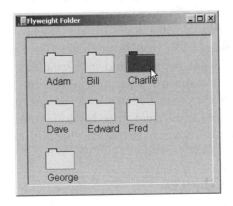

Figure 20-4   The VB.Net Flyweight program.

Flyweight Uses in VB

Flyweights are not frequently used at the application level in VB. They are more of a system resource management technique used at a lower level. However, there are a number of stateless objects that get created in Internet programming that are somewhat analogous to Flyweights. It is generally useful to recognize that this technique exists so you can use it if you need it.

Some objects within the VB language could be implemented under the covers as Flyweights. For example, if there are two instances of a String constant with identical characters, they could refer to the same storage location. Similarly, it might be that two Integer or Float constants that contain the same value could be implemented as Flyweights, although they probably are not.

Sharable Objects

The *Smalltalk Companion* points out that sharable objects are much like Flyweights, although the purpose is somewhat different. When you have a very large object containing a lot of complex data, such as tables or bitmaps, you would want to minimize the number of instances of that object. Instead, in such cases, you'd return one instance to every part of the program that asked for it and avoid creating other instances.

A problem with such sharable objects occurs when one part of a program wants to change some data in a shared object. You then must decide whether to change the object for all users, prevent any change, or create a new instance with the changed data. If you change the object for every instance, you may have to notify them that the object has changed.

Sharable objects are also useful when you are referring to large data systems outside of VB, such as databases. The Dbase class we developed previously in the Façade pattern could be a candidate for a sharable object. We might not want a number of separate connections to the database from different program modules, preferring that only one be instantiated. However, should several modules in different threads decide to make queries simultaneously, the Database class might have to queue the queries or spawn extra connections.

Copy-on-Write Objects

The Flyweight pattern uses just a few object instances to represent many different objects in a program. All of them normally have the same base properties as intrinsic data and a few properties that represent extrinsic data that vary with each manifestation of the class instance. However, it could occur that some of these instances eventually take on new intrinsic properties (such as shape or folder tab position) and require a new specific instance of the class to represent them. Rather than creating these in advance as special subclasses, it is possible to copy the class instance and change its intrinsic properties when the program flow indicates that a new separate instance is required. The class copies this itself when the change becomes inevitable, changing those intrinsic properties in the new class. We call this process "copy-on-write" and can build this into Flyweights as well as a number of other classes, such as the Proxy, which we discuss next.

THOUGHT QUESTION

If Buttons can appear on several different tabs of a TabDialog, but each of them controls the same one or two tasks, is this an appropriate use for a Flyweight?

Programs on the CD-ROM

\Flyweight\Flywt	VB6 folders
\Flyweight\Vbnet	VB7 Flyweight folders

CHAPTER 21

The Proxy Pattern

The Proxy pattern is used when you need to represent an object that is complex or time consuming to create, by a simpler one. If creating an object is expensive in time or computer resources, Proxy allows you to postpone this creation until you need the actual object. A Proxy usually has the same methods as the object it represents, and once the object is loaded, it passes on the method calls from the Proxy to the actual object.

There are several cases where a Proxy can be useful.

1. An object, such as a large image, takes a long time to load.

2. The results of a computation take a long time to complete, and you need to display intermediate results while the computation continues.

3. The object is on a remote machine, and loading it over the network may be slow, especially during peak network load periods.

4. The object has limited access rights, and the proxy can validate the access permissions for that user.

Proxies can also be used to distinguish between requesting an instance of an object and the actual need to access it. For example, program initialization may set up a number of objects that may not all be used right away. In that case, the proxy can load the real object only when it is needed.

Let's consider the case of a large image that a program needs to load and display. When the program starts, there must be some indication that an image is to be displayed so that the screen lays out correctly, but the actual image display can be postponed until the image is completely loaded. This is particularly important in programs such as word processors and Web browsers that lay out text around the images even before the images are available.

An image proxy can note the image and begin loading it in the background while drawing a simple rectangle or other symbol to represent the image's extent on the screen before it appears. The proxy can even delay loading the image at all until it receives a paint request and only then begin the process.

Sample Code

In this example, we create a simple program to display an image on a Image control when it is loaded. Rather than loading the image directly, we use a class we call ImageProxy to defer loading and draw a rectangle until loading is completed.

```
'Displays an image during and after computation
Private impr As ImageProxy
'--------
Private Sub Form_Load()
  Set impr = New ImageProxy
End Sub
'--------
Private Sub Loadit_Click()
'start the image fetch or computation
 Timer1.Enabled = True
 impr.startImage
End Sub
'--------
Private Sub Timer1_Timer()
'get an image to display
  Image1.Picture = LoadPicture(impr.getImage)
End Sub
```

Note that we create the instance of the ImageProxy just as we would have for an Image. The ImageProxy class sets up the image loading and creates an Imager object to follow the loading process. It returns a class that implements the Imager interface.

```
'Class imager
Public Function getImage() As String
End Function
```

In this simple case, the ImageProxy class just delays five seconds and then switches from the preliminary image to the final image.

```
'Class ImageProxy
Private stTime As Variant
Private started As Boolean
Private img As Imager
'--------
```

```
Public Sub startImage()
  started = True     'image fetch starting
  stTime = Time      'log the time
End Sub
'--------
Public Function isReady() As Boolean
 'return true after image delay— here 5 seconds
 Dim tim As Variant
 tim = DateDiff("s", stTime, Time)
  If tim > 5 And started Then
    isReady = True
  Else
    isReady = False
  End If
End Function
'--------
Public Function getImage() As String
 'return an image from the prelim or final image class
 If isReady Then
   Set img = New FinalImage
 End If
 getImage = img.getImage
End Function
'--------
Private Sub Class_Initialize()
  started = False
  Set img = New QuickImage
End Sub
```

We implement the Imager interface in two tiny classes we called QuickImage and FinalImage. One gets a small gif image and the other a larger (and presumably slower) jpeg image.

```
'Class QuickImage
Implements Imager
Private Function Imager_getImage() As String
 Imager_getImage = App.Path & "\box.gif"
End Function

'Class FinalImage
Implements Imager
Private Function Imager_getImage() As String
 Imager_getImage = App.Path & "\flowrtree.jpg"
End Function
```

The program's two states are illustrated in Figure 21-1.

Figure 21-1   The proxy image display on the left is shown until the image loads as shown on the right.

Writing a Proxy in VB.Net

We will illustrate the same image proxy in VB7. Since the PictureBox's Image property requires an Image as an argument, we will change our Imager interface to return an Image type.

```
Public Interface Imager
    Function getImage() As Image
End Interface
```

In VB7, Image is an abstract class, and the Bitmap, Cursor, Icon, and Metafile classes are derived from it. So the actual class we will usually return is derived from Image. The QuickImage class returns a Bitmap from a gif file

```
Public Class QuickImage
    Implements Imager
    '-----
    Public Function getImage() As Image _
            Implements Imager.getImage
        Return New bitmap("Box.gif")
    End Function
End Class
```

and the FinalImage class returns a bitmap from a jpeg file.

```
Public Class FinalImage
    Implements Imager
    '-----
    Public Function getImage() As Image _
```

```
        Implements Imager.getImage
        Return New Bitmap("flowrtree.jpg")
    End Function
End Class
```

The main difference in the way we obtain images in this program is in our ImageProxy class. Timers are handled quite differently in VB7, using a Timer-Callback class that defines the method to be called when the timer ticks. This is much the same as the way we add other event handlers.

```
Public Class ImageProxy
    Private done As Boolean
    Private tm As Timer
    '-----
    Public Sub New()
        done = False
        'set up timer that ticks once after 5 seconds
        tm = New Timer( _
        New TimerCallback(AddressOf tCallback), _
                        Me, 5000, 0)
    End Sub
```

The timer callback defines that the tCallback method will be called.

```
Public Sub tCallback(ByVal obj As Object)
        'set done flag and turn off timer
        done = True
        tm.Dispose()
End Sub
```

And this method sets the done flag and turns off the timer.

When you go to fetch an image, you initially get the quick image, and after five seconds, if you call the method again, you get the final image.

```
    Public Function getImage() As Image
        Dim img As Imager
        'return quick image until ready
        If isReady Then
            img = New FinalImage()
        Else
            img = New QuickImage()
        End If
        Return img.getImage
    End Function
```

This program works so that when you first click on the form's load button, you get the quick image for five seconds after the first click. After five seconds, if you click the button again, you get the final jpeg image.

Proxies in VB

Since VB6 is primarily a client-writing language, you will find VB6 Proxies less common than in client-server systems. However, you see much more proxy-like behavior in VB7, which is crafted for network and Internet use. For example, the ADO database connection classes are all effectively proxies.

You can use VB6 to create server-side WebClass objects and Active Server Pages (ASPs) that themselves utilize VB-like code. However, it is not common to have VB6 running as both the server and client system, and thus Proxies are less likely to be used. Even in Visual Studio.NET, where you can use VB7 or one or more other languages to create server code, the client-side code is more frequently HTML, and proxies would not normally occur. However, server-side classes in any convenient languages can benefit from proxies whenever the server-side program is time consuming to complete.

Copy-on-Write

You can also use proxies is to keep copies of large objects that may or may not change. If you create a second instance of an expensive object, a Proxy can decide there is no reason to make a copy yet. It simply uses the original object. Then, if the program makes a change in the new copy, the Proxy can copy the original object and make the change in the new instance. This can be a great time and space saver when objects do not always change after they are instantiated.

Comparison with Related Patterns

Both the Adapter and the Proxy constitute a thin layer around an object. However, the Adapter provides a different interface for an object, while the Proxy provides the same interface for the object but interposes itself where it can postpone processing or data transmission effort.

A Decorator also has the same interface as the object it surrounds, but its purpose is to add additional (sometimes visual) function to the original object. A proxy, by contrast, controls access to the contained class.

 THOUGHT QUESTION

You have designed a server that connects to a database. If several clients connect to your server at once, how might Proxies be of help?

Programs on the CD-ROM

`\Proxy`	VB6 Image proxy
`\Proxy\VBNet`	VB7 image proxy

Summary of Structural Patterns

Part 3 covered the following structural patterns.

The **Adapter** pattern is used to change the interface of one class to that of another one.

The **Bridge** pattern is designed to separate a class's interface from its implementation so you can vary or replace the implementation without changing the client code.

The **Composite** pattern is a collection of objects, any one of which may be either itself a Composite or just a leaf object.

The **Decorator** pattern, a class that surrounds a given class, adds new capabilities to it and passes all the unchanged methods to the underlying class.

The **Façade** pattern groups a complex set of objects and provides a new, simpler interface to access those data.

The **Flyweight** pattern provides a way to limit the proliferation of small, similar instances by moving some of the class data outside the class and passing it in during various execution methods.

The **Proxy** pattern provides a simple placeholder object for a more complex object that is in some way time consuming or expensive to instantiate

PART 4

Behavioral Patterns

Behavioral patterns are most specifically concerned with communication between objects. In Part 4, we examine the following.

The **Chain of Responsibility** allows a decoupling between objects by passing a request from one object to the next in a chain until the request is recognized.

The **Command pattern** utilizes simple objects to represent execution of software commands and allows you to support logging and undoable operations.

The **Interpreter pattern** provides a definition of how to include language elements in a program.

The **Iterator pattern** formalizes the way we move through a list of data within a class.

The **Mediator pattern** defines how communication between objects can be simplified by using a separate object to keep all objects from having to know about each other.

The **Memento pattern** defines how you might save the contents of an instance of a class and restore it later.

The **Observer pattern** defines the way a number of objects can be notified of a change,

The **State pattern** allows an object to modify its behavior when its internal state changes.

The **Strategy pattern** encapsulates an algorithm inside a class.

The **Template Method pattern** provides an abstract definition of an algorithm.

The **Visitor pattern** adds polymorphic functions to a class noninvasively.

CHAPTER 22

Chain of Responsibility

The Chain of Responsibility pattern allows a number of classes to attempt to handle a request without any of them knowing about the capabilities of the other classes. It provides a loose coupling between these classes; the only common link is the request that is passed between them. The request is passed along until one of the classes can handle it.

One example of such a chain pattern is a Help system like the one shown in Figure 22-1. This is a simple application where different kinds of help could be useful, where every screen region of an application invites you to seek help but in which there are window background areas where more generic help is the only suitable result.

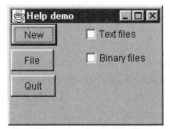

Figure 22-1   A simple application where different kinds of help could be useful

When you select an area for help, that visual control forwards its ID or name to the chain. Suppose you selected the "New" button. If the first module can handle the New button, it displays the help message. If not, it forwards the request to the next module. Eventually, the message is forwarded to an "All buttons" class that can display a general message about how buttons work. If there is no general button help, the message is forwarded to the general help module that tells you how the system works in general. If that doesn't exist, the message is lost, and no information is displayed. This is illustrated in Figure 22-2.

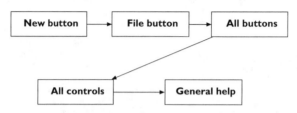

Figure 22-2   A simple Chain of Responsibility

There are two significant points we can observe from this example: first, the chain is organized from most specific to most general, and second, there is no guarantee that the request will produce a response in all cases. We will see shortly that you can use the Observer pattern to provide a way for a number of classes to be notified of a change.

Applicability

The Chain of Responsibility is a good example of a pattern that helps keep knowledge separate of what each object in a program can do. In other words, it reduces the coupling between objects so that they can act independently. This also applies to the object that constitutes the main program and contains instances of the other objects. You will find this pattern helpful in the following situations.

- There are several objects with similar methods that could be appropriate for the action the program is requesting. However, it is more appropriate for the objects to decide which one is to carry out the action than it is for you to build this decision into the calling code.
- One of the objects may be most suitable, but you don't want to build in a series of if-else or switch statements to select a particular object.
- There might be new objects that you want to add to the possible list of processing options while the program is executing.
- There might be cases when more than one object will have to act on a request, and you don't want to build knowledge of these interactions into the calling program.

Sample Code

The help system we just described is a little involved for a first example. Instead, let's start with a simple visual command-interpreter program (Figure 22-3) that illustrates how the chain works. This program displays the results of typed-in commands. While this first case is constrained to keep the example code tractable, we'll see that this Chain of Responsibility pattern is commonly used for parsers and even compilers.

In this example, the commands can be any of the following.

- Image filenames
- General filenames
- Color names
- All other commands

In the first three cases, we can display a concrete result of the request, and in the fourth case, we can only display the request text itself.

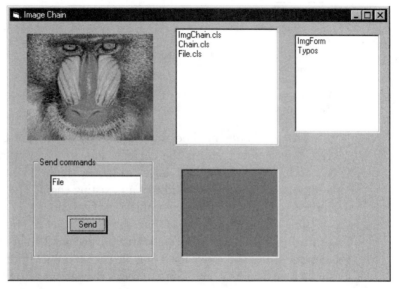

Figure 22-3 A simple visual command interpreter program that acts on one of four panels, depending on the command you type in.

In the preceding example system, we do the following.

1. We type in "Mandrill" and see a display of the image Mandrill.jpg.

2. Then we type in a filename, and that filename is displayed in the center list box.

3. Next, we type in "blue," and that color is displayed in the lower center panel.

Finally, if we type in anything that is neither a filename nor a color, that text is displayed in the final, right-hand list box. This is shown in Figure 22-4.

Figure 22-4   How the command chain works for the program in Figure 22-3

To write this simple chain of responsibility program, we start with an abstract Chain class.

```
'Interface class Chain
'--------
Public Sub addChain(c As Chain)
End Sub
'--------
Public Sub sendToChain(mesg As String)
End Sub
'--------
Public Function getChain() As Chain
End Function
'--------
Public Sub setControl(c As Control)
End Sub
'--------
Public Function hasChain() As Boolean
End Function
```

The *addChain* method adds another class to the chain of classes. The *getChain* method returns the current class to which messages are being forwarded. These two methods allow us to modify the chain dynamically and add additional classes in the middle of an existing chain. The *sendToChain* method forwards a message to the next object in the chain.

Our main program assembles the Chain classes and sets a reference to a control into each of them. We start with the ImgChain class, which takes the message string and looks for a .jpg file of that name. If it finds one, it displays it in the Image control, and if not, it sends the command on to the next element in the chain.

```
'Class ImgChain
Implements Chain
Private chn As Chain
Private hasLink As Boolean
Private fl As File
Private img As Image
'--------
Private Sub Chain_addChain(c As Chain)
  Set chn = c
  hasLink = True
End Sub
'--------
Private Function Chain_getChain() As Chain
```

```
    Set Chain_getChain = chn
End Function
'--------
Private Function Chain_hasChain() As Boolean
  Chain_hasChain = hasLink
End Function
'--------
Private Sub Chain_sendToChain(mesg As String)
  fl.setFilename App.Path & "\" & mesg & ".jpg"
  If fl.exists Then
    img.Picture = LoadPicture(fl.getFilename)
  Else
    chn.sendToChain mesg
  End If
End Sub
'--------
Private Sub Chain_setControl(c As Control)
  Set img = c
End Sub
'--------
Private Sub Class_Initialize()
  hasLink = False
  Set fl = New File
End Sub
```

In a similar fashion, the ColorChain class simply interprets the message as a color name and displays it if it can. This example only interprets three colors, but you could implement any number.

```
Private Sub Chain_sendToChain(mesg As String)
Dim colr As Long, found As Boolean
  found = True
  Select Case LCase(mesg) 'look for a color name
    Case "red"
      colr = vbRed
    Case "blue"
      colr = vbBlue
    Case "green"
      colr = vbGreen
    Case Else
    'if not found send it on
      If hasLink Then
        chn.sendToChain mesg
        found = False    'not found
      End If
  End Select
  'if found change the color
  If found Then
    pc.BackColor = colr
  End If
End Sub
```

The List Boxes

Both the file list and the list of unrecognized commands are ListBoxes. If the message matches part of a filename, the filename is displayed in the fileList box, and if not, the message is sent on to the NoComd chain element.

```
Private Sub Chain_sendToChain(mesg As String)
Dim fls As String
  ChDir App.Path     'current directory
  fls = Dir(mesg & "*.*")    'look for match
  If Len(fls) > 0 Then
    lst.AddItem fls       'add it to list
  Else
    If hasLink Then
      chn.sendToChain mesg  'or send to Nocmd class
    End If
  End If
End Sub
```

The NoCmd Chain class is very similar. It, however, has no class to which to send data.

```
'Class NoCmd
Implements Chain
Private lst As ListBox
'--------
Private Sub Chain_addChain(c As Chain)
End Sub
'--------
Private Function Chain_getChain() As Chain
End Function
'--------
Private Function Chain_hasChain() As Boolean
  Chain_hasChain = False
End Function
'--------
Private Sub Chain_sendToChain(mesg As String)
  lst.AddItem mesg
End Sub
'--------
Private Sub Chain_setControl(c As Control)
  Set lst = c
End Sub
```

Finally, we link these classes together in the Form_Load routine to create the Chain.

```
'set up Chain of Responsibility
Dim colr As Chain
Dim fls As Chain
Dim nocom As Chain
```

```
'Image chain
Set chn = New ImgChain
chn.setControl imgJpg
'Color chain
Set colr = New ColorChain
colr.setControl pcColor
chn.addChain colr
'File chain
Set fls = New FileChain
fls.setControl lsFiles
colr.addChain fls
'No Command
Set nocom = New NoCmd
nocom.setControl lsNocomds
fls.addChain nocom
```

You can see the relationship between these classes in the UML diagram in Figure 22-5.

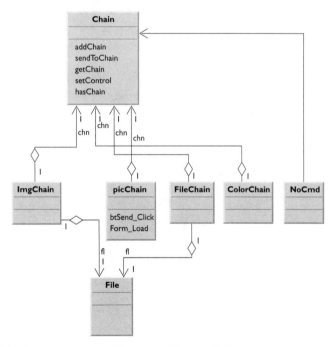

Figure 22-5   The class strcuture of the Chain of Responsibility program

The Sender class is the initial class that implements the Chain interface. It receives the button clicks and obtains the text from the text field. It passes the command on to the Imager class, the FileList class, the ColorImage class, and finally to the RestList class. Note that FileList is a subclass of RestList and implements the Chain interface because the parent RestList class does.

Programming a Help System

As we noted at the beginning of this discussion, help systems provide good examples of how the Chain of Responsibility pattern can be used. Now that we've outlined a way to write such chains, we'll consider a help system for a window with several controls. The program (Figure 22-6) pops up a help dialog message when the user presses the F1 (help) key. The message depends on which control is selected when the F1 key is pressed.

Figure 22-6   A simple help demonstration

In this example, the user has selected the Quit key, which does not have a specific help message associated with it. Instead, the chain forwards the help request to a general button help object that displays the message shown on the right.

To write this help chain system, we begin with a general Chain interface class that has empty implementations of all of the Chain interface methods.

```
'Interface class Chain
'--------
Public Sub addChain(c As Chain)
End Sub
'--------
Public Sub sendToChain(c As Control)
End Sub
'--------
Public Function getChain() As Chain
End Function
'--------
Public Function hasChain() As Boolean

End Function
```

Note that this chain does not need to have a copy of a reference to any kind of control. This is passed in using the sendToChain method.

Then you need to create specific classes for each of the help message categories you want to produce. As we illustrated earlier, we want help messages for the following.

- The New button
- The File button
- A general button
- A general visual control (covering the check boxes)

In VB, one control will always have the focus, and thus we don't need a case for the Window itself. Therefore, we write the above four classes and combine them into a chain as follows.

```
Private Sub Form_Load()
Dim butc As Chain
Dim filc As Chain
Dim cchn As Chain
'create chain of responsibility
  Set chn = New NewChain
  Set filc = New FileChain
  Set butc = New ButtonChain
  Set cchn = New ControlChain
  chn.addChain filc
  filc.addChain butc
  butc.addChain cchn
End Sub
```

Receiving the Help Command

Now we need to assign keyboard listeners to look for the F1 keypress. At first, you might think we need five such listeners—for the three buttons and the two check boxes. However, we can make control arrays of the buttons and the check boxes, and then we need to listend for a KeyDown event in two places, and both call the same method.

```
Private chn As Chain
'--------
Private Sub btNew_KeyDown(Index As Integer, keyCode As Integer, _
          Shift As Integer)
  callChain btNew(Index), keyCode
End Sub
'--------
Private Sub callChain(c As Control, keyCode As Integer)
If keyCode = vbKeyF1 Then    'respond to F1 only
  chn.sendToChain c
End If
End Sub
```

For the File button, the chain class is implemented as follows.

```
Implements Chain
Private chn As Chain
Private hasLink As Boolean
'--------
Private Sub Chain_addChain(c As Chain)
  Set chn = c
  hasLink = True
End Sub
'--------
Private Function Chain_getChain() As Chain
  Set Chain_getChain = chn
End Function
'--------
Private Function Chain_hasChain() As Boolean
  Chain_hasChain = hasLink
End Function
'--------
Private Sub Chain_sendToChain(c As Control)
  If c.Caption = "File" Then
    MsgBox "Use to open a file"
  Else
    If hasLink Then
      chn.sendToChain c
    End If
  End If
End Sub
'--------
Private Sub Class_Initialize()
  hasLink = False
End Sub
```

At first you might think that you could just as easily have made a separate KeyDown event method for each of the controls on the form, instead of having only a couple of such events and sending them all through the same chain. And, in fact, that is how VB programs are usually written. The advantage to this Chain of Responsibility approach is that you can decide the order in which controls are checked for membership in various classes and control and easily change this order within your program. This provides a considerably more versatile and flexible system than if each control called its own event method. We show the complete class diagram for this help system in Figure 22-7.

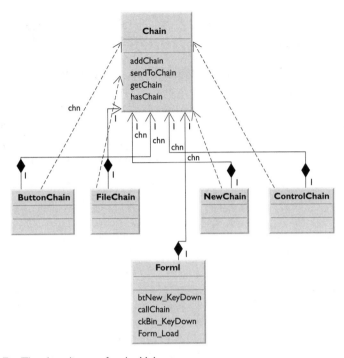

Figure 22-7   The class diagram for the Help system

A Chain or a Tree?

Of course, a Chain of Responsibility does not have to be linear. The *Smalltalk Companion* suggests that it is more generally a tree structure with a number of specific entry points all pointing upward to the most general node, as shown in Figure 22-8.

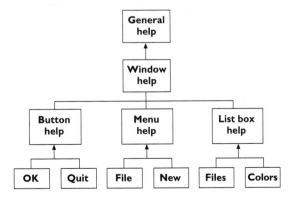

Figure 22-8   The chain of responsibility implemented as a tree structure

However, this sort of structure seems to imply that each button, or its handler, knows where to enter the chain. This can complicate the design in some cases and may preclude the need for the chain at all.

Another way of handling a tree-like structure is to have a single entry point that branches to the specific button, menu, or other widget types and then "unbranches," as previously, to more general help cases. There is little reason for that complexity—you could align the classes into a single chain, starting at the bottom, and going left to right and up a row at a time until the entire system had been traversed, as shown in Figure 22-9.

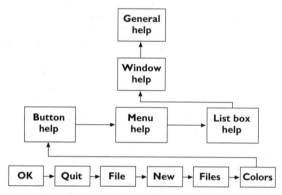

Figure 22-9   The same chain of responsibility implemented as a linear chain

Chain of Responsibility in VB.NET

We can implement the Chain of Responsibility in VB7 in a very similar manner. However, it is convenient to make the Chain class an abstract class instead of an interface. Remember that an abstract class has one or more methods that must be implemented in the derived classes. We mark this method as MustOverride and mark the class as MustInherit, as we illustrate here.

```
Public MustInherit Class Chain
    Protected chn As Chain
    Private hasLink As Boolean
    '-----
    Public Sub New()
        hasLink = False
    End Sub
    '-----
    Public Sub addChain(ByVal c As chain)
        chn = c
        haslink = True   'mark as available
    End Sub
    '-----
```

```
        'will fill this in in derived classes
        Public MustOverride Sub sendToChain(_
                            ByVal mesg As String)
        '-----
        Public Function getChain() As chain
            Return chn
        End Function
        '-----
        Public Function hasChain() As Boolean
            Return hasLink
        End Function
End Class
```

Then we can easily derive classes, and we only need to implement the send-ToChain method. For example, here is the FileChain class.

```
Public Class FileChain
    Inherits Chain
    Private flist As ListBox
    '-----
    Public Sub new(ByVal lbox As ListBox)
        MyBase.new()
        flist = lbox
    End Sub
    '-----
    Public Overrides Sub sendToChain( _
                        ByVal mesg As String)
        Dim fname As String
        Dim files As File()
        fname = mesg & "*.*"
        files = Directory.GetFilesInDirectory( _
            Directory.CurrentDirectory, fname)
        'add them all to the listbox
        If files.Length > 0 Then
            Dim i As Integer
            For i = 0 To files.Length - 1
                flist.Items.Add(files(i).Name)
            Next
        Else
            If haschain Then
                chn.sendToChain(mesg)
            End If
        End If
    End Sub
End Class
```

Since we initialize the chains in their constructors, the code in the form constructor that sets them up is a little simpler.

```
Private Sub setUpChain()
        Dim clrchain As New ColorChain(pnlcolor)
        Dim flchain As New FileChain(lsfiles)
```

```
        Dim nochain As New NoCmd(lsnocomd)

        chn = New ImageChain(picImage)
        chn.addChain(clrchain)
        clrchain.addChain(flchain)
        flchain.addChain(nochain)
    End Sub
```

The final display is shown in Figure 22-10.

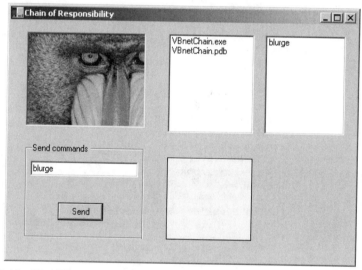

Figure 22-10   The VB7 version of the image Chain of Responsibility

Kinds of Requests

The request or message passed along the Chain of Responsibility may well be a great deal more complicated than just the string or Control that we conveniently used on these examples. The information could include various data types or a complete object with a number of methods. Since various classes along the chain may use different properties of such a request object, you might end up designing an abstract Request type and any number of derived classes with additional methods.

Examples in VB

Under the covers, VB form windows receive various events, such as Mouse-Move, and then forward them to the controls the form contains. However, only the final control ever receives the message in VB, whereas in some other languages, each containing control does as well. This is a clear implementation of Chain of Responsibility pattern. We could also argue that, in general, the VB.NET class inheritance structure itself exemplifies this pattern. If you call for a method to be executed in a deeply derived class, that method is passed up the inheritance chain until the first parent class containing that method is found. The fact that further parents contain other implementations of that method does not come into play.

We will also see that the Chain of Responsibility is ideal for implementing Interpreters and use one in the Interpreter pattern we discuss later.

Consequences of the Chain of Responsibility

1. The main purpose for this pattern, like a number of others, is to reduce coupling between objects. An object only needs to know how to forward the request to other objects.

2. Each VB object in the chain is self-contained. It knows nothing of the others and only need decide whether it can satisfy the request. This makes both writing each one and constructing the chain very easy.

3. You can decide whether the final object in the chain handles all requests it receives in some default fashion or just discards them. However, you do have to know which object will be last in the chain for this to be effective.

4. Finally, since VB cannot provide multiple inheritance, the basic Chain class needs to be an interface rather than an abstract class so the individual objects can inherit from another useful hierarchy, as we did here by deriving them all from Control. This disadvantage of this approach is that you often have to implement the linking, sending, and forwarding code in each module separately or, as we did here, by subclassing a concrete class that implements the Chain interface.

 THOUGHT QUESTION

Suggest how you might use a Chain of Responsibility to implement an e-mail filter.

Programs on the CD-ROM

\Chain\HelpChain	VB6 program showing how a help system can be implemented
\Chain\PicChain	VB6 chain of file and image displays
\Chain\VBNetChain	VB7 chain of file and image displays

CHAPTER 23

The Command Pattern

The Chain of Responsibility forwards requests along a chain of classes, but the Command pattern forwards a request only to a specific object. It encloses a request for a specific action inside an object and gives it a known public interface. It lets you give the client the ability to make requests without knowing anything about the actual action that will be performed and allows you to change that action without affecting the client program in any way.

Motivation

When you build a VB user interface, you provide menu items, buttons, check boxes, and so forth to allow the user to tell the program what to do. When a user selects one of these controls, the program receives a clicked event, which it receives into a special routine in the user interface. Let's suppose we build a very simple program that allows you to select the menu items File|Open, File|Red, and File|Exit, and click on a button marked Red that turns the background of the window red. The File|Red menu item also turns the background red. This program is shown in Figure 23-1.

The program consists of the File Menu object with the mnuOpen, mnuRed, and mnuExit MenuItems added to it. It also contains one button called btnRed. During the design phase, clicking on any of these items creates a little method in the Form class that gets called when the control is clicked.

As long as there are only a few menu items and buttons, this approach works fine, but when you have dozens of menu items and several buttons, the Form module code can get pretty unwieldy. In addition, the red command is carried out both from the button and the menu.

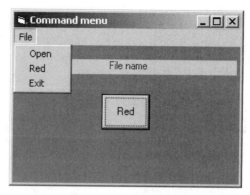

Figure 23-1   A simple program that receives events from the button and menu items

Command Objects

One way to ensure that every object receives its own commands directly is to use the Command pattern and create individual Command objects. A Command object always has an Execute() method that is called when an action occurs on that object. Most simply, a Command object implements at least the following interface.

```
'Class Command
Public Sub Execute()
End Sub
```

One objective of using this interface is to separate the user interface code from the actions the program must carry out, as shown here.

```
Private Sub mnuexit_Click()
  exitCmd.Execute
End Sub
'-------
Private Sub mnuOpen_Click()
  flCmd.Execute
End Sub
```

Then we can provide an Execute method for each object that carries out the desired action, thus keeping the knowledge of what to do inside the object where it belongs, instead of having another part of the program make these decisions.

One important purpose of the Command pattern is to keep the program and user interface objects completely separate from the actions that they initiate. In other words, these program objects should be completely separate from each other and should not have to know how other objects work. The user interface receives a command and tells a Command object to carry out whatever duties it has been instructed to do. The UI does not and should not need to know what tasks will be executed. This decouples the UI class from the execution of specific commands, making it possible to modify or completely change the action code without changing the classes containing the user interface.

The Command object can also be used when you need to tell the program to execute the command when the resources are available rather than immediately. In such cases, you are *queuing* commands to be executed later. Finally, you can use Command objects to remember operations so you can support Undo requests.

Building Command Objects

There are several ways to go about building Command objects for a program like this, and each has some advantages. We'll start with the simplest one: creating new classes and implementing the Command interface in each. Here is an example of the exit class.

```
'Class Exit command
Implements Command
Private Sub Command_Execute()
   End
End Sub
```

Then both the File|Exit command and the Form_Unload event can call it.

```
Private Sub Form_Unload(Cancel As Integer)
 exitCmd.Execute
End Sub
'-----
Private Sub mnuexit_Click()
   exitCmd.Execute
End Sub
```

You also have only one localized place to change what takes place if, for example, you want to add an "Are you sure?" message box.

This certainly lets us simplify the user interface code, but it does require that we create and instantiate a new class for each action we want to execute. Further, because VB has fairly stringent type checking, we need to create two references to these objects, one as a specific class and one as a Command object.

```
Private exitCmd As Command
Private exitCl As ExitClass
'the exit command class
Set exitCl = New ExitClass
Set exitCmd = exitCl         'as command
```

Classes that require specific parameters to work need to have those parameters passed in the init method or in a set method. For example, the File|Open command requires that you pass it an instance of the CommonDialog object and the label where the filename will be displayed.

```
'and the file|open class
Set opner = New Opener
opner.init cDlg, Label1 'send it the common dialog and label
Set flCmd = opner
```

Similarly, our RedCommand object needs the Form to set its background to red.

```
'create the red command class
Set redCl = New RedClass
redCl.setForm Me
Set redCmd = redCl 'as a command
```

This can then be called both from the menu and button click event methods.

```
Private Sub btnRed_Click()
 redCmd.Execute
End Sub
'-----
Private Sub mnuRed_Click()
 redCmd.Execute
End Sub
```

Arrays of Commands

When you have a program with an array of similar controls, such as a series of buttons or radio buttons, you can create a parallel array of command objects and simply execute the right one. For example, you might have a program to display either or both sexes in a list of kids.

For example, the program in Figure 23-2 allows you to select the girls, the boys, or show all the kids at once.

You can create the three radio buttons as a control array when you design the program. Then you can simply create three command objects and put them in a Collection. When a radio button is clicked, you just pick that command and execute it.

```
'all button clicks come here
Private Sub opSex_Click(Index As Integer)
Dim cmd As Command
'execute the command from the Collection
```

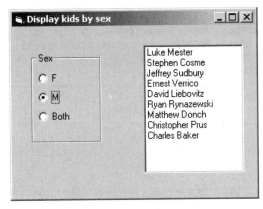

Figure 23-2 A program that displays kids by sex or all at once

```
Set cmd = buttons(Index + 1)
cmd.Execute
End Sub
```

In this program we create a Kids object containing a Collection of individual swimmers.

```
'Class kids
Private kds As New Collection
Private Index As Integer
Private sex As String
Private sw As Swimmer
'-----
Public Sub add(sw As Swimmer)
  kds.add sw
End Sub
'-----
Public Sub setSex(sx As String)
 sex = sx
 moveFirst
End Sub
'-----
Public Sub moveFirst()
 Index = 1
 Set sw = kds(Index)
End Sub
'-----
Public Sub readKids(fname As String)
  'details on CDROM
End Sub
'-----
'returns true if there are any more kids
'of the current sex
Public Function hasMoreElements() As Boolean
```

```
    Set sw = kds(Index)
    If sw.getSex = sex Or sex = "" Then
     hasMoreElements = Index < kds.Count
    Else
     nextElement
     hasMoreElements = Index < kds.Count
    End If
End Function
'-----
'moves to the next kids of that sex
Public Function nextElement() As Swimmer
   Set sw = kds(Index)
   If sex <> "" Then
     While sw.getSex <> sex And Index <= kds.Count
       Set sw = kds(Index)
       If sw.getSex <> sex Then Index = Index + 1
     Wend
     If sw.getSex = sex Then
       Set nextElement = sw
       Index = Index + 1
     Else
       Index = Index + 1
     End If
   Else
     Set nextElement = kds(Index)
     Index = Index + 1
   End If
End Function
```

Then we create a PickKids class that implements the Command interface that returns a Collection of the kids who match the criterion.

```
'Class pickKids
Implements Command
Private kds As Kids
Private lst As ListBox
Private sex As String
'-----
Public Sub init(sx As String, kidds As Kids, list As ListBox)
 Set kds = kidds
 sex = sx
 Set lst = list
End Sub
'-----
Private Sub loadList()
'loads the list box with the selected kids
Dim sw As Swimmer
lst.Clear
kds.setSex sex
kds.moveFirst
While kds.hasMoreElements
  Set sw = kds.nextElement
```

```
    lst.AddItem sw.getName
Wend
End Sub
'-----
'the command is executed here
Private Sub Command_Execute()
  loadList
End Sub
```

With this simple infrastructure, we can create three instances of the Pick-Kids class and select the right one, depending on the button that the user clicks.

```
Dim pk As PickKids

Set kds = New Kids
Set buttons = New Collection
kds.readKids "Swimmers.txt"

'create 3 instances of PickKids
'for each of the 3 option selections
Set pk = New PickKids
pk.init "F", kds, lsKids
buttons.add pk  'and add to the collection

Set pk = New PickKids
pk.init "M", kds, lsKids
buttons.add pk

Set pk = New PickKids
pk.init "", kds, lsKids
buttons.add pk
```

Again, the advantage here is that the user interface no longer plays a tangled role in providing the actual execution of commands. Instead, it simply executes the command without ever knowing what it is or whether the programmer had changed the character of that command.

Consequences of the Command Pattern

The main disadvantage of the Command pattern seems to be a proliferation of little classes that clutter up the program. However, even in the case where we have separate click events, we usually call little private methods to carry out the actual function. It turns out that these private methods are just about as long as our little classes, so there is frequently little difference in complexity between building the command classes and just writing more methods. The main difference is that the Command pattern produces little classes that are much more readable.

Providing Undo

Another of the main reasons for using Command design patterns is that they provide a convenient way to store and execute an Undo function. Each command object can remember what it just did and restore that state when requested to do so if the computational and memory requirements are not too overwhelming. At the top level, we simply redefine the Command interface to have two methods.

```
'Class Command
Public Sub Execute()
End Sub
'-----
Public Sub Undo()
End Sub
'-----
Public Function isUndo() As Boolean
End Function
```

Then we have to design each command object to keep a record of what it last did so it can undo it. This can be a little more complicated than it first appears, since having a number of interleaved Commands being executed and then undone can lead to some hysteresis. In addition, each command will need to store enough information about each execution of the command that it can know what specifically has to be undone.

The problem of undoing commands is actually a multipart problem. First, you must keep a list of the commands that have been executed, and second, each command has to keep a list of its executions. To illustrate how we use the Command pattern to carry out undo operations, let's consider the program shown in Figure 23-3 that draws successive red or blue lines on the screen, using two buttons to draw a new instance of each line. You can undo the last line you drew with the undo button.

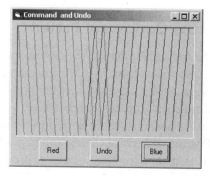

Figure 23-3   A program that draws red and blue lines each time you click the Red and Blue buttons

If you click on Undo several times, you'd expect the last several lines to disappear no matter what order the buttons were clicked in, as shown in Figure 23-4.

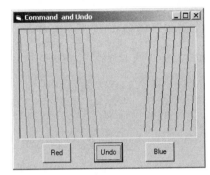

Figure 23-4   The same program as in Figure 23-3 after the Undo button has been clicked several times

Thus, any undoable program needs a single sequential list of all the commands that have been executed. Each time we click on any button, we add its corresponding command to the list.

```
Private Sub btDraw_Click(Index As Integer)
Dim cmd As Command
'get the command and execute it
 Set cmd = buttons(Index + 1)
 cmd.Execute
 ud.add cmd        'Add to undo collection
 Refresh           'repaint screen
End Sub
```

Further, the list to which we add the Command objects is maintained inside the Undo command object so it can access that list conveniently.

```
Option Explicit
'Class UndoCommand
Implements Command
Private undoList As Collection
'-----
Public Sub init()
Set undoList = New Collection
End Sub
'-----
Public Sub add(cmd As Command)
If Not (cmd.isUndo) Then
   undoList.add cmd
End If
End Sub
'-----
```

```
Private Sub Command_Execute()
Dim Index As Integer
Dim cmd As Command
Index = undoList.Count
If undoList.Count > 0 Then
  Set cmd = undoList(Index)
  cmd.Undo
  undoList.Remove Index
End If
End Sub
'-----
Private Function Command_isUndo() As Boolean
Command_isUndo = True
End Function
'-----
Private Sub Command_Undo()
'do nothing
End Sub
```

The undoCommand object keeps a list of *Commands*, not a list of actual data. Each command object has its unDo method called to execute the actual undo operation. Note that since the undoCommand object implements the Command interface, it, too, needs to have an unDo method. However, the idea of undoing successive unDo operations is a little complex for this simple example program. Consequently, you should note that the *add* method adds all Commands to the list *except* the undoCommand itself, since we have just defined undoing an unDo command as doing nothing. For this reason, our new Command interface includes an isUndo method that returns false for the RedCommand and BlueCommand objects and true for the UndoCommand object.

The redCommand and blueCommand classes simply use different colors and start at opposite sides of the window, although both implement the revised Command interface. Each class keeps a list of lines to be drawn in a Collection as a series of *drawData* objects containing the coordinates of each line. Undoing a line from either the red or the blue line list simply means removing the last *drawData* object from the *drawList* collection. Then either command forces a repaint of the screen.

```
Implements Command
'Class RedCommand
Private drawList As Collection
Private x As Integer, y As Integer, dx As Integer, dy As Integer
Private pic As PictureBox
'-----
Public Sub init(pict As PictureBox)
  Set pic = pict
  Set drawList = New Collection
```

```
  x = 0
  dx = 200
  y = 0
  dy = 0
End Sub
'-----
Private Sub Command_Execute()
 Dim dl As DrawData
 Set dl = New DrawData
 dl.init x, y, dx, dy    'create a new DrawData object
 drawList.add dl         'and add it to the list
 x = x + dx              'next one has these values
 y = y + dy
 pic.Refresh             'repaint screen window
End Sub
'-----
Private Function Command_isUndo() As Boolean
 Command_isUndo = False
End Function
'-----
Private Sub Command_Undo()
'undo last draw
 Dim Index As Integer
 Dim dl As DrawData
 Index = drawList.Count
 If Index > 0 Then
    Set dl = drawList(Index)
    drawList.Remove Index
    x = dl.getX
    y = dl.getY
 End If
 pic.Refresh
End Sub
'-----
Public Sub draw()
'draw entire list of lines
Dim h As Integer, w As Integer
Dim i As Integer
Dim dl As DrawData
h = pic.Height
w = pic.Width

For i = 1 To drawList.Count
 Set dl = drawList(i)
 pic.Line (dl.getX, dl.getY)-(dl.getX + dx, dl.getdY + h), vbRed
Next i
End Sub
```

Note that the *draw* method in the *drawCommand* class redraws the entire list of lines the command object has stored. These two draw methods are called from the paint method of the form.

```
Private Sub Form_Paint()
 rc.draw     'redraw red lines
 bc.draw     'redraw blue lines
End Sub
```

The set of classes we use in this Undo program is shown in Figure 23-5.

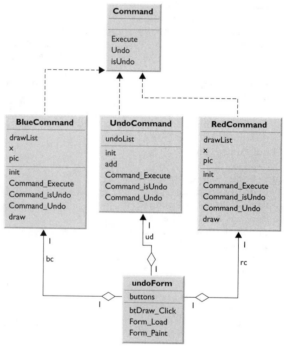

Figure 23-5   The classes used to implement Undo in a Command pattern implementation

The Command Pattern in VB.NET

While you can write more or less the same code in VB7, the availability of inheritance provides some additional advantages. If you reconsider our original program with File|Open, File|Exit, and a Red button, you can create derived Menu objects that also implement the Command interface. Here, our command interface initially contains only the Execute method.

```
Public Interface Command
    Sub Execute()
End Interface
```

One difference here is that we can derive our RedButton class directly from Button and have it also implement the Command interface.

```
Public Class redButton
    Inherits System.Windows.Forms.Button
    Implements Command
    Private frm As Form

    Public Sub setForm(ByVal frm_ As Form)
        frm = frm_
    End Sub
    Public Sub Execute() Implements BtnMenu.Command.Execute
        Dim clr As Color
        clr = Me.BackColor
        frm.BackColor = Color.Red
        Me.BackColor = clr
    End Sub
End Class
```

Recall that in order to create a control that is derived from a Windows control and that will still work with the Form designer in Visual Studio, we add UserControl and then change the code so the control is derived from Button. Then, after compiling the program once, the new cmdButton control will appear on the bottom of the toolbar. You can use this to create a button on the form.

To create a MenuItem that also implements the Command interface, you can use the MainMenu control on the toolbar and name it MenuBar. The designer is shown in Figure 23-6.

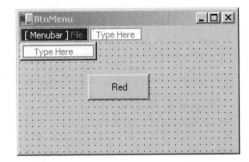

Figure 23-6   The menu designer interface

We derive the OpenMenu and ExitMenu classes from the MenuItem class. However, we have to add these in the program code, since there is no way to add them in the Form Designer. Here is the ExitMenu class.

```
Public class ExitMenu
    inherits MenuItem
    implements Command

Private frm as Form
'-----
```

```
    Public Sub New(ByVal frm_ As Form)
        MyBase.New("Exit")
        frm = frm_
    End Sub
    '-----
    Public Sub Execute() Implements Command.Execute
        frm.close()
    End Sub
End Class
```

One other major difference in VB7 is that you don't have to have separate click methods for each event. Instead, you can add the same event handler to each button and menu item. This handler simply calls the commands.

```
Private Sub commandHandler( _
        ByVal sender As System.Object, _
        ByVal e As System.EventArgs)
        Dim cmd As Command
        cmd = CType(sender, Command)
        cmd.Execute()
    End Sub
```

Here is how you register this method as the event handler.

```
Private Sub init()
        evh = New EventHandler(AddressOf commandHandler)
        AddHandler rdbutn.Click, evh
        rdbutn.setForm(Me)
        mnMain = New MainMenu()
        mnFile = New MenuItem("File")
        mnOpen = New FileOpen()
        mnQuit = New ExitMenu(Me)
        mnMain.MenuItems.AddRange(New MenuItem() {mnFile})
        mnFile.MenuItems.AddRange(New MenuItem() {mnOpen, mnQuit})
        Me.Menu = mnMain
        AddHandler mnOpen.Click, evh
        AddHandler mnQuit.Click, evh
    End Sub
```

The CommandHolder Interface

Now, while it is advantageous to encapsulate the action in a Command object, binding that object into the element that causes the action (such as the menu item or button) is not exactly what the Command pattern is about. Instead, the Command object really ought to be separate from the invoking client so you can vary the invoking program and the details of the command action separately. Rather than having the command be part of the menu or button, we can make the menu and button classes *containers* for a Command object that exists separately. We thus make these UI elements implement a CommandHolder interface.

```
Public Interface CommandHolder
    Function getCommand() As Command
End Interface
```

This simple interface says that there is a way to obtain that object to call its Execute method. We put the command object into the menu object as part of the constructor. This is particularly important where we have several ways of calling the same action, such as when we have both a Red button and a Red menu item. In such a case, you would certainly not want the same code to be executed inside both the MenuItem and the Buttn classes. Instead, you should fetch references to the same command object from both classes and execute that command.

Then we create cmdMenu class, which implements this interface.

```
Public Class CmdMenu
    Implements CommandHolder
    Inherits MenuItem
    Protected comd As Command
    '-----
    Public Sub New(ByVal lbl As String, _
                ByVal cmd As Command, ByVal evh As EventHandler)
        MyBase.New(lbl)
        AddHandler Click, evh
        comd = cmd
    End Sub
    '-----
    Public Function getCommand() As Command _
                Implements CommandHolder.getCommand
        Return comd
    End Function
End Class
```

This actually simplifies our program. We don't have to create a separate menu class for each action we want to carry out. We just create instances of the menu and pass them different Command objects.

```
Private Sub init()
        'called from the New constructor
        evh = New EventHandler(AddressOf CommandHandler)
        AddHandler rdButn.Click, evh
        rdButn.setCommand(New RedCommand(Me))
        mnMain = New MainMenu()
        mnFile = New MenuItem("File")
        mnOpen = New CmdMenu("Open", New FileOpenCommand(), evh)
        mnQuit = New CmdMenu("Exit", New ExitCommand(Me), evh)
        mnMain.MenuItems.AddRange(New MenuItem() {mnFile})
```

```
    mnFile.MenuItems.AddRange(New MenuItem() {mnOpen, mnQuit})
    Me.Menu = mnMain
    AddHandler mnOpen.Click, evh
    AddHandler mnQuit.Click, evh
End Sub
```

Creating the cmdButton class is analogous, and we can use the same RedCommand instance we just created.

```
    redbutton.setCommand(redc)
```

We still have to create separate Command objects, but they are no longer part of the user interface classes. For example, the FileCommand class is just this.

```
Public Class FileOpenCommand
    Implements Command
    'Command object to show file-open dialog
    Public Sub New()
        MyBase.New()
    End Sub
    '-----
    Public Sub Execute() Implements Command.Execute
        Dim fd As OpenFileDialog
        fd = New OpenFileDialog()
        fd.ShowDialog()
    End Sub
End Class
```

Then our action method needs to obtain the actual command object from the UI object that caused the action and execute that command.

```
Public Sub CommandHandler(ByVal sender As Object, _
        ByVal e As EventArgs)
    Dim cmdh As CommandHolder
    Dim cmd As Command
    cmdh = CType(sender, CommandHolder)
    cmd = cmdh.getCommand
    cmd.Execute()
End Sub
```

This is only slightly more complicated than our original routine and again keeps the action separate from the user interface elements. We can see the relations between theses classes and interfaces clearly in the UML diagram in Figure 23-7.

Here you see that redButton and cmdMenu implement the Command-Holder interface and that there are three instances of cmdMenu in the UI class ComdHolder. Figure 21-7 also shows the classes ExitCommand, RedCommand, and FileCommand, which implement the Command interface and are instantiated in the ComdHolder UI class. This is finally the complete implementation of the Command pattern that we have been inching toward.

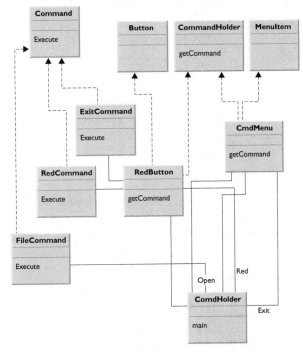

Figure 23-7 A class structure for three different objects that all implement the Command interface and two that implement the CommandHolder interface

Handling Undo Commands in VB.NET

The UndoCommand version of the Command pattern is quite analogous. The command interface now becomes the following.

```
Public Interface Command
    Sub Execute()
    Sub Undo()
    Function isUndo() As Boolean
End Interface
```

We need only create one command button by deriving it from UserControl, as we did previously.

```
Public Class CmdButton
    Inherits System.WinForms.Button
    Implements CommandHolder
    Private cmd As Command
```

```
Public Sub New()
    MyBase.New
    'This call is required by the Win Form Designer.
    InitializeComponent
End Sub


'-----
Public Sub setCommmand(ByVal Comd As Command)
    cmd = comd
End Sub
'-----
Public Function getCommand() As Command _
        Implements CommandHolder.getCommand
    Return cmd
End Function
End Class
```

Then we create three instances of it for the Red, Blue and Undo buttons. The command objects for Red, Blue, and Undo differ slightly, since we must use a graphics object for drawing. Here is the BlueCommand.

```
Public class BlueCommand
  Implements Command

Private drawList As ArrayList
Protected colr as Color
Protected x, y , dx, dy As Integer
Private pic As PictureBox
    '-----
    Public Sub New(ByVal pict As PictureBox)
        MyBase.New()
        pic = pict
        drawList = New ArrayList()
        x = pic.Width
        Colr = color.Blue
        dx = -20
        y = 0
        dy = 0
    End Sub
    '-----
    Public Sub Execute() Implements Command.Execute
        Dim dl As DrawData
        dl = New DrawData(x, y, dx, dy)
        drawList.add(dl)
        x = x + dx
        y = y + dy
        pic.Refresh()
    End Sub
    '-----
    Public Function isUndo() As Boolean _
            Implements Command.IsUndo
        Return False
```

```
        End Function
        '-----
        Public Sub Undo() Implements Command.Undo
            Dim Index As Integer
            Dim dl As DrawData
            Index = drawList.Count - 1
            If Index >= 0 Then
                dl = CType(drawList(index), DrawData)
                drawList.RemoveAt(Index)
                x = dl.getX
                y = dl.getY
            End If
            pic.Refresh()
        End Sub
        '-----
        Public Sub draw(ByVal g As Graphics)
            Dim h, w As Integer
            Dim i As Integer
            Dim dl As DrawData

            Dim rpen As New Pen(Color.FromARGB(255, colr), 1)
            h = pic.Height
            w = pic.Width

            For i = 0 To drawList.Count - 1
                dl = CType(drawList(i), DrawData)
                g.drawLine(rpen, dl.getX, dl.getY, _
                        dl.getX + dx, dl.getdY + h)
            Next i
        End Sub
End Class
```

Then the command listener in the main form class is as follows.

```
Public Sub CommandHandler(ByVal sender As Object, _
                        ByVal e As EventArgs)
        Dim cmdh As CommandHolder
        Dim cmd As Command
        'get the command
        cmdh = CType(sender, commandholder)
        cmd = cmdh.getCommand
        undoc.add(cmd) 'add it to the undo list
        cmd.Execute()
    End Sub
```

We add a paint event handler to the picture box.

```
AddHandler Pict.Paint, _
New PaintEventHandler(AddressOf painthandler)
```

The paint handler routine just calls the red and blue command's draw methods.

```
Public Sub PaintHandler(ByVal sender As Object, _
        ByVal e As PaintEventArgs)
    Dim g As Graphics = e.Graphics
    redc.draw(g)
    bluec.draw(g)
End Sub
```

The Command Pattern in the VB Language

There is still another way to approach this. If you give every control its own EventHandler class, you are in effect creating individual command objects for each of them.

THOUGHT QUESTIONS

1. Mouse clicks on list box items and on radio buttons also constitute commands. Clicks on multiselect list boxes could also be represented as commands. Design a program including these features.

2. A lottery system uses a random number generator constrained to integers between 1 and 50. The selections are made at intervals selected by a random timer. Each selection must be unique. Design command patterns to choose the winning numbers each week.

Programs on the CD-ROM

\Command\ButtonMenu	VB6 Buttons and menus using Command pattern
\Command\RadioCommands	VB6 program showing Commands applied to radio buttons
\Command\Undo	VB6 program showing line drawing and Undo
\Command\VBNet\ButtonMenu	VB7 menus and button commands
\Command\VBNet\ComdHolder	VB7 program showing CommandHolder interface
\Command\VBNet\UndoComd	VB7 program showing line drawing and undo

CHAPTER 24

The Interpreter Pattern

Some programs benefit from having a language to describe operations they can perform. The Interpreter pattern generally describes defining a grammar for that language and using that grammar to interpret statements in that language.

Motivation

When a program presents a number of different but somewhat similar cases it can deal with, it can be advantageous to use a simple language to describe these cases and then have the program interpret that language. Such cases can be as simple as the sort of Macro language recording facilities a number of office suite programs provide or as complex as Visual Basic for Applications (VBA). VBA is not only included in Microsoft Office products, but it can be embedded in any number of third-party products quite simply.

One of the problems we must deal with is how to recognize when a language can be helpful. The Macro language recorder simply records menu and keystroke operations for later playback and just barely qualifies as a language; it may not actually have a written form or grammar. Languages such as VBA, on the other hand, are quite complex, but they are far beyond the capabilities of the individual application developer. Further, embedding commercial languages usually require substantial licensing fees, which makes them less attractive to all but the largest developers.

Applicability

As the *SmallTalk Companion* notes, recognizing cases where an Interpreter can be helpful is much of the problem, and programmers without formal language/compiler training frequently overlook this approach. There are not large numbers of such cases, but there are three general places where languages are applicable.

1. *When you need a command interpreter to parse user commands.* The user can type queries of various kinds and obtain a variety of answers.

2. *When the program must parse an algebraic string.* This case is fairly obvious. The program is asked to carry out its operations based on a computation where the user enters an equation of some sort. This frequently occurs in mathematical-graphics programs where the program renders a curve or surface based on any equation it can evaluate. Programs like *Mathematica* and graph drawing packages such as *Origin* work in this way.

3. *When the program must produce varying kinds of output.* This case is a little less obvious but far more useful. Consider a program that can display columns of data in any order and sort them in various ways. These programs are frequently referred to as Report Generators, and while the underlying data may be stored in a relational database, the user interface to the report program is usually much simpler than the SQL language that the database uses. In fact, in some cases, the simple report language may be interpreted by the report program and translated into SQL.

A Simple Report Example

Let's consider a simplified report generator that can operate on five columns of data in a table and return various reports on these data. Suppose we have the following results from a swimming competition.

The five columns are *frname, lname, age, club* and *time*. If we consider the complete race results of 51 swimmers, we realize that it might be convenient to sort these results by club, by last name, or by age. Since there are a number of useful reports we could produce from these data in which the order of the columns changes as well as the sorting, a language is one useful way to handle these reports.

We'll define a very simple nonrecursive grammar of this sort.

```
Print lname frname club time Sortby club Thenby time
```

Amanda McCarthy	12	WCA	29.28
Jamie Falco	12	HNHS	29.80
Meaghan O'Donnell	12	EDST	30.00
Greer Gibbs	12	CDEV	30.04
Rhiannon Jeffrey	11	WYW	30.04
Sophie Connolly	12	WAC	30.05
Dana Helyer	12	ARAC	30.18

For the purposes of this example, we define these three verbs.

```
Print
Sortby
Thenby
```

And we'll define the five column names we listed earlier.

```
Frname
Lname
Age
Club
Time
```

For convenience, we'll assume that the language is case insensitive. We'll also note that the simple grammar of this language is punctuation free and amounts in brief to the following.

Print var[var] [sortby var [thenby var]]

Finally, there is only one main verb, and while each statement is a declaration, there is no assignment statement or computational ability in this grammar.

Interpreting the Language

Interpreting the language takes place in three steps.

1. Parsing the language symbols into tokens.

2. Reducing the tokens into actions.

3. Executing the actions.

We parse the language into tokens by simply scanning each statement with a StringTokenizer and then substituting a number for each word. Usually parsers push each parsed token onto a *stack* we will use that technique here. We implement the Stack class using an Arraylist—where we have *push, pop, top,* and *nextTop* methods to examine and manipulate the stack contents.

After parsing, our stack could look like this.

type	token
Var	Time
Verb	Thenby
Var	Club
Verb	Sortby
Var	Time
Var	Club
Var	Frname
verb	Lname

<-top of stack

However, we quickly realize that the "verb" *Thenby* has no real meaning other than clarification, and it is more likely that we'd parse the tokens and skip the *Thenby* word altogether. Our initial stack then, looks like this.

```
Time
Club
Sortby
Time
Club
Frname
Lname
Print
```

Objects Used in Parsing

Because the Interpreter pattern relies so heavily on having parsing objects that all derived from the same base class, we will illustrate this pattern in VB7 initially. While you can write this pattern using VB6 interfaces, as we will see, it is more difficult to present and explain.

In this parsing procedure, we do not push just a numeric token onto the stack but a *ParseObject* that has the both a type and a value property.

```
Public Class ParseObject

    Public Const VERB As Integer = 1000
    Public Const VAR As Integer = 1010
    Public Const MULTVAR As Integer = 1020
    Protected value As Integer
    Protected type As Integer

    Public Sub New(ByVal val As Integer, _
                   ByVal typ As Integer)
        MyBase.New()
        value = val
        type = typ
    End Sub
    '----
    Public Function getValue() As Integer
        Return value
    End Function
    '----
    Public Function get_Type() As Integer
        Return type
    End Function

End Class
```

These objects can take on the type VERB or VAR. Then we extend this object into ParseVerb and ParseVar objects, whose value fields can take on PRINT or SORT for ParseVerb and FRNAME, LNAME, and so on for ParseVar. For later use in reducing the parse list, we then derive *Print* and *Sort* objects from ParseVerb.

This gives us a simple hierarchy shown in Figure 24-1.

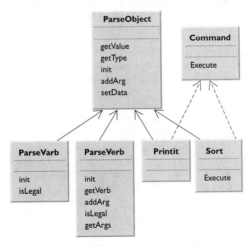

Figure 24-1 A simple parsing hierarchy for the Interpreter pattern

The parsing process is just the following simple code, using the String-Tokenizer and the parse objects. Part of the main Parser class is shown here.

```
Public Class Parser
    Implements Command
    Private stk As Stack
    Private actionList As ArrayList
    Private kdata As KidData
    Private dat As Data
    Private ptable As Listbox
    Private chn As Chain

Public Sub New(ByVal line As String, _
        ByVal k As KidData, ByVal pt As ListBox)
        stk = New Stack()
        setData(k, pt)
        'actions accumulate here
        actionList = New ArrayList()
        buildStack(line)
        buildChain()    'construct interpreter chain
End Sub
    '-------------------------------------
    Private Sub buildStack(ByVal line As String)
        'parse input tokens and build stack
        Dim tok As StringTokenizer = _
            New StringTokenizer(line)
        While (tok.hasMoreElements())
            Dim token As ParseObject = _
            tokenize(tok.nextToken())
            stk.push(token)
        End While
End Sub
    '-------------------------------------------
Public Sub setData(ByVal k As KidData, _
        ByVal pt As listbox)
        dat = New Data(k.getData())
        ptable = pt
End Sub
    '----------------------------------------
Protected Function tokenize(ByVal s As String) As _
                ParseObject
  Dim obj As ParseObject
  Dim typ As Integer
  Try
    obj = getVerb(s)
    typ = obj.get_Type 'this will throw null exception
  Catch e As NullReferenceException
    obj = getVar(s)
  End Try

  Return obj
End Function
    '-------------------------------------------
  Protected Function getVerb(ByVal s As String) _
```

```
                    As ParseVerb
            Dim v As ParseVerb
            v = New ParseVerb(s, dat, ptable)
            If (v.isLegal()) Then

                Return v.getVerb(s)
            Else
                Return Nothing
            End If
        End Function
        '---------------------------------------
    Protected Function getVar(ByVal s As String) _
                As ParseVar
            Dim v As ParseVar
            v = New ParseVar(s)
            If (v.isLegal()) Then
                Return v
            End If
        End Function

End Class
```

The ParseVerb and ParseVar classes return objects with isLegal set to true if they recognize the word.

```
Public Class ParseVerb
    Inherits ParseObject
    Protected Const PRINT As Integer = 100
    Protected Const SORTBY As Integer = 110
    Protected Const THENBY As Integer = 120
    Protected args As ArrayList
    Protected kd As Data
    Protected pt As listbox
    '-------
    Public Sub New(ByVal s As String, _
            ByVal kd_ As Data, ByVal pt_ As ListBox)
        args = New Arraylist()
        s = s.ToLower()
        value = -1
        type = VERB
        kd = kd_
        pt = pt_
        Select Case s
            Case "print"
                value = PRINT
            Case "sortby"
                value = SORTBY
        End Select
    End Sub
    '-----
    Public Function getVerb(ByVal s As String) _
                As ParseVerb
        Select Case value
```

```
            Case PRINT
                Return New Print(s, kd, pt)
            Case SORTBY
                Return New Sort(s)
            Case Else
                Return Nothing
        End Select
    End Function
```

Reducing the Parsed Stack

The tokens on the stack have this form.

```
Var
Var
Verb
Var
Var
Var
Var
Verb
```

We reduce the stack a token at a time, folding successive Vars into a Mult-Var class until the arguments are folded into the verb objects, as we show in Figure 24-2.

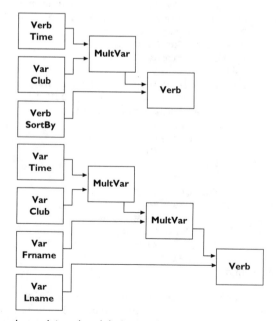

Figure 24-2   How the stack is reduced during parsing

When the stack reduces to a verb, this verb and its arguments are placed in an action list; when the stack is empty, the actions are executed.

Creating a Parser class that is a Command object and executing it when the Go button is pressed on the user interface carries out this entire process.

```
Private Sub Compute_Click(ByVal sender As System.Object, _
        ByVal e As System.EventArgs) Handles Compute.Click
    parse() 'call the parser
End Sub
    '-----
    Private Sub parse()
        'parse the command in the text box
        Dim par As New Parser( _
                txCommand.Text, kdata, lsResults)
        par.Execute()
    End Sub
```

The parser itself just reduces the tokens, as the preceding shows. It checks for various pairs of tokens on the stack and reduces each pair to a single one for each of five different cases.

Implementing the Interpreter Pattern

It would certainly be possible to write a parser for this simple grammar as just a series of *if* statements. For each of the six possible stack configurations, reduce the stack until only a verb remains. Then, since we have made the Print and Sort verb classes Command objects, we can just Execute them one by one as the action list is enumerated.

However, the real advantage of the Interpreter pattern is its flexibility. By making each parsing case an individual object, we can represent the parse tree as a series of connected objects that reduce the stack successively. Using this arrangement, we can easily change the parsing rules without much in the way of program changes: We just create new objects and insert them into the parse tree.

According to the Gang of Four, these are the names for the participating objects in the Interpreter pattern:

- **AbstractExpression**—declares the abstract Interpret operation.
- **TerminalExpression**—interprets expressions containing any of the terminal tokens in the grammar.
- **NonTerminalExpression**—interprets all of the nonterminal expressions in the grammar.
- **Context**—contains the global information that is part of the parser—in this case, the token stack.
- **Client**—builds the syntax tree from the preceding expression types and invokes the Interpret operation.

The Syntax Tree

The syntax tree we construct to carry out the parsing of the stack we just showed can be quite simple. We just need to look for each of the stack configurations we defined and reduce them to an executable form. In fact, the best way to implement this tree is using a Chain of Responsibility, which passes the stack configuration along between classes until one of them recognizes that configuration and acts on it. You can decide whether a successful stack reduction should end that pass or not. It is perfectly possible to have several successive chain members work on the stack in a single pass. The processing ends when the stack is empty. We see a diagram of the individual parse chain elements in Figure 24-3.

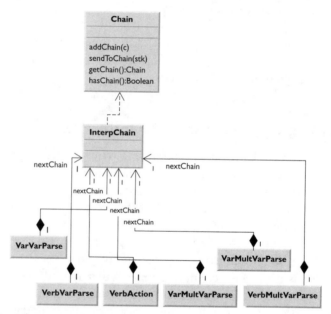

Figure 24-3   How the classes that perform the parsing interact.

In this class structure, we start with the AbstractExpression interpreter class *InterpChain*.

```
Public MustInherit Class InterpChain
    Implements Chain

    Private nextChain As chain
    Protected stk As Stack
'-------------------------------------------
Public Sub addtoChain(ByVal c As Chain) _
    Implements Chain.addToChain
```

```
            nextChain = c      'next in chain of resp
End Sub
'----------------------------------------
Public MustOverride Function interpret() As Boolean
'----------------------------------------
Public Function getChain() As Interpreter.Chain _
        Implements Interpreter.Chain.getChain
    Return nextChain
End Function
'----------------------------------------
Public Sub sendToChain(ByVal stk_ As Stack) _
        Implements Chain.sendToChain
    stk = stk_
    If (Not interpret) Then  'interpret stack
        'Otherwise, pass request along chain
        nextChain.sendToChain(stk)
    End If
End Sub
'----------------------------------------
Protected Sub addArgsToVerb()
    Dim v As ParseObject = CType(stk.pop(), parseobject)
    Dim verb As ParseVerb = CType(stk.pop(), parseverb)
    verb.addArgs(v)
    stk.push(verb)
End Sub
'----------------------------------------
  Protected Function topStack(ByVal c1 As Integer, _
          ByVal c2 As Integer) As Boolean
    Dim pobj1, pobj2 As ParseObject
    pobj1 = stk.top
    pobj2 = stk.nextTop
  Return (pobj1.get_Type() = c1) And (pobj2.get_Type() = c2)
  End Function
End Class
```

This class also contains the methods for manipulating objects on the stack. Each of the subclasses implements the *interpret* operation differently and reduces the stack accordingly. For example, the complete VarVarParse class reduces two variables on the stack in succession to a single MultVar object.

```
Public Class VarVarParse
    Inherits InterpChain

Public Overrides Function interpret() As Boolean
    If (topStack(ParseObject.VAR, ParseObject.VAR)) Then
            'reduce (Var Var) to Multvar
        Dim v As ParseVar = CType(stk.pop(), ParseVar)
        Dim v1 As ParseVar = CType(stk.pop(), ParseVar)
        Dim mv As MultVar = New MultVar(v1, v)
        stk.push(mv)
      Return True
```

```
      Else
         Return False
      End If
   End Function
End Class
```

Thus, in this implementation of the pattern, the stack constitutes the Context participant. Each of the first five subclasses of *InterpChain* are NonTerminal-Expression participants, and the ActionVerb class that moves the completed verb and action objects to the actionList constitutes the TerminalExpression participant.

The client object is the Parser class that builds the stack object list from the typed-in command text and constructs the Chain of Responsibility from the various interpreter classes. We showed most of the Parser class above already. However, it also implements the Command pattern and sends the stack through the chain until it is empty and then executes the verbs that have accumulated in the action list when its Execute method is called.

```
'executes parse and interpretation of command line
   Public Sub Execute() Implements Command.Execute
      Dim i As Integer
      While (stk.hasMoreElements())
         chn.sendToChain(stk)
      End While
      'now execute the verbs
      For i = 0 To actionList.Count - 1
         Dim v As Verb = CType(actionList(i), Verb)
         v.setData(dat, ptable)
         v.Execute()
      Next i
   End Sub
```

The final visual program is shown in Figure 24-4.

Building an Interpreter in VB6

Writing an interpreter in VB6 is a bit more challenging because we don't have the convenience of inheriting many methods that the parser classes have in common. We will still organize the parser using the same classes and using the Chain of Responsibility pattern to send the stack from one to the next until the stack pattern is matched. However, we have to flatten out our class hierarchy to a much simpler single level one, since VB6 does not conveniently allow classes that implement one interface to then be used as interfaces themselves.

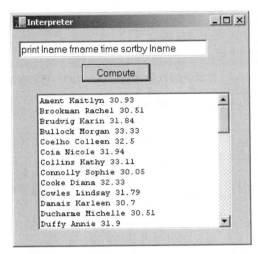

Figure 24-4 The Interpreter pattern operating on the simple command in the text field

Thus, we might have started with the Chain interface and build from it.

```
'Interface class Chain
'--------
Public Sub addChain(c As Chain)
End Sub
'--------
Public Sub sendToChain(stk As Stack)
End Sub
'--------
Public Function getChain() As Chain
End Function
'--------
Public Function hasChain() As Boolean
End Function
```

Since we derive our Interpreter chain class from Chain by having it implement the Chain interface, we flatten the hierarchy and have the InterpChain class be the interface that all the remaining classes implement. Further, since a number of classes call the addArgsToVerb method, we put it in this class and let the derived classes create an instance of the base class and call that method.

```
'Class InterpChain
'Implements Chain but does it directly
Private stk As Stack
Private nextChain As InterpChain
Private has_chain As Boolean
'-----
```

```
Public Sub init(stk_ As Stack)
  Set stk = stk_
End Sub
'-----
Public Sub addToChain(c As InterpChain)
  Set nextChain = c
  has_chain = True
End Sub
'-----
Public Sub sendToChain(stk As Stack)
End Sub
'-----
Public Function interpret() As Boolean
End Function
'-----
Public Sub addArgsToVerb()
   Dim v As ParseObject
   Set v = stk.pop()      'get one off stack
   Dim vo As ParseObject
   Set vo = stk.pop()
   vo.addArg v            'add to next once
   stk.push vo            'and put it back
End Sub
```

Using this interface, we can write each of the six stack reduction parsers.
Here is the VarVarParse class that reduces two variables on the stack to a single
MultVar variable.

```
'Class VarVarParse
Implements InterpChain
    Private nextChain As InterpChain
    Private stk As Stack
    Private ichain As New InterpChain
    Private has_chain As Boolean
'-----
Private Sub InterpChain_addArgsToVerb()
 ichain.addArgsToVerb
End Sub
'-----
Private Sub InterpChain_addToChain(c As InterpChain)
 Set nextChain = c  'next in chain
 has_chain = True
End Sub
'-----
Public Sub init(stk_ As Stack)
 Set stk = stk_
 ichain.init stk     'used to call addArgsToVerb
End Sub
'-----
Private Function InterpChain_getChain() As InterpChain
```

```
        Set InterpChain_getChain = nextChain
End Function
'-----
Private Function InterpChain_hasChain() As Boolean
 InterpChain_hasChain = has_chain
End Function
'-----
Private Sub InterpChain_init(stk_ As Stack)
 Set stk = stk_
 init stk_
End Sub
'-----
Private Function InterpChain_interpret() As Boolean
 Dim v As ParseObject, v1 As ParseObject, mv As Multvar
 If (stk.topStack(VAR_TYPE, VAR_TYPE)) Then
        'reduce (Var Var) to Multvar
        Set v = stk.pop()
        Set v1 = stk.pop()
        Set mv = New Multvar
        mv.init v1, v
        stk.push mv
        InterpChain_interpret = True
   Else
        InterpChain_interpret = False
   End If
End Function
'-----
Private Sub InterpChain_sendToChain(stk_ As Stack)
'try interpreting the top of the stack
 If Not InterpChain_interpret Then
    'if no match, pass it on
    nextChain.sendToChain stk_
  End If
End Sub
'-----
Private Function InterpChain_topStack(ByVal c1 As Integer, _
        ByVal c2 As Integer) As Boolean
 InterpChain_topStack = stk.topStack(c1, c2)
End Function
```

The Parse Objects

In our VB7, we created objects representing each of the stack reduction states: ParseObject, ParseVar, ParseVerb, Verb, Sort, and Print. We derived the Parsevar and ParseVerb classes from ParseObject and the Command object Verb from ParseVerb. Then we derived Print and Sort from Verb. In the VB6 version, we have to flatten this hierarchy as well and have all these classes implement the ParseObject interface so we can use them interchangeably.

```
'Interface ParseObject
'All objects passed around interpreter implement this interface
 '-----
 Public Function getValue() As Integer
 End Function
 '-----
 Public Function getType() As Integer
 End Function
 '-----
 Public Sub init()
 End Sub
 '-----
 Public Sub addArg(p As ParseObject)
 End Sub
 '-----
 Public Sub setData(dt As data, ByVal pt As ListBox)
 End Sub
```

In VB6, we must rename the Print class to Printit, since VB6 has a single name space and Print is a reserved word. Both our Printit and Sort classes also implement the Command pattern, so they can be executed from the action list stack.

This interpreter works much as the previous one once we have gotten all the classes reduced to being ParseObjects. The user string is tokenized and converted into ParseObjects of type ParseVar or ParseVerb. Then the stack is reduced by combining adjacent ParseVars into MultVars and Var-Verb or MultVar-Verb combined into Verbs that contain the list of variables to operate on. When the top of the stack is a verb, it is removed and placed on the action list. When the stack is empty, the action list is executed, treating each verb as a Command with an Execute method.

Consequences of the Interpreter Pattern

Whenever you introduce an interpreter into a program, you need to provide a simple way for the program user to enter commands in that language. It can be as simple as the Macro record button we noted earlier, or it can be an editable text field like the one in the preceding program.

However, introducing a language and its accompanying grammar also requires fairly extensive error checking for misspelled terms or misplaced grammatical elements. This can easily consume a great deal of programming effort unless some template code is available for implementing this checking. Further, effective methods for notifying the users of these errors are not easy to design and implement.

In the preceding Interpreter example, the only error handling is that keywords that are not recognized are not converted to ParseObjects and pushed onto the stack. Thus, nothing will happen because the resulting stack sequence probably cannot be parsed successfully, or if it can, the item represented by the misspelled keyword will not be included.

You can also consider generating a language automatically from a user interface of radio and command buttons and list boxes. While it may seem that having such an interface obviates the necessity for a language at all, the same requirements of sequence and computation still apply. When you have to have a way to specify the order of sequential operations, a language is a good way to do so, even if the language is generated from the user interface.

The Interpreter pattern has the advantage that you can extend or revise the grammar fairly easily once you have built the general parsing and reduction tools. You can also add new verbs or variables easily once the foundation is constructed. However, as the syntax of the grammar becomes more complex, you run the risk of creating a hard-to-maintain program.

While interpreters are not all that common in solving general programming problems, the Iterator pattern we take up next is one of the most common ones you'll be using.

THOUGHT QUESTION

Design a system to compute the results of simple quadratic expressions such as

```
4x^2 + 3x - 4
```

where the user can enter x or a range of x's and can type in the equation.

Programs on the CD-ROM

\Interpreter\VBNet	VB7 interpreter
\Interpreter	VB6 interpreter

CHAPTER 25

The Iterator Pattern

The Iterator is one of the simplest and most frequently used of the design patterns. The Iterator pattern allows you to move through a list or collection of data using a standard interface without having to know the details of the internal representations of that data. In addition, you can also define special iterators that perform some special processing and return only specified elements of the data collection.

Motivation

The Iterator is useful because it provides a defined way to move through a set of data elements without exposing what is taking place inside the class. Since the Iterator is an *interface,* you can implement it in any way that is convenient for the data you are returning. *Design Patterns* suggests that a suitable interface for an Iterator might be the following.

```
Public Interface Iterator
      public Function First() as Object
      public Function  Next() as Object
      public Function isDone() as Boolean
      public Function CurrentItem() as Object
End Interface
```

Here you can move to the top of the list, move through the list, find out if there are more elements, and find the current list item. This interface is easy to implement and it has certain advantages, but a number of other similar interfaces are possible. For example, when we discussed the Composite pattern, we introduced the Subords class for looping through all of the subordinates any employee may have. The interface we used can be reduced in VB7 terms to the following.

```
Public Interface Iterator
  Public Sub moveFirst()
  Public Function hasMoreElements() as Boolean
  Public Function nextElement() as Object
End Interface
```

This also allows us to loop through a list of zero or more elements in some internal list structure without our having to know how that list is organized inside the class.

One disadvantage of this Enumeration over similar constructs in C++ and Smalltalk is the strong typing of the VB7 language. This prevents the *hasMoreElements()* method from returning an object of the actual type of the data in the collection. Instead, you must convert the returned Object type to the actual type of the data in the collection. Thus, while the Iterator or Enumeration interface is intended to be polymorphic, this is not directly possible in VB7.

Sample VB6 Code

Let's reuse the list of swimmers, clubs, and times we described in Chapter 22, and add some enumeration capabilities to the KidData class. This class is essentially a collection of Kids, each with a name, club, and time, and these Kid objects are stored in a Collection.

```
'Class Kids
Implements Iterator
Private kidList As Collection
Private index As Integer

Public Sub init(Filename As String)
  Dim sline As String      'line read in
  Dim vbf As New vbFile    'file class
  Dim kd As Kid            'kid object
  Set kidList = New Collection
  vbf.OpenForRead Filename     'open the file
  While Not vbf.fEof           'read in the lines
    sline = vbf.readLine
    Set kd = New Kid
    kd.init sline                'convert to kid
    kidList.Add kd               'Add to collection
  Wend
  vbf.closeFile
  Iterator_moveFirst           'move to top of list
End Sub
```

To obtain an enumeration of all the Kids in the collection, we simply use the methods of the Iterator interface we just defined.

```
Private Function Iterator_hasMoreElements() As Boolean
 Iterator_hasMoreElements = index < kidList.Count
End Function
'-----
Private Sub Iterator_moveFirst()
 index = 1
End Sub
'-----
Private Function Iterator_nextElement() As Object
 Set Iterator_nextElement = kidList(index)
 index = index + 1
End Function
```

Reading in the data and displaying a list of names is quite easy. We initialize the Kids class with the filename and have it build the collection of kid objects. Then we treat the Kids class as an instance of Iterator and move through it to get out the kids and display their names.

```
'Class KidForm
Dim kidz As Kids            'same as iter

Private Sub Form_Load()
 Dim iter As Iterator       'same as kidz
 Dim kd As Kid

 Set kidz = New Kids
 'initialize the collection class
 'and read in the data file
 kidz.init App.Path & "\50free.txt"

 'treat collection class as iterator
 Set iter = kidz
 While iter.hasMoreElements  'load into listbox
   Set kd = iter.nextElement
   List1.AddItem kd.getFrname & " " & kd.getLname
 Wend
End Sub
```

Fetching an Iterator

Another slightly more flexible way to handle iterators in a class is to provide the class with a getIterator method that returns instances of an iterator for that class's data. This is somewhat more flexible because you can have any number of iterators active simultaneously on the same data. Our KidIterator class can then be the one that implements our Iterator interface.

```
'Class KidIterator
Implements Iterator
```

```
Private index As Integer
Private kidList As Collection
'-----
Public Sub init(col As Collection)
 index = 1
 Set kidList = col
End Sub
'-----
Private Function Iterator_hasMoreElements() As Boolean
 Iterator_hasMoreElements = index < kidList.Count
End Function
'-----
Private Sub Iterator_moveFirst()
 index = 1
End Sub
'-----
Private Function Iterator_nextElement() As Object
 Set Iterator_nextElement = kidList(index)
 index = index + 1
End Function
```

We can fetch iterators from the main KidList class by creating them as needed.

```
Public Function getIterator() As Iterator
 Dim kiter As New KidIterator    'create an iterator
   kiter.init kidList            'initialize it
   Set getIterator = kiter       'and return it
End Function
```

Filtered Iterators

While having a clearly defined method of moving through a collection is helpful, you can also define filtered Iterators that perform some computation on the data before returning it. For example, you could return the data ordered in some particular way or only those objects that match a particular criterion. Then, rather than have a lot of very similar interfaces for these filtered iterators, you simply provide a method that returns each type of enumeration with each one of these enumerations having the same methods.

The Filtered Iterator

Suppose, however, that we wanted to enumerate only those kids who belonged to a certain club. This necessitates a special Iterator class that has access to the data in the KidData class. This is very simple because the methods we just defined give us that access. Then we only need to write an Iterator that returns kids belonging to a specified club.

```
'Class KidClubIterator
Implements Iterator
Private index As Integer
Private kidList As Collection
Private club As String
'-----
Public Sub init(col As Collection, clb As String)
 index = 1
 Set kidList = col
 club = clb
End Sub
'-----
Private Function Iterator_hasMoreElements() As Boolean
 Dim more As Boolean
 Dim kd As Kid
 more = index <= kidList.Count
 If more Then
   Set kd = kidList(index)
   While more And kd.getClub <> club
     Set kd = kidList(index)
     index = index + 1
     more = index <= kidList.Count
   Wend
 End If
 Iterator_hasMoreElements = more
End Function
'-----
Private Sub Iterator_moveFirst()
index = 1
End Sub
'-----
Private Function Iterator_nextElement() As Object
 Set Iterator_nextElement = kidList(index)
 index = index + 1
End Function
```

All of the work is done in the *hasMoreElements()* method, which scans through the collection for another kid belonging to the club specified in the constructor and saves that kid in the *kid* variable or sets it to *null*. Then it returns either true or false. The *nextElement()* method returns that next kid variable.

Finally, we need to add a method to KidData to return this new filtered Enumeration.

```
Public Function getClubIterator(clb As String) As Iterator
Dim kiter As New KidClubIterator     'create an iterator
 kiter.init kidList, clb              'initialize it
 Set getClubIterator = kiter         'and return it
End Function
```

This simple method passes the collection to the new Iterator class kid-ClubIterator along with the club initials. A simple program is shown in Figure 25-1 that displays all of the kids on the left side. It fills a combo box with a list of the clubs and then allows the user to select a club and fills the right-hand list box with those belonging to a single club. The class diagram is shown in Figure 25-2. Note that the *elements* method in KidData supplies an Enumeration and the kidClub class is in fact itself an Enumeration class.

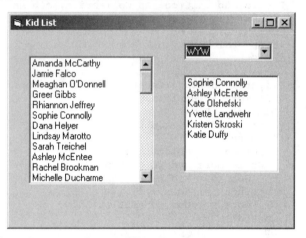

Figure 25-1   A simple program illustrating filtered enumeration

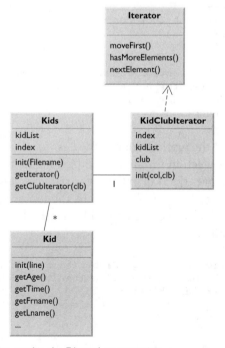

Figure 25-2   The classes used in the Filtered enumeration

Iterators in VB.NET

You can write virtually the same code in VB7 as you could in VB6 with the slight changes in how interfaces are declared. For example, the KidClubIterator we wrote for VB6 varies in VB7 only in that we change Collections to ArrayLists, change to zero-based arrays, use constructors instead of init methods, and simplify the code slightly, using the return statement. Here is the revised KidClubIterator class.

```
Public Class KidClubIterator
    Implements Iterator
    Private index As Integer
    Private kidList As arraylist
    Private club As String
    '-----
    Public Sub New(ByRef col As ArrayList, _
            ByRef clb As String)
        MyBase.New()
        index = 0
        kidList = col
        club = clb
    End Sub
    '-----
    Public Function hasMoreElements() As Boolean _
            Implements Iterator.hasMoreElements
        Dim more As Boolean
        Dim kd As Kid
        more = index < kidList.Count()
        If more Then
            kd = CType(kidList.Item(index), kid)
            While more And kd.getClub <> club
                kd = CType(kidList.Item(index), kid)
                index = index + 1
                more = index < kidList.Count()
            End While
        End If
        Return more
    End Function
    '-----
    Public Sub moveFirst() Implements Iterator.moveFirst
        index = 0
    End Sub
    '-----
    Private Function nextElement() As Object _
        Implements Iterator.nextElement
        index = index + 1
        Return kidList.Item(index - 1)
    End Function
End Class
```

However, you can also write iterators using the standard VB.Net IEnumerator interface, which amounts to the following.

```
Function MoveNext() as Boolean
Sub Reset()
Property ReadOnly Current as Object
```

If you rewrite your KidIterator class to use these methods, the code looks like this.

```
Private index As Integer
Private kidList As ArrayList
'-----
Public Sub New(ByVal col As Arraylist)
    index = 0
    kidList = col
End Sub
'-----
Public Function MoveNext() As Boolean _
    Implements IEnumerator.MoveNext
    index = index + 1
    Return index < kidList.Count
End Function
'-----
Public Sub Reset() Implements _
        IEnumerator.Reset
    index = 0
End Sub
'-----
Public ReadOnly Property Current() As Object _
    Implements IEnumerator.Current
    Get
        Return kidList.Item(index)
    End Get
End Property
End Class
```

If you have a class like our Kids class that can return an instance of an enumerator, it is said to implement the IEnumerable interface.

```
Public Function GetEnumerator() As IEnumerator _
Implements IEnumerable.GetEnumerator
```

Consequences of the Iterator Pattern

1. *Data modification.* The most significant question iterators may raise is the question of iterating through data while it is being changed. If your code is wide ranging and only occasionally moves to the next element, it is possible that an element might be added or deleted from the underlying collection

while you are moving through it. It is also possible that another thread could change the collection. There are no simple answers to this problem. If you want to move through a loop using an Enumeration and delete certain items, you must be careful of the consequences. Deleting or adding an element might mean that a particular element is skipped or accessed twice, depending on the storage mechanism you are using.

2. *Privileged access.* Enumeration classes may need to have some sort of privileged access to the underlying data structures of the original container class so they can move through the data. If the data is stored in an Arraylist or Hashtable, this is pretty easy to accomplish, but if it is in some other collection structure contained in a class, you probably have to make that structure available through a *get* operation. Alternatively, you could make the Iterator a derived class of the containment class and access the data directly.

3. *External versus Internal Iterators.* The *Design Patterns* text describes two types of iterators: external and internal. Thus far, we have only described external iterators. Internal iterators are methods that move through the entire collection, performing some operation on each element directly without any specific requests from the user. These are less common in VB, but you could imagine methods that normalized a collection of data values to lie between 0 and 1 or converted all of the strings to a particular case. In general, external iterators give you more control because the calling program accesses each element directly and can decide whether to perform an operation on it.

Programs on the CD-ROM

\Iterator\SimpleIter	VB6 kid list using Iterator
\Iterator\FilteredIterator	VB6 filtered iterator by team name
\Iterator\FilteredIterator\VBNet	VB7 filtered iterator

CHAPTER 26

The Mediator Pattern

When a program is made up of a number of classes, the logic and computation is divided logically among these classes. However, as more of these isolated classes are developed in a program, the problem of communication between these classes becomes more complex. The more each class needs to know about the methods of another class, the more tangled the class structure can become. This makes the program harder to read and harder to maintain. Further, it can become difficult to change the program, since any change may affect code in several other classes. The Mediator pattern addresses this problem by promoting looser coupling between these classes. Mediators accomplish this by being the only class that has detailed knowledge of the methods of other classes. Classes inform the Mediator when changes occur, and the Mediator passes on the changes to any other classes that need to be informed.

An Example System

Let's consider a program that has several buttons, two list boxes, and a text entry field, as shown in Figure 26-1.

When the program starts, the Copy and Clear buttons are disabled.

1. When you select one of the names in the left-hand list box, it is copied into the text field for editing, and the *Copy* button is enabled.

2. When you click on *Copy,* that text is added to the right-hand list box, and the *Clear* button is enabled, as we see in Figure 26-2.

3. If you click on the *Clear* button, the right-hand list box and the text field are cleared, the list box is deselected, and the two buttons are again disabled.

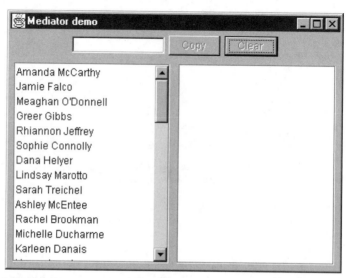

Figure 26-1   A simple program with two lists, two buttons, and a text field that will interact

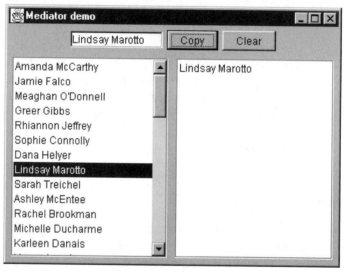

Figure 26-2   When you select a name, the buttons are enabled, and when you click on Copy, the name is copied to the right list box.

User interfaces such as this one are commonly used to select lists of people or products from longer lists. Further, they are usually even more complicated than this one, involving insert, delete, and undo operations as well.

Interactions between Controls

The interactions between the visual controls are pretty complex, even in this simple example. Each visual object needs to know about two or more others, leading to quite a tangled relationship diagram, as shown in Figure 26-3.

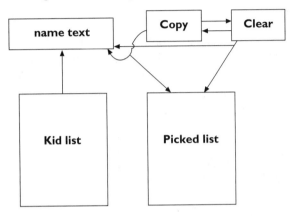

Figure 26-3 A tangled web of interactions between classes in the simple visual interface we presented in Figures 26-1 and 26-2

The Mediator pattern simplifies this system by being the only class that is aware of the other classes in the system. Each of the controls with which the Mediator communicates is called a Colleague. Each Colleague informs the Mediator when it has received a user event, and the Mediator decides which other classes should be informed of this event. This simpler interaction scheme is illustrated in Figure 26-4.

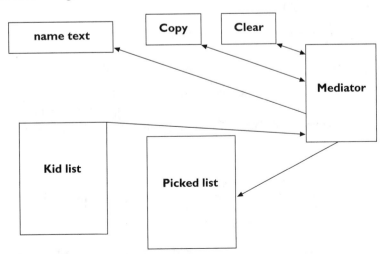

Figure 26-4 A Mediator class simplifies the interactions between classes.

The advantage of the Mediator is clear: It is the only class that knows of the other classes and thus the only one that would need to be changed if one of the other classes changes or if other interface control classes are added.

Sample Code

Let's consider this program in detail and decide how each control is constructed. The main difference in writing a program using a Mediator class is that each class needs to be aware of the existence of the Mediator. You start by creating an instance of the Mediator and then pass the instance of the Mediator to each class in its init method.

```
Set med = New Mediator
med.registerKidList lsKids
med.registerPicked lsPicked
med.registerText txName
med.init
```

Our two buttons use accompanying Command pattern classes and register themselves with the Mediator during their initialization. Here is the Copy-Command class.

```
'Class CopyCommand
Implements Command
Private med As Mediator

Public Sub init(md As Mediator, cpBut As CommandButton)
 Set med = md
 med.registerCopy cpBut
End Sub

Private Sub Command_Execute()
 med.copyClicked
End Sub
```

The Clear button is exactly analogous.

The Kid name list is based on the one we used in the last two examples but expanded so that the data loading of the list takes place in the Mediator's init method.

```
Public Sub init()
 'init method for Mediator
 Dim kds As New Kids     'Kids class instabce
 Dim kd As Kid
 Dim iter As Iterator

 kds.init App.Path & "\50free.txt"   'read in file
 Set iter = kds.getIterator          'get iterator
```

```
While iter.hasMoreElements      'put names in list box
   Set kd = iter.nextElement
   kidList.AddItem kd.getFrname & " " & kd.getLname
Wend
clearClicked
End Sub
```

The text field is even simpler, since all we have to do is register it with the Mediator. The complete Form_Load event for the list box is shown here with all the registration and command classes.

```
Private Sub Form_Load()
  Set med = New Mediator          'create mediator
  Set cpyCmd = New CopyCommand    'copy command class
  cpyCmd.init med, btCopy

  Set clrCmd = New ClearCommand   'clear command class
  clrCmd.init med, btClear

  med.registerKidList lsKids      'register lists
  med.registerPicked lsPicked     'and text box
  med.registerText txName
  med.init                        'set all to beginning state
End Sub
```

The general point of all these classes is that each knows about the Mediator and tells the Mediator of its existence so the Mediator can send commands to it when appropriate.

The Mediator itself is very simple. It supports the Copy, Clear, and Select methods and has register methods for each of the controls.

```
Option Explicit
'Class Mediator
Private copyButton As CommandButton
Private clearButton As CommandButton
Private txtBox As TextBox
Private kidList As ListBox
Private pickedList As ListBox
'-----
Public Sub registerCopy(cpBut As CommandButton)
   Set copyButton = cpBut     'copy button
End Sub
'-----
Public Sub copyClicked()
  pickedList.AddItem txtBox.Text 'add text to picked list
  clearButton.Enabled = True     'enable clear button
  kidList.ListIndex = -1         'deselect list item
End Sub
'-----
Public Sub registerClear(clrBut As CommandButton)
   Set clearButton = clrBut      'clear button
```

```
End Sub
'-----
Public Sub clearClicked()
  txtBox.Text = ""                 'clear text bos
  copyButton.Enabled = False       'disable buttons
  clearButton.Enabled = False
  pickedList.Clear                 'clear picked list
  kidList.ListIndex = -1           'deselect list item
End Sub
'-----
Public Sub registerText(txt As TextBox)
  Set txtBox = txt                 'text box
End Sub
'-----
Public Sub registerKidList(klist As ListBox)
  Set kidList = klist              'kid list
End Sub
'-----
Public Sub registerPicked(plist As ListBox)
  Set pickedList = plist           'picked list
End Sub
'-----
Public Sub listClicked()
 Dim i As Integer
 i = kidList.ListIndex
 If (i >= 0) Then
    txtBox.Text = kidList.Text
 End If
 copyButton.Enabled = True
End Sub
'-----
Public Sub init()
 'init method for Mediator
 Dim kds As New Kids      'Kids class instance
 Dim kd As Kid
 Dim iter As Iterator

 kds.init App.Path & "\50free.txt"  'read in file
 Set iter = kds.getIterator          'get iterator
 While iter.hasMoreElements          'put names in list box
    Set kd = iter.nextElement
    kidList.AddItem kd.getFrname & " " & kd.getLname
 Wend
 clearClicked                        'Set to initial state
End Sub
```

Initialization of the System

One further operation that is best delegated to the Mediator is the initialization of all the controls to the desired state. When we launch the program, each control must be in a known, default state, and since these states may change as the program evolves, we simply create an *init* method in the Mediator, which sets them all to the desired state. In this case, that state is the same as the one achieved by the Clear button, and we simply call that method this.

```
clearClicked        'Set to initial state
```

Mediators and Command Objects

The two buttons in this program use command objects. Just as we noted earlier, this makes processing of the button click events quite simple.

```
Private Sub btClear_Click()
 med.clearClicked
End Sub
'-----
Private Sub btCopy_Click()
 med.copyClicked
End Sub
'-----
Private Sub lsKids_Click()
 med.listClicked
End Sub
```

In either case, however, this represents the solution to one of the problems we noted in the Command pattern chapter: Each button needed knowledge of many of the other user interface classes in order to execute its command. Here, we delegate that knowledge to the Mediator, so the Command buttons do not need any knowledge of the methods of the other visual objects. The class diagram for this program is shown in Figure 26-5, illustrating both the Mediator pattern and the use of the Command pattern.

The Mediator in VB.Net

You can create a Mediator in much the same way in VB7, but you can take advantage of inheritance to make your work easier. The Copy and Clear buttons and the Kid name list can all be subclassed from the standard controls so that they support the Command interface and register themselves with the Mediator during the constructor. This makes the derived button classes very easy to write.

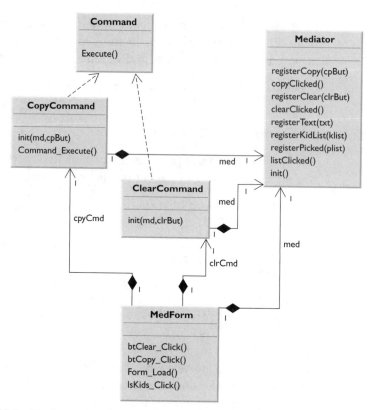

Figure 26-5   The interactions between the Command objects and the Mediator object

```
Public Class CpyButton
    Inherits System.Windows.Forms.Button
    Implements Command
    Private med As Mediator
    Public Sub setMediator(ByVal md As Mediator)
        med = md
        med.register(Me)
    End Sub
    '----
    'tell the Mediator we've been clicked
    Public Sub Execute() Implements Command.Execute
        med.copyClicked()
    End Sub
End Class
```

Further, since VB7 supports polymorphism, we can have a register method
in the Mediator with different argument types for each control we want to register. These methods are shown here.

```
Public Overloads Sub register(ByVal cpb As CopyButton)
    cpbutton = cpb
```

```
End Sub
'-----
Public Overloads Sub register(ByVal clr _
            As ClearButton)
    clrbutton = clr
End Sub
'-----
Public Overloads Sub register(ByVal kd _
            As KidsListBox)
    klist = kd
End Sub
'-----
Public Overloads Sub register(ByVal pick As ListBox)
    pklist = pick
End Sub
'-----
Public Overloads Sub register(ByVal tx As TextBox)
    txkids = tx
End Sub
```

The remainder of the Mediator manipulates the various controls as before.

```
Public Sub kidPicked()
    'copy text from list to textbox
    txkids.Text = klist.Text
    'copy button enabled
    cpbutton.Enabled = True
End Sub
'-----
Public Sub copyClicked()
    'copy name to picked list
    pklist.Items.Add(txkids.Text)
    'clear button enabled
    clrbutton.Enabled = True
    klist.SelectedIndex = -1
End Sub
'-----
Public Sub clearClicked()
    'disable buttons and clear list
    cpbutton.Enabled = False
    clrbutton.Enabled = False
    pklist.Items.Clear()
End Sub
'-----
```

Initialization

When we create the controls, we start by creating an instance of the Mediator. Then as the buttons and list box controls are created, they can register themselves inside the constructor for each derived control.

```
Private Sub init()
        'called from New constructor
        Dim evh As EventHandler
        evh = New EventHandler(AddressOf CommandHandler)

        med = New Mediator()
        btCopy.setMediator(med)
        btClear.setMediator(med)
        kList.setMediator(med)
        'register remaining controls
        med.register(txName)
        med.register(lsPicked)
        med.init()         'initialize mediator
```

During initialization, the Mediator reads in the data file and puts the kid's
names in the kidList list box. Note that the Kids class does the reading as before,
using the vbFile class, and that the Mediator just provides the filename and
loads the list once the file is read.

```
Public Sub init()
        'initializes the Mediator's objects
        Dim kd As Kid
        clearClicked()  'set to defaults
        'read in datafile and load list
        kds = New Kids(Application.StartupPath & "\50free.txt")
        Dim iter As Iterator = kds.getIterator
        'Note we use the iterator here
        While (iter.hasMoreElements)
            kd = CType(iter.nextElement, Kid)
            klist.Items.Add(kd.getFrname + " " + kd.getLname)
        End While
    End Sub
```

Handling the Events for the New Controls

We create the new classes CopyButton, ClearButton, and KidListBox, and rather
than declaring them as WithEvents, we simply add an event handler to each of
them, which is the same simple handler in all three cases, and include this handler
registration in the Forms init method called from its constructor.

```
AddHandler btCopy.Click, evh
AddHandler btClear.Click, evh
AddHandler kList.SelectedIndexChanged, evh
```

Now, the two buttons clicks and selecting a kid in the Listbox all call the
CommandHandler. Since all three classes implement the Command interface,
our command handler reduces to just two lines of code.

```
Public Sub CommandHandler(ByVal sender As Object, _
            ByVal e As System.EventArgs)
    Dim cmd As Command = CType(sender, Command)
    cmd.Execute()
End Sub
```

You can appreciate the simplification VB7 makes in using a Mediator by examining the UML diagram shown in Figure 26-6.

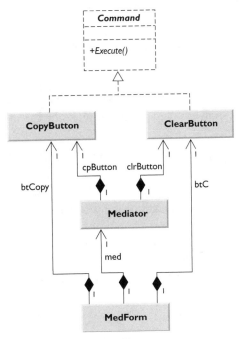

Figure 26-6   The UML diagram for the VB7 Mediator pattern

Consequences of the Mediator Pattern

1. The Mediator pattern keeps classes from becoming entangled when actions in one class need to be reflected in the state of another class.

2. Using a Mediator makes it easy to change a program's behavior. For many kinds of changes, you can merely change or subclass the Mediator, leaving the rest of the program unchanged.

3. You can add new controls or other classes without changing anything except the Mediator.

4. The Mediator solves the problem of each Command object needing to know too much about the objects and methods in the rest of a user interface.

5. The Mediator can become a "god class," having too much knowledge of the rest of the program. This can make it hard to change and maintain. Sometimes you can improve this situation by putting more of the function into the individual classes and less into the Mediator. Each object should carry out its own tasks, and the Mediator should only manage the interaction between objects.

6. Each Mediator is a custom-written class that has methods for each Colleague to call and knows what methods each Colleague has available. This makes it difficult to reuse Mediator code in different projects. On the other hand, most Mediators are quite simple, and writing this code is far easier than managing the complex object interactions any other way.

Single Interface Mediators

The Mediator pattern described here acts as a kind of Observer pattern, observing changes in each of the Colleague elements, with each element having a custom interface to the Mediator. Another approach is to have a single interface to your Mediator and pass to that method various objects that tell the Mediator which operations to perform.

In this approach, we avoid registering the active components and create a single action method with different polymorphic arguments for each of the action elements.

```
Public Sub action(mv As MoveButton)
Public Sub action(clrButton As ClearButton)
Public Sub action(klst as KidList)
```

Thus, we need not register the action objects, such as the buttons and source list boxes, since we can pass them as part of generic *action* methods.

In the same fashion, you can have a single Colleague interface that each Colleague implements, and each Colleague then decides what operation it is to carry out.

Implementation Issues

Mediators are not limited to use in visual interface programs; however, it is their most common application. You can use them whenever you are faced with the problem of complex intercommunication between a number of objects.

Programs on the CD-ROM

`\Mediator`	VB6 Mediator
`\Mediator\VBNet`	VB7 Mediator

CHAPTER 27

The Memento Pattern

In this chapter, we discuss how to use the Memento pattern to save data about an object so you can restore it later. For example, you might like to save the color, size, pattern, or shape of objects in a drafting or painting program. Ideally, it should be possible to save and restore this state without making each object take care of this task and without violating encapsulation. This is the purpose of the Memento pattern.

Motivation

Objects normally shouldn't expose much of their internal state using public methods, but you would still like to be able to save the entire state of an object because you might need to restore it later. In some cases, you could obtain enough information from the public interfaces (such as the drawing position of graphical objects) to save and restore that data. In other cases, the color, shading, angle, and connection relationships to other graphical objects need to be saved, and this information is not readily available. This sort of information saving and restoration is common in systems that need to support Undo commands.

If all of the information describing an object is available in public variables, it is not that difficult to save them in some external store. However, making these data public makes the entire system vulnerable to change by external program code, when we usually expect data inside an object to be private and encapsulated from the outside world.

The Memento pattern attempts to solve this problem in some languages by having privileged access to the state of the object you want to save. Other objects have only a more restricted access to the object, thus preserving their encapsulation. In VB6, however, there is no such thing as privileged access and we will see this is true only to a limited degree in VB7.

This pattern defines three roles for objects.

1. The **Originator** is the object whose state we want to save.

2. The **Memento** is another object that saves the state of the Originator.

3. The **Caretaker** manages the timing of the saving of the state, saves the Memento, and, if needed, uses the Memento to restore the state of the Originator.

Implementation

Saving the state of an object without making all of its variables publicly available is tricky and can be done with varying degrees of success in various languages. *Design Patterns* suggests using the C++ *friend* construction to achieve this access, and the *Smalltalk Companion* notes that it is not directly possible in Smalltalk. In Java, this privileged access is possible using the package protected mode. In VB6, like Smalltalk, this is not directly possible. The *friend* keyword is available in both VB6 and VB7, but all that means is any class method labeled as *friend* will only be accessible within the project. If you make a library from such classes, the methods marked as friends will not be exported and available. Instead, we will define a property to fetch and store the important internal values and make use of no other properties for any purpose in that class. For consistency, we'll use the friend keyword on these properties, but remember that this linguistic use of *friend* is not very restrictive.

Sample Code

Let's consider a simple prototype of a graphics drawing program that creates rectangles and allows you to select them and move them around by dragging them with the mouse. This program has a toolbar containing three buttons—Rectangle, Undo, and Clear—as we see in Figure 27-1.

The Rectangle button is a toolbar ToggleButton that stays selected until you click the mouse to draw a new rectangle. Once you have drawn the rectangle, you can click in any rectangle to select it, as we see in Figure 27-2.

Once it is selected, you can drag that rectangle to a new position, using the mouse, as shown in Figure 27-3.

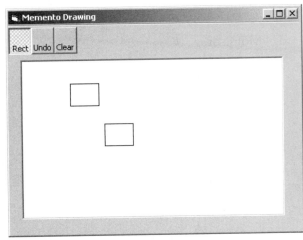

Figure 27-1 A simple graphics drawing program that allows you to draw rectangles, undo their drawing, and clear the screen

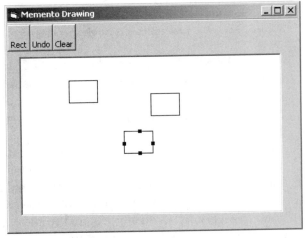

Figure 27-2 Selecting a rectangle causes "handles" to appear, indicating that it is selected and can be moved.

The Undo button can undo a succession of operations. Specifically, it can undo moving a rectangle, and it can undo the creation of each rectangle. There are five actions we need to respond to in this program.

1. Rectangle button click

2. Undo button click

3. Clear button click

4. Mouse click

5. Mouse drag

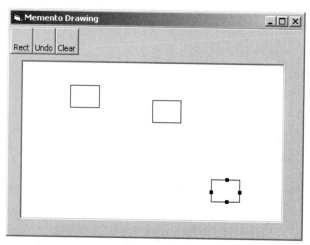

Figure 27-3   The same selected rectangle after dragging

The three buttons can be constructed as Command objects, and the mouse click and drag can be treated as commands as well. Since we have a number of visual objects that control the display of screen objects, this suggests an opportunity to use the Mediator pattern, and that is, in fact, the way this program is constructed.

We will create a Caretaker class to manage the Undo action list. It can keep a list of the last *n* operations so they can be undone. The Mediator maintains the list of drawing objects and communicates with the Caretaker object as well. In fact, since there could be any number of actions to save and undo in such a program, a Mediator is virtually required so there is a single place to send these commands to the Undo list in the Caretaker.

In this program, we save and undo only two actions: creating new rectangles and changing the position of rectangles. Let's start with our visRectangle class, which actually draws each instance of the rectangles.

```
'Class VisRectangle
Dim x As Integer, y As Integer, w As Integer, h As Integer
Private rect As Rectangle
Private selected As Boolean
'-----
Public Sub init(xp As Integer, yp As Integer)
  x = xp      'save coordinates
  y = yp
  w = 40      'default size
```

```
   h = 30
   saveAsRect 'keep in rectangle class as well
 End Sub
 '-----
 'Property methods used to save and restore state
 Friend Property Get rects() As Rectangle
   Set rects = rect
 End Property
 '-----
 Friend Property Set rects(rc As Rectangle)
   x = rc.x
   y = rc.y
   w = rc.w
   h = rc.h
   saveAsRect
 End Property
 '-----
 Public Sub setSelected(b As Boolean)
   selected = b
 End Sub
 '-----
 'save values in Rectangle class
 Private Sub saveAsRect()
   Set rect = New Rectangle
   rect.init x, y, w, h
 End Sub
 '-----
 'draw rectangle and handles
 Public Sub draw(Pic As PictureBox)
 'draw rectangle
   Pic.Line (x, y)-(x + w, y + h), , B
   If selected Then    'draw handles
     Pic.Line (x + w / 2, y - 2)- _
       (x + w / 2 + 4, y + 2), , BF
     Pic.Line (x - 2, y + h / 2)- _
       (x + 2, y + h / 2 + 4), , BF
     Pic.Line (x + (w / 2), y + h - 2)- _
       (x + (w / 2) + 4, y + h + 2), , BF
     Pic.Line (x + (w - 2), y + (h / 2))- _
       (x + (w + 2), y + (h / 2) + 4), , BF
   End If
 End Sub
 '-----
 Public Function contains(xp As Integer, yp As Integer) As Boolean
   contains = rect.contains(xp, yp)
 End Function
 '-----
 Public Sub move(xpt As Integer, ypt As Integer)
   x = xpt
   y = ypt
   saveAsRect
 End Sub
```

We also use a Rectangle class that contains Get and Let properties for the x, y, w, and h values and a *contains* method.

Drawing the rectangle is pretty straightforward. Now, let's look at our simple Memento class that we use to store the state of a rectangle.

```
'Class Memento
Private x As Integer, y As Integer
Private w As Integer, h As Integer
Private rect As Rectangle
Private visRect As VisRectangle
'-----
Public Sub init(vrect As VisRectangle)
'save the state of a visual rectangle
 Set visRect = vrect
 Set rect = vrect.rects
 x = rect.x
 y = rect.y
 w = rect.w
 h = rect.h
End Sub
'-----
Public Sub restore()
'restore the state of a visual rectangle
 rect.x = x
 rect.y = y
 rect.h = h
 rect.w = w
 Set visRect.rects = rect
End Sub
```

When we create an instance of the Memento class, we pass it the visRectangle instance we want to save, using the init method. It copies the size and position parameters and saves a copy of the instance of the visRectangle itself. Later, when we want to restore these parameters, the Memento knows which instance to which it must restore them, and it can do it directly, as we see in the *restore()* method.

The rest of the activity takes place in the Mediator class, where we save the previous state of the list of drawings as an integer on the undo list.

```
Public Sub createRect(ByVal x As Integer, ByVal y As Integer)
Dim count As Integer
Dim v As VisRectangle
 unpick              'make sure no rectangle is selected
 If startRect Then  'if rect button is depressed
    count = drawings.count
    caretakr.add count 'Save previous drawing list size
    Set v = New VisRectangle   'create a rectangle
    v.init x, y
    drawings.add v                'add new element to list
```

```
        startRect = False        'done with this rectangle
        rect.setSelected False   'unclick button
        canvas.Refresh
    Else
        pickRect x, y  'if not pressed look for rect to select
    End If
End Sub
```

On the other hand, if you click on the panel when the Rectangle button has not been selected, you are trying to select an existing rectangle. This is tested here.

```
Public Sub pickRect(x As Integer, y As Integer)
'save current selected rectangle
'to avoid double save of undo
  Dim lastPick As Integer
  Dim v As VisRectangle
  Dim i As Integer
  If selectedIndex > 0 Then
    lastPick = selectedIndex
    End If
    unpick   'undo any selection
    'see if one is being selected
    For i = 1 To drawings.count
      Set v = drawings(i)
      If v.contains(x, y) Then 'did click inside a rectangle
        selectedIndex = i      'save it
        rectSelected = True
        If selectedIndex <> lastPick Then 'but not twice
          caretakr.rememberPosition drawings(selectedIndex)
        End If
        v.setSelected True     'turn on handles
        repaint                'and redraw
      End If
    Next i
End Sub
```

The Caretaker class remembers the previous position of the rectangle in a Memento object and adds it to the undo list.

```
Public Sub rememberPosition(vrect As VisRectangle)
    Dim m As Memento
    Set m = New Memento
    m.init vrect
    undoList.add m
End Sub
```

The Caretaker class manages the undo list. This list is a Collection of integers and Memento objects. If the value is an integer, it represents the number of drawings to be drawn at that instant. If it is a Memento, it represents the previous state of a visRectangle that is to be restored. In other words, the undo list can undo the adding of new rectangles and the movement of existing rectangles.

Our undo method simply decides whether to reduce the drawing list by one or to invoke the *restore* method of a Memento.

```
Public Sub undo()
Dim obj As Object
  If undoList.count > 0 Then
    'get last element in undo list
      Set obj = undoList(undoList.count)
      undoList.remove undoList.count    'and remove it
      If Not (TypeOf obj Is Memento) Then
          removeLast              'remove Integer
      Else
          remove obj              'remove Memento
      End If
  End If
End Sub
```

This Undo method requires that all the elements in the Collection be objects rather than a mixture of integers and Memento objects. So we create a small wrapper class to convert the integer count into an object.

```
'Class intClass
'treats an integer as an object
Private intg As Integer
Public Sub init(a As Integer)
  intg = a
End Sub
'-----
Property Get integ() As Integer
  integ = intg
End Property
```

Instances of this class are created when we add an integer to the undo list.

```
Public Sub add(intObj As Integer)
        Dim integ As intClass
        Set integ = New intClass
        integ.init intObj
        undoList.add integ
      End Sub
```

The two remove methods either reduce the number of drawings or restore the position of a rectangle.

```
    Private Sub removeLast()
      drawings.remove drawings.count
    End Sub
    '-----
```

```
Private Sub remove(obj As Memento)
 obj.restore
End Sub
```

A Cautionary Note

While it is helpful in this example to detect the differences between a Memento of a rectangle position and an integer specifying the addition of a new drawing, this is in general an absolutely terrible example of OO programming. You should *never* need to check the type of an object to decide what to do with it. Instead, you should be able to call the correct method on that object and have it do the right thing.

A more correct way to have written this example would be to have both the intClass and what we are calling the Memento class both have their own restore methods and have them both be members of a general Memento class (or interface). We take this approach in the State example pattern in the next chapter.

Command Objects in the User Interface

We can also use the Command pattern to help in simplifying the code in the user interface. The three buttons are toolbar buttons that are of the class MSComctlLib.Button. We create parallel command object classes for each of the buttons and have them carry out the actions in conjunction with the mediator.

```
Private Sub Form_Load()
 Set med = New Mediator      'create the mediator
 med.init
 med.registerCanvas Pic
 Set rectB = New RectButton      'rectangle button
 rectB.init med, tbar.Buttons(1)
 Set ubutn = New UndoButton      'undo button
 ubutn.init med, tbar.Buttons(2)
 Set clrb = New ClearButton      'clear button
 clrb.init med
 Set commands = New Collection   'make a list of them
 commands.add rectB
 commands.add ubutn
 commands.add clrb
End Sub
```

Then the command interpretation devolves to just a few lines of code, since all the buttons call the same click event already.

```
Private Sub tbar_ButtonClick(ByVal Button As
MSComctlLib.Button)
 Dim i As Integer
```

```
 Dim cmd As Command
 i = Button.Index         'get which button
 Set cmd = commands(i)    'get that command
 cmd.Execute              'execute it
End Sub
```

The RectButton command class is where most of the activity takes place.

```
'Class RectButton
Implements Command
Private bt As MSComctlLib.Button
Private med As Mediator
'-----
Public Sub init(md As Mediator, but As MSComctlLib.Button)
 Set bt = but
 Set med = md
 med.registerRectButton Me
End Sub
'-----
Private Sub Command_Execute()
 If bt.Value = tbrPressed Then
    med.startRectangle
 End If
End Sub
'-----
Public Sub setSelected(sel As Boolean)
 If sel Then
    bt.Value = tbrPressed
 Else
    bt.Value = tbrUnpressed
 End If
End Sub
```

Handling Mouse and Paint Events

We also must catch the mouse down, up, and move events and pass them on to
the Mediator to handle.

```
Private Sub Pic_MouseDown(Button As Integer, _
       Shift As Integer, x As Single, y As Single)
 mouse_down = True
 med.createRect x, y
End Sub
Private Sub Pic_MouseMove(Button As Integer, _
       Shift As Integer, x As Single, y As Single)
 If mouse_down Then
    med.drag x, y
 End If
End Sub
Private Sub Pic_MouseUp(Button As Integer, Shift As Integer, _
```

```
    x As Single, y As Single)
 mouse_down = False
End Sub
```

Whenever the Mediator makes a change, it calls for a refresh of the picture box, which in turn calls the Paint event. We then pass this back to the Mediator to draw the rectangles in their new positions.

```
Private Sub Pic_Paint()
 med.reDraw Pic
End Sub
```

The complete class structure is diagrammed in Figure 27-4.

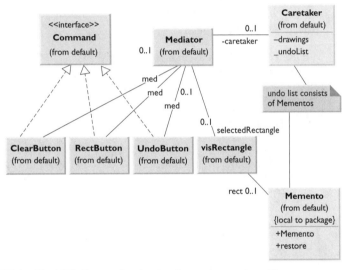

Figure 27-4 The UML diagram for the drawing program using a Memento

Writing a Memento in VB.NET

We can write almost the same code in VB7. We will use the same *friend* keyword to indicate the somewhat restricted nature of the properties and save and restore rectangle state. For our visRectangle class, we can declare the rect property as having a friend modifier.

```
'Property methods used to save and restore state
    Friend Property rects() As vbpatterns.Rectangle
        Set
            x = value.x
            y = value.y
            w = value.w
```

```
        h = value.h
        saveAsRect()
    End Set
  Get
        Return rect
    End Get
End Property
```

As in VB6, this approach is almost the same as having public access to the method, with the exception that if you compile the code into a library, these methods are not visible. So while this friend property is much less restrictive than the C++ friend modifier, it is still slightly restrictive.

The remainder of the program can be written in much the same way as for VB6. The visRectangle class's draw method is only slightly different, since it uses the Graphics object,

```
'draw rectangle and handles
Public Sub draw(ByVal g As Graphics)
'draw rectangle
 g.DrawRectangle(bpen, x, y, w, h)

 If selected Then    'draw handles
   g.fillrectangle(bbrush, x + w / 2, y - 2, 4, 4)
   g.FillRectangle(bbrush, x - 2, y + h / 2, 4, 4)
   g.FillRectangle(bbrush, x + (w / 2), y + h - 2, 4, 4)
   g.FillRectangle(bbrush, x + (w - 2), y + (h / 2), 4, 4)
 End If
End Sub
```

However, the Memento saves and restores a Rectangle object in much the same way.

You can build a toolbar and create ToolbarButtons in VB7 using the IDE, but if you do, it is difficult to subclass them to make them into command objects. There are two possible solutions. First, you can keep a parallel array of Command objects for the RectButton, the UndoButton, and the Clear button and call them in the toolbar click routine.

You should note, however, that the toolbar buttons do not have an Index property, and you cannot just ask which one has been clicked by its index and relate it to the command array. Instead, we can use the getHashCode property of each tool button to get a unique identifier for that button and keep the corresponding command objects in a Hashtable keyed off these button hash codes. We construct the Hashtable as follows.

```
Private Sub init()
        'called from New constructor
        med = New Mediator(Pic)      'create Mediator
```

```
        commands = New Hashtable()  'and Hash table
        'create the command objects
        Dim rbutn As New RectButton(med, Tbar.Buttons(0))
        Dim ubutn As New UndoButton(med, Tbar.Buttons(1))
        Dim clrbutn As New Clearbutton(med)
        'add them to the hashtable using the button hash values
        commands.Add(btRect.GetHashCode, rbutn)
        commands.Add(btundo.GetHashCode, ubutn)
        commands.Add(btClear.GetHashCode, clrbutn)
        AddHandler Pic.Paint, _
            New PaintEventHandler(AddressOf paintHandler)
    End Sub
```

We can use these hash codes to get the right command object when the buttons are clicked.

```
Protected Sub tBar_ButtonClick(ByVal sender As Object, _
        ByVal e As ToolBarButtonClickEventArgs)
    Dim cmd As Command
    Dim tbutn As ToolBarButton = e.button
    cmd = CType(commands(tbutn.GetHashCode), Command)
    cmd.Execute()
End Sub
```

The VB7 version is shown in Figure 27-5.

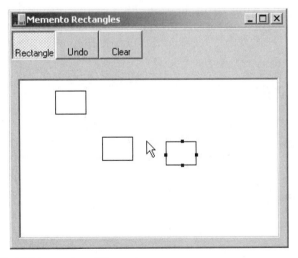

Figure 27-5   The VB.Net version of Memento

Alternatively, you could create the toolbar under IDE control but add the tool buttons to the collection programmatically and use derived buttons with a Command interface instead. We illustrate this approach in the State pattern.

Consequences of the Memento

The Memento provides a way to preserve the state of an object while preserving encapsulation in languages where this is possible. Thus, data to which only the Originator class should have access effectively remain private. It also preserves the simplicity of the Originator class by delegating the saving and restoring of information to the Memento class.

On the other hand, the amount of information that a Memento has to save might be quite large, thus taking up fair amounts of storage. This further has an effect on the Caretaker class that may have to design strategies to limit the number of objects for which it saves state. In our simple example, we impose no such limits. In cases where objects change in a predictable manner, each Memento may be able to get by with saving only incremental changes of an object's state.

In our example code in this chapter, we have to use not only the Memento but the Command and Mediator patterns as well. This clustering of several patterns is very common, and the more you see of good OO programs, the more you will see these pattern groupings.

 THOUGHT QUESTION

Mementos can also be used to restore the state of an object when a process fails. If a database update fails because of a dropped network connection, you should be able to restore the data in your cached data to their previous state. Rewrite the Database class in the Façade chapter to allow for such failures.

Programs on the CD-ROM

\Memento	VB6 Memento
\Memento\VBNet	VB7 Memento

CHAPTER 28

The Observer Pattern

In this chapter we discuss how you can use the Observer pattern to present data in several forms at once. In our new, more sophisticated windowing world, we often would like to display data in more than one form at the same time and have all of the displays reflect any changes in that data. For example, you might represent stock price changes both as a graph and as a table or list box. Each time the price changes, we'd expect both representations to change at once without any action on our part.

We expect this sort of behavior because there are any number of Windows applications, like Excel, where we see that behavior. Now there is nothing inherent in Windows to allow this activity, and, as you may know, programming directly in Windows in C or C++ is pretty complicated. In VB, however, we can easily use the Observer Design Pattern to make our program behave this way.

The Observer pattern assumes that the object containing the data is separate from the objects that display the data and that these display objects *observe* changes in that data. This is simple to illustrate, as we see in Figure 28-1.

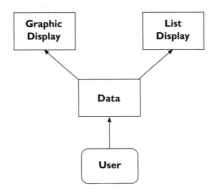

Figure 28-1   Data are displayed as a list and in some graphical mode.

When we implement the Observer pattern, we usually refer to the data as the Subject and each of the displays as an Observer. Each of these observers registers its interest in the data by calling a public method in the Subject. Then each observer has a known interface that the subject calls when the data change. We could define these interfaces as follows.

```
'Interface Observer
Public Sub sendNotify(mesg As String)
End Sub
'-----
'Interface Subject
Public Sub registerInterest(obs As Observer)
End Sub
```

The advantages of defining these abstract interfaces is that you can write any sort of class objects you want as long as they implement these interfaces and that you can declare these objects to be of type Subject and Observer no matter what else they do.

Watching Colors Change

Let's write a simple program to illustrate how we can use this powerful concept. Our program shows a display form containing three radio buttons named Red, Green, and Blue, as shown in Figure 28-2.

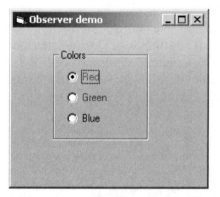

Figure 28-2   A simple control panel to create red, green, or blue "data"

Note that our main form class implements the Subject interface. That means that it must provide a public method for registering interest in the data in this class. This method is the *registerInterest* method, which just adds Observer objects to a Collection.

```
Private Sub Subject_registerInterest(obs As Observer)
 observers.Add obs
End Sub
```

Now we create two observers, one that displays the color (and its name) and
another that adds the current color to a list box.

```
Private Sub Form_Load()
 Set observers = New Collection
 'create list observer
 Dim lso As New lsObserver
 lso.init Me
 lso.Show
 'create color fram observer
 Dim cfr As New ColorFrame
 cfr.init Me
 cfr.Show

End Sub
```

When we create our ColorForm window, we register our interest in the data
in the main program.

```
'Class ColorForm
Implements Observer
Public Sub init(s As Subject)
 s.registerInterest Me
End Sub

Private Sub Observer_sendNotify(mesg As String)
Pic.Cls
 Select Case LCase(mesg)
  Case "red"
   Pic.BackColor = vbRed
   Case "green"
   Pic.BackColor = vbGreen
   Case "blue"
   Pic.BackColor = vbBlue
   End Select
  Pic.PSet (300, 600)
  Pic.Print mesg
End Sub
```

Our list box window is also an observer, and all it has to do is add the color
name to the list. The entire class is shown here.

```
'Class ListObserver
Implements Observer
```

```
Public Sub init(s As Subject)
  s.registerInterest Me
End Sub
'-----
Private Sub Observer_sendNotify(mesg As String)
 'add color names to list
 lsColors.AddItem mesg
End Sub
```

Meanwhile, in our main program, every time someone clicks on one of the radio buttons, it calls the *sendNotify* method of each Observer who has registered interest in these changes by simply running through the objects in the Observer's Collection.

```
Private Sub btColor_Click(Index As Integer)
 Dim i As Integer
 Dim mesg As String
 Dim obs As Observer
 mesg = btColor(Index).Caption     'get the button label
 'send it to all the observers
 For i = 1 To observers.Count
   Set obs = observers(i)
   obs.sendNotify mesg
 Next i
End Sub
```

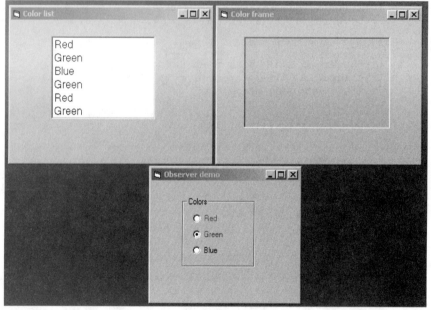

Figure 28-3   The data control pane generates data that is displayed simultaneously as a colored panel and as a list box. This is a candidate for an Observer pattern.

In the case of the ColorForm observer, the sendNotify method changes the background color and the text string in the form Picturebox. In the case of the ListForm observer, however, it just adds the name of the new color to the list box. We see the final program running in Figure 28-3.

Writing an Observer in VB.NET

In VB7, we still use the Observer and Subject interfaces to define the interaction between the data and the displays of that data.

```
Public Interface Observer
    Sub sendNotify(ByVal mesg As String)
End Interface
'-----
Public Interface Subject
    Sub registerInterest(ByVal obs As observer)
End Interface
```

As in the preceding, the main program with its three radio buttons constitutes the Subject or data class and notifies the observers when the data changes. To make the programming simpler, we add the same event handler to all three radio buttons.

```
Dim evh As EventHandler = _
        New EventHandler(AddressOf radioHandler)
    AddHandler opRed.Click, evh
    AddHandler opblue.Click, evh
    AddHandler opgreen.Click, evh
```

Then we send the text of their label to the observers.

```
Protected Sub RadioHandler(ByVal sender As Object, _
                     ByVal e As EventArgs)
Dim i As Integer
Dim rbut As RadioButton = CType(sender, RadioButton)
 For i = 0 To observers.Count - 1
    Dim obs As Observer = CType(observers(i), observer)
    obs.sendNotify(rbut.Text)
 Next i
End Sub
```

The list box observer is essentially identical, where we add the text to the list box.

```
Public Class listObs
    Inherits System.WinForms.Form
    Implements Observer
    Public Sub New(ByVal subj As Subject)
```

```
            MyBase.New()
            listObs = Me
            InitializeComponent()
            subj.registerInterest(Me)
        End Sub
        '-----
    Public Sub sendNotify(ByVal mesg As String) _
                        Implements Observer.sendNotify
        lscolors.Items.Add(mesg)
    End Sub
End Class
```

The Color window observer is a little different in that we paint the text in the paint event handler and change the background color directly in the notify event method.

```
Public Class ColForm
    Inherits System.WinForms.Form
    Implements Observer
    Private colname As String
    Dim fnt As Font
    Dim bBrush As SolidBrush
    '-----
    Public Sub New(ByVal subj As Subject)
        Me.new()    'Call base constructor
        subj.registerInterest(Me)
        fnt = New Font("arial", 18, Drawing.FontStyle.Bold)
        bBrush = New SolidBrush(Color.Black)
        AddHandler Pic.Paint, _
            New PaintEventHandler(AddressOf paintHandler)
    End Sub
        '-----
    Public Sub sendNotify(ByVal mesg As System.String) _
                        Implements VBNetObserver.Observer.sendNotify
        colname = mesg
        Select Case mesg.ToLower
            Case "red"
                pic.BackColor = color.Red '
            Case "blue"
                pic.BackColor = color.Blue
            Case "green"
                pic.BackColor = color.Green
        End Select
    End Sub
    '-----
    Private Sub paintHandler(ByVal sender As Object, _
                        ByVal e As PaintEventArgs)
        Dim g As Graphics = e.Graphics
        g.DrawString(colname, fnt, bbrush, 20, 40)
    End Sub
End Class
```

The Message to the Media

Now, what kind of notification should a subject send to its observers? In this carefully circumscribed example, the notification message is the string representing the color itself. When we click on one of the radio buttons, we can get the caption for that button and send it to the observers. This, of course, assumes that all the observers can handle that string representation. In more realistic situations, this might not always be the case, especially if the observers could also be used to observe other data objects. Here we undertake two simple data conversions.

1. We get the label from the radio button and send it to the observers.

2. We convert the label to an actual color in the ColorFrame observer.

In more complicated systems, we might have observers that demand specific, but different, kinds of data. Rather than have each observer convert the message to the right data type, we could use an intermediate Adapter class to perform this conversion.

Another problem observers may have to deal with is the case where the data of the central subject class can change in several ways. We could delete points from a list of data, edit their values, or change the scale of the data we are viewing. In these cases we either need to send different change messages to the observers or send a single message and then have the observer ask which sort of change has occurred.

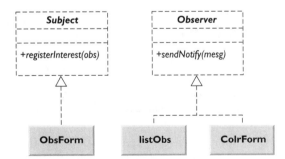

Figure 28-4   The Observer interface and Subject interface implementation of the Observer pattern

Consequences of the Observer Pattern

Observers promote abstract coupling to Subjects. A subject doesn't know the details of any of its observers. However, this has the potential disadvantage of successive or repeated updates to the Observers when there are a series of incremental changes to the data. If the cost of these updates is high, it may be necessary to introduce some sort of change management so the Observers are not notified too soon or too frequently.

When one client makes a change in the underlying data, you need to decide which object will initiate the notification of the change to the other observers. If the Subject notifies all the observers when it is changed, each client is not responsible for remembering to initiate the notification. On the other hand, this can result in a number of small successive updates being triggered. If the clients tell the Subject when to notify the other clients, this cascading notification can be avoided, but the clients are left with the responsibility of telling the Subject when to send the notifications. If one client "forgets," the program simply won't work properly.

Finally, you can specify the kind of notification you choose to send by defining a number of update methods for the Observers to receive, depending on the type or scope of change. In some cases, the clients will thus be able to ignore some of these notifications.

THOUGHT QUESTION

The VB6 version of our observer example puts up three separate windows. However, unlike the VB7 version, closing one of the windows does not close the other two and end the program. How could you use an observer to ensure that the program shuts down as desired?

Programs on the CD-ROM

\Observer	VB6 Observer
\Observer\VBNet	VB7 Observer

CHAPTER 29

The State Pattern

The State pattern is used when you want to have an object represent the state of your application and switch application states by switching objects. For example, you could have an enclosing class switch between a number of related contained classes and pass method calls on to the current contained class. *Design Patterns* suggests that the State pattern switches between internal classes in such a way that the enclosing object appears to change its class. In VB, at least, this is a bit of an exaggeration, but the actual purpose to which the classes are applied can change significantly.

Many programmers have had the experience of creating a class that performs slightly different computations or displays different information based on the arguments passed into the class. This frequently leads to some types of *select case* or *if-else* statements inside the class that determine which behavior to carry out. It is this inelegance that the State pattern seeks to replace.

Sample Code

Let's consider the case of a drawing program similar to the one we developed for the Memento class. Our program will have toolbar buttons for Select, Rectangle, Fill, Circle, and Clear. We show this program in Figure 29-1.

Each one of the tool buttons does something rather different when it is selected and you click or drag your mouse across the screen. Thus, the *state* of the graphical editor affects the behavior the program should exhibit. This suggests some sort of design using the State pattern.

Initially we might design our program like this, with a Mediator managing the actions of five command buttons, as shown in Figure 29-2. However, this initial design puts the entire burden of maintaining the state of the program on the Mediator, and we know that the main purpose of a Mediator is to

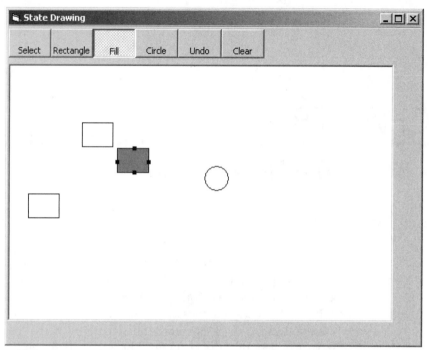

Figure 29-1   A simple drawing program we will use for illustrating the State pattern

coordinate activities between various controls, such as the buttons. Keeping the
state of the buttons and the desired mouse activity inside the Mediator can make
it unduly complicated, as well as leading to a set of *If* or *Select* tests that make the
program difficult to read and maintain.

Further, this set of large, monolithic conditional statements might have to
be repeated for each action the Mediator interprets, such as mouseUp, mouse-
Drag, rightClick, and so forth. This makes the program very hard to read and
maintain.

Instead, let's analyze the expected behavior for each of the buttons.

1. If the Select button is selected, clicking inside a drawing element should cause
    it to be highlighted or appear with "handles." If the mouse is dragged and a
    drawing element is already selected, the element should move on the screen.

2. If the Rect button is selected, clicking on the screen should cause a new rect-
    angle drawing element to be created.

3. If the Fill button is selected and a drawing element is already selected, that
    element should be filled with the current color. If no drawing is selected,
    then clicking inside a drawing should fill it with the current color.

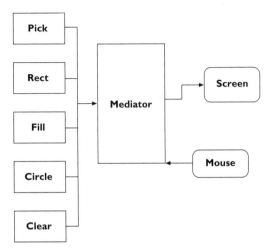

Figure 29-2   One possible interaction between the classes needed to support the simple drawing program

4. If the Circle button is selected, clicking on the screen should cause a new circle drawing element to be created.

5. If the Clear button is selected, all the drawing elements are removed.

There are some common threads among several of these actions we should explore. Four of them use the mouse click event to cause actions. One uses the mouse drag event to cause an action. Thus, we really want to create a system that can help us redirect these events based on which button is currently selected.

Let's consider creating a State object that handles mouse activities.

```
'Interface State
Public Sub mouseDown(X As Integer, Y As Integer)
End Sub
'-----
Public Sub mouseUp(X As Integer, Y As Integer)
End Sub
'-----
Public Sub mouseDrag(X As Integer, Y As Integer)
End Sub
```

We'll include the mouseUp event in case we need it later. Then we'll create four derived State classes for Pick, Rect, Circle, and Fill and put instances of all of them inside a StateManager class that sets the current state and executes methods on that state object. In *Design Patterns,* this StateManager class is referred to as a *Context.* This object is illustrated in Figure 29-3.

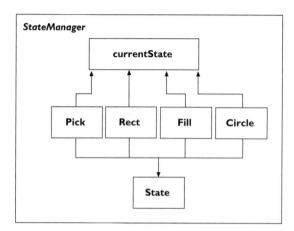

Figure 29-3   A StateManager class that keeps track of the current state

A typical State object simply overrides (in VB6, implements and fills out) those event methods that it must handle specially. For example, this is the complete Rectangle state object.

```
'Class RectState
Implements State
Private med As Mediator
Public Sub init(md As Mediator)
 Set med = md
End Sub
'-----
Private Sub State_mouseDown(X As Integer, Y As Integer)
Dim vr As New VisRectangle
 vr.init X, Y
 med.addDrawing vr
End Sub
'-----
Private Sub State_mouseDrag(X As Integer, Y As Integer)
End Sub
'-----
Private Sub State_mouseUp(X As Integer, Y As Integer)
End Sub
```

The RectState object simply tells the Mediator to add a rectangle drawing to the drawing list. Similarly, the Circle state object tells the Mediator to add a circle to the drawing list.

```
'Class CircleState
Implements State
Private med As Mediator
'-----
Public Sub init(md As Mediator)
 Set med = md
```

```
End Sub
'-----
Private Sub State_mouseDown(X As Integer, Y As Integer)
  Dim c As visCircle
  Set c = New visCircle
  c.init X, Y
  med.addDrawing c
End Sub
'-----
Private Sub State_mouseDrag(X As Integer, Y As Integer)
End Sub
'-----
Private Sub State_mouseUp(X As Integer, Y As Integer)
End Sub
```

The only tricky button is the Fill button because we have defined two actions for it.

1. If an object is already selected, fill it.

2. If the mouse is clicked inside an object, fill that one.

In order to carry out these tasks, we need to add the *selectOne* method to our base State interface. This method is called when each tool button is selected.

```
'Interface State
Public Sub mouseDown(X As Integer, Y As Integer)
End Sub
'-----
Public Sub mouseUp(X As Integer, Y As Integer)
End Sub
'-----
Public Sub mouseDrag(X As Integer, Y As Integer)
End Sub
'-----
Public Sub selectOne(d As Drawing)
End Sub
```

The Drawing argument is either the currently selected Drawing or null if none is selected. In this simple program, we have arbitrarily set the fill color to red, so our Fill state class becomes the following.

```
'Class FillState
Implements State
Private med As Mediator
Private color As ColorConstants
'-----
Public Sub init(md As Mediator)
  Set med = md
  color = vbRed
End Sub
```

```
'-----
Private Sub State_mouseDown(X As Integer, Y As Integer)
  Dim drawings As Collection
  Dim i As Integer
  Dim d As Drawing
    'Fill drawing if you click inside one
    Set drawings = med.getDrawings()
    For i = 1 To drawings.Count
       Set d = drawings(i)
       If d.contains(X, Y) Then
          d.setFill color 'fill drawing
        End If
     Next i
End Sub
'-----
Private Sub State_mouseDrag(X As Integer, Y As Integer)
End Sub
'-----
Private Sub State_mouseUp(X As Integer, Y As Integer)
End Sub
'-----
Private Sub State_selectOne(d As Drawing)
'Fill drawing if selected
   d.setFill color 'fill that drawing
End Sub
```

Switching between States

Now that we have defined how each state behaves when mouse events are sent to it, we need to examine how the StateManager switches between states. We create an instance of each state, and then we simply set the currentState variable to the state indicated by the button that is selected.

```
'Class StateManager
Private currentState As State
Private rState As RectState
Private aState As ArrowState
Private cState As CircleState
Private fState As FillState
'-----
Public Sub init(med As Mediator)
'create an instance of each state
  Set rState = New RectState
  Set cState = New CircleState
  Set aState = New ArrowState
  Set fState = New FillState
    'and initialize them
  rState.init med
  cState.init med
  aState.init med
```

```
    fState.init med
    'set default state
    Set currentState = aState
End Sub
```

Note that in this version of the StateManager, we create an instance of each state during the constructor and copy the correct one into the state variable when the set methods are called. It would also be possible to create these states on demand. This might be advisable if there are a large number of states that each consume a fair number of resources.

The remainder of the state manager code simply calls the methods of whichever state object is current. This is the critical piece—there is no conditional testing. Instead, the correct state is already in place, and its methods are ready to be called.

```
Public Sub mouseDown(X As Integer, Y As Integer)
 currentState.mouseDown X, Y
End Sub
'-----
Public Sub mouseUp(X As Integer, Y As Integer)
 currentState.mouseUp X, Y
End Sub
'-----
Public Sub mouseDrag(X As Integer, Y As Integer)
 currentState.mouseDrag X, Y
End Sub
'-----
Public Sub selectOne(d As Drawing, c As ColorConstants)
    currentState.selectOne d
End Sub
```

How the Mediator Interacts with the State Manager

We mentioned that it is clearer to separate the state management from the Mediator's button and mouse event management. The Mediator is the critical class, however, since it tells the StateManager when the current program state changes. The beginning part of the Mediator illustrates how this state change takes place. Note that each button click calls one of these methods and changes the state of the application. The remaining statements in each method simply turn off the other toggle buttons so only one button at a time can be depressed.

```
'Class Mediator
    Private startRect As Boolean
    Private selectedIndex As Integer
    Private rectb As RectButton
    Private dSelected As Boolean
    Private drawings As Collection
```

```
      Private undoList As Collection
      Private rbutton As RectButton
      Private filbutton As FillButton
      Private circButton As CircleButton
      Private arrowButton As PickButton
      Private canvas As PictureBox
      Private selectedDrawing As Integer
      Private stmgr As StateManager
  '-----
  Public Sub init(Pic As PictureBox)
     startRect = False
     dSelected = False
     Set drawings = New Collection
     Set undoList = New Collection
     Set stmgr = New StateManager
     stmgr.init Me
     Set canvas = Pic
  End Sub
  '-----
  Public Sub startRectangle()
     stmgr.setRect
     arrowButton.setSelected (False)
     circButton.setSelected (False)
     filbutton.setSelected (False)
  End Sub
  '-----
  Public Sub startCircle()
     Dim st As State
     stmgr.setCircle
     rectb.setSelected False
     arrowButton.setSelected False
     filbutton.setSelected False
  End Sub
```

As we did in the discussion of the Memento pattern, we create a series of
button Command objects paralleling the toolbar buttons and keep them in an
array to be called when the toolbar button click event occurs.

```
Private Sub Form_Load()
 Set buttons = New Collection
 'create an instance of the Mediator
 Set med = New Mediator
 med.init Pic
 'Create the button command objects
 'give each of them access to the Mediator
 Set pickb = New PickButton
 pickb.init med, tbar.buttons(1)
 Set rectb = New RectButton
 rectb.init med, tbar.buttons(2)
 Set filb = New FillButton
 filb.init med, tbar.buttons(3)
 Set cb = New CircleButton
 cb.init med, tbar.buttons(4)
```

```
Set clrb = New ClearButton
clrb.init med

Set undob = New UndoButton
undob.init med
'keep a Collection of the button Command objects
buttons.Add pickb
buttons.Add rectb
buttons.Add filb
buttons.Add cb
buttons.Add undob
buttons.Add clrb
End Sub
```

These Execute methods in turn call the preceding *startXxx* methods.

```
Private Sub tbar_ButtonClick(ByVal Button As MSComctlLib.Button)
 Dim i As Integer
 Dim cmd As Command
 'find out which button was clicked
 i = Button.index
 'get that command object
 Set cmd = buttons(i)
 cmd.Execute    'and execute it
End Sub
```

The class diagram for this program illustrating the State pattern in this application is illustrated in two parts. The State section is shown in Figure 29-4.
    The connection of the Mediator to the buttons is shown in Figure 29-5.

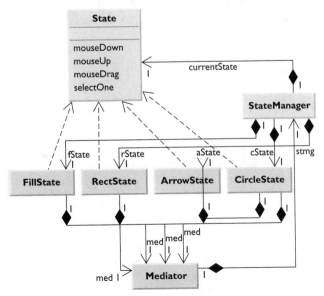

Figure 29-4 The StateManager and the Mediator

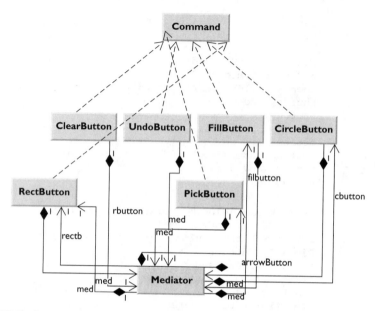

Figure 29-5   Interaction between the buttons and the Mediator

Handling the Fill State

The Fill State object is only slightly more complex because we have to handle two cases. The program will fill the currently selected object if one exists or fill the next one that you click on. This means there are two State methods we have to fill in for these two cases, as we see here.

```
'Class FillState
Implements State
Private med As Mediator
'-----
Public Sub init(md As Mediator)
 Set med = md
End Sub
'-----
Private Sub State_mouseDown(x As Integer, y As Integer)
  Dim drawings As Collection
  Dim i As Integer
  Dim d As Drawing
    'Fill drawing if you click inside one
    i = med.findDrawing(x, y)
    If i > 0 Then
      Set d = med.getDrawing(i)
      d.setFill True 'fill drawing
    End If
End Sub
```

```
'-----
Private Sub State_mouseDrag(x As Integer, y As Integer)
End Sub
'-----
Private Sub State_mouseUp(x As Integer, y As Integer)
End Sub
'-----
Private Sub State_selectOne(d As Drawing)
'Fill drawing if selected
    d.setFill True 'fill that drawing
End Sub
```

Handling the Undo List

Now we should be able to undo each of the actions we carry out in this drawing program, and this means that we keep them in an undo list of some kind. These are the actions we can carry out and undo.

1.   Creating a rectangle

2.   Creating a circle

3.   Moving a rectangle or circle

4.   Filling a rectangle or circle

In our discussion of the Memento pattern, we indicated that we would use a Memento object to store the state of the rectangle object and restore its position from that Memento as needed. This is generally true for both rectangles and circles, since we need to save and restore the same kind of position information. However, the addition of rectangles or circles and the filling of various figures are also activities we want to be able to undo. And, as we indicated in the previous Memento discussion, the idea of checking for the type of object in the undo list and performing the correct undo operation is a really terrible idea.

```
'really terrible programming approach
   Set obj = undoList(undoList.count)
   undoList.remove undoList.count    'and remove it
   If Not (TypeOf obj Is Memento) Then
       drawings.remove drawings.count
   Else
       obj.restore
   End If
```

Instead, let's define the Memento as an interface.

```
'Interface Memento
Public Sub init(d As Drawing)
End Sub
```

```
'-----
Public Sub restore()
'restore the state of an object
End Sub
```

Then all of the objects we add into the undo list will implement the Memento interface and will have a restore method that performs some operation. Some kinds of Mementos will save and restore the coordinates of drawings, and others will simply remove drawings or undo fill states.

First, we will have both our circle and rectangle objects implement the Drawing interface.

```
'Interface Drawing
Public Sub setSelected(b As Boolean)
End Sub
'-----
Public Sub draw(g As PictureBox)
End Sub
'-----
Public Sub move(xpt As Integer, ypt As Integer)
End Sub
'-----
Public Function contains(X As Integer, Y As Integer) As Boolean
End Function
'-----
Public Sub setFill(b as Boolean)
End Sub
'-----
'Property methods used to save and restore state
Property Get rects() As Rectangle
End Property
'-----
Property Set rects(rc As Rectangle)
End Property
```

The Memento we will use for saving the state of a Drawing will be similar to the one we used in the Memento chapter, except that we specifically make it implement the Memento interface.

```
'Class DrawMemento
Implements Memento
Private X As Integer, Y As Integer
Private w As Integer, h As Integer
Private rect As Rectangle
Private visDraw As Drawing
'-----
Private Sub Memento_init(d As Drawing)
'save the state of a visual rectangle
 Set visDraw = d
 Set rect = visDraw.rects
```

```
X = rect.X
Y = rect.Y
w = rect.w
h = rect.h
End Sub
'-----
Private Sub Memento_restore()
'restore the state of a drawing object
 rect.X = X
 rect.Y = Y
 rect.h = h
 rect.w = w
 Set visDraw.rects = rect
End Sub
```

Now for the case where we just want to remove a drawing from the list to be redrawn, we create a class to remember that index of that drawing and remove it when its *restore* method is called.

```
'Class DrawInstance
Implements Memento
'treats a drawing index as an object
Private intg As Integer
Private med As Mediator
Public Sub init(a As Integer, md As Mediator)
 intg = a         'remember the index
 Set med = md
End Sub
Property Get integ() As Integer
 integ = intg
End Property
'-----
Private Sub Memento_init(d As Drawing)
End Sub
'-----
Private Sub Memento_restore()
 'remove that drawing from the list
 med.removeDrawing intg
End Sub
```

We handle the FillMemento in just the same way, except that its restore method turns off the fill flag for that drawing element.

```
'Class FillMemento
Implements Memento
Private index As Integer
Private med As Mediator
'-----
Public Sub init(a As Integer, md As Mediator)
 index = a
 Set med = md
End Sub
```

```
'-----
Private Sub Memento_init(d As Drawing)
End Sub
'-----
Private Sub Memento_restore()
Dim d As Drawing
 Set d = med.getDrawing(index)
 d.setFill False
End Sub
```

Filling Circles in VB6

VB6 does not have a way to draw filled circles that is analogous to the way we draw filled rectangles. Instead, circles are filled if the Picturebox control's Fill-Style is set appropriately. However, in that case, it fills *all* circles you draw, whether you want to or not. Therefore, for VB6, we approximate filling the circles by drawing concentric circles inside the original circle and then drawing an inscribed filled rectangle as well.

```
If filled Then
  For i = r To 1 Step -1
    Pic.Circle (xc, yc), i, fillColor
  Next i
  Pic.Line (x + 4, y + 4)-(x + w - 6, y + w - 6), fillColor, BF
End If
```

A State Pattern in VB.NET

The State pattern in VB7 is similar to that in VB6. We use the same interfaces for the Memento and Drawing classes.

```
Public Interface Memento
    Sub restore()
End Interface

Public Interface Drawing
    Sub setSelected(ByVal b As Boolean)
    Sub draw(ByVal g As Graphics)
    Sub move(ByVal xpt As Integer, ByVal ypt As Integer)
    Function contains(ByVal x As Integer, _
            ByVal y As Integer) As Boolean
    Sub setFill(ByVal b As Boolean)
    Property rects() As vbpatterns.Rectangle
End Interface
```

However, there is some advantage in creating a State class with empty methods and overriding only those that a particular derived State class will require. So our base State class is as follows.

```
Public Class State
    Public Overridable Sub mouseDown(ByVal x As Integer,_
                                ByVal y As Integer)
    End Sub
    '-----
    Public Overridable Sub mouseUp(ByVal x As Integer, _
                                ByVal y As Integer)
    End Sub
    '-----
    Public Overridable Sub mouseDrag(ByVal x As Integer, _
                                ByVal y As Integer)
    End Sub
    '-----
    Public Overridable Sub selectOne(ByVal d As Drawing)
    End Sub
End Class
```

Then our derived state classes need only override the methods important to them. For example, the RectState class only responds to MouseDown.

```
Public Class RectState
    Inherits State
    Private med As Mediator
    Public Sub New(ByVal md As Mediator)
        med = md
    End Sub
    '-----
    Public Overrides Sub mouseDown(ByVal x As Integer, _
        ByVal y As Integer)
        Dim vr As New VisRectangle(x, y)
        med.addDrawing(vr)
    End Sub
End Class
```

We can take some useful advantage of inheritance in designing our visRectangle and visCircle classes. We make visRectangle *implement* the Drawing interface and then have visCircle *inherit* from visRectangle. This allows us to reuse the setSelected, setFill, and move methods and the rects properties. In addition, we can split off the drawHandle method and use it in both classes. The revised visRectangle class looks like this.

```
Public Class VisRectangle
    Implements Drawing
    Protected x, y, w, h As Integer
    Private rect As vbpatterns.Rectangle
    Protected selected As Boolean
    Protected filled As Boolean
    Protected bBrush As SolidBrush
    Protected rBrush As SolidBrush
    Protected bPen As Pen
```

```
    Private fillColor As Color
    '-----
    Public Sub New(ByVal xp As Integer, _
                ByVal yp As Integer)
        x = xp        'save coordinates
        y = yp
        w = 40        'default size
        h = 30
        fillColor = Color.Red
        bbrush = New SolidBrush(color.Black)
        rbrush = New SolidBrush(fillcolor)
        bPen = New Pen(color.Black)
        saveAsRect() 'keep in rectangle class as well
    End Sub
    '-----
    Protected Sub saveAsRect()
        rect = New vbpatterns.Rectangle(x, y, w, h)
    End Sub
    '-----
    Public Function contains(ByVal xp As Integer, _
        ByVal yp As Integer) As Boolean _
            Implements Drawing.contains
        Return rect.contains(xp, yp)
    End Function
    '-----
    Public Overridable Sub draw(ByVal g As Graphics) _
        Implements Drawing.draw
        'draw rectangle
        If filled Then
            g.FillRectangle(rbrush, x, y, w, h)
        End If
        g.DrawRectangle(bpen, x, y, w, h)
        If selected Then    'draw handles
            drawHandles(g)
        End If
    End Sub
    '-----
Protected Sub drawHandles(ByVal g As Graphics)
    'Draws handles on sides of square or circle
    g.fillrectangle(bBrush, (x + w \ 2), (y - 2), 4, 4)
    g.FillRectangle(bbrush, x - 2, y + h \ 2, 4, 4)
    g.FillRectangle(bbrush, x + (w \ 2), y + h - 2, 4, 4)
    g.FillRectangle(bbrush, x + (w - 2), y + (h \ 2), 4, 4)
End Sub
    '-----
    Public Overridable Sub move(ByVal xpt As Integer, _
        ByVal ypt As System.Integer) _
            Implements VBNetState.Drawing.move
    'Moves drawing to new coordinates
        x = xpt
        y = ypt
        saveAsRect()
    End Sub
    '-----
```

```
    Friend Property rects() As vbPatterns.Rectangle _
        Implements Drawing.rects
    'Allows changing of remembered state
        Set
            x = value.x
            y = value.y
            w = value.w
            h = value.h
            saveAsRect()
        End Set
        Get
            Return rect
        End Get
    End Property
    '-----
    Public Sub setFill(ByVal b As Boolean) _
        Implements Drawing.setFill
        filled = b
    End Sub
    '-----
    Public Sub setSelected(ByVal b As Boolean) _
        Implements VBNetState.Drawing.setSelected
        selected = b
    End Sub
End Class
```

However, our visCircle class only needs to override the draw method and have a slightly different constructor.

```
Public Class VisCircle
    Inherits VisRectangle
    Private r As Integer
    '-----
    Public Sub New(ByVal xp As Integer, _
            ByVal yp As Integer)
        MyBase.New(xp, yp)
        r = 15
        w = 30
        h = 30
        saveAsRect()
    End Sub
    '-----
    Public Overrides Sub draw(ByVal g As Graphics)
        'Fill the circle if flag set
        If filled Then
            g.FillEllipse(rbrush, x, y, w, h)
        End If
        g.DrawEllipse(bpen, x, y, w, h)
        If selected Then
            drawHandles(g)
        End If
    End Sub
End Class
```

Note that since we have made the x, y, and filled variables Protected, we can refer to them in the derived visCircle class without declaring them at all. Note that there is a valid fill method in VB7 to fill circles (ellipses).

The Mediator, Memento, and StateManager classes are essentially identical to those we wrote for VB6. However, we can simplify the overall program a great deal by creating derived classes from the ToolBarButton class and making them implement the Command interface as well.

```
'A toolbar button class that also
'has a command interface
Public Class CmdToolbarButton
    Inherits System.WinForms.ToolBarButton
    Implements Command
    Protected med As Mediator
    Protected selected As Boolean
    Public Sub New(ByVal caption As String, _
                ByVal md As mediator)
        MyBase.New()
        Me.Text = caption
        med = md
        InitializeComponent()
    End Sub
    '-----
    Public Overridable Sub setSelected(ByRef b As Boolean)
        selected = b
    End Sub
    '-----
    Public Overridable Sub Execute() _
        Implements Command.Execute
    End Sub
End Class
```

We then can derive our RectButton, CircleButton, ClearButton, Undo-Button, FillButton, and PickButton classes from the CmdToolBarButton class and give each of them the appropriate Execute method. The RectButton class is just that straightforward.

```
Public Class RectButton
    Inherits CmdToolbarButton
    '-----
    Public Sub New(ByVal md As Mediator)
        MyBase.New("Rectangle", md)
        Me.Style = ToolBarButtonStyle.ToggleButton
        med.registerRectButton(Me)
    End Sub
    '-----
    Public Overrides Sub Execute()
        med.startrectangle()
    End Sub
End Class
```

The only disadvantage to this approach is that you have to add the buttons to the toolbar programmatically instead of using the designer. However, this just amounts to adding the buttons to a collection. We create the empty toolbar in the designer, giving it the name Tbar, and then add the buttons to it.

```
Private Sub init()
        'called from New constructir
        'create a Mediator
        med = New Mediator(Pic)
        'create the buttons
        RctButton = New RectButton(med)
        ArowButton = New PickButton(med)
        CircButton = New CircleButton(med)
        flbutton = New FillButton(med)
        undoB = New UndoButton(med)
        clrb = New ClearButton(med)
        'add the buttons into the toolbar
        TBar.Buttons.Add(ArowButton)
        TBar.Buttons.Add(RctButton)
        TBar.Buttons.Add(CircButton)
        TBar.Buttons.Add(flbutton)
        'include a separator
        Dim sep As New ToolBarButton()
        sep.Style = ToolBarButtonStyle.Separator
        TBar.Buttons.Add(sep)
        TBar.Buttons.Add(undoB)
        TBar.Buttons.Add(clrb)
    End Sub
```

This makes the processing of the button clicks completely object oriented because we do not have to know which button was clicked. They are all Command objects, and we just call their execute methods.

```
'process button commands
    Private Sub TBar_ButtonClick( _
            ByVal sender As System.Object, _
            ByVal e As ToolBarButtonClickEventArgs) _
            Handles TBar.ButtonClick
        Dim cmd As Command
        Dim tbutn As ToolBarButton = e.Button
        cmd = CType(tbutn, Command) 'get the command object
        cmd.Execute()              'and execute it
    End Sub
```

Mediators and the God Class

One real problem with programs with this many objects interacting is putting too much knowledge of the system into the Mediator so it becomes a "god class." In the preceding example, the Mediator communicates with the six

buttons, the drawing list, and the StateManager. We could write this program
another way so that the button Command objects communicate with the State-
Manager and the Mediator only deals with the buttons and the drawing list.
Here, each button creates an instance of the required state and sends it to the
StateManager. This we will leave as an exercise for the reader.

Consequences of the State Pattern

1. The State pattern creates a subclass of a basic State object for each state an
    application can have and switches between them as the application changes
    between states.

2. You don't need to have a long set of conditional *if* or *switch* statements
    associated with the various states, since each is encapsulated in a class.

3. Since there is no variable anywhere that specifies which state a program is
    in, this approach reduces errors caused by programmers forgetting to test
    this state variable

4. You could share state objects between several parts of an application,
    such as separate windows, as long as none of the state objects have specific
    instance variables. In this example, only the FillState class has an instance
    variable, and this could be easily rewritten to be an argument passed in each
    time.

5. This approach generates a number of small class objects but in the process
    simplifies and clarifies the program.

6. In VB, all of the States must implement a common interface, and they must
    thus all have common methods, although some of those methods can be
    empty. In other languages, the states can be implemented by function point-
    ers with much less type checking and, of course, greater chance of error.

State Transitions

The transition between states can be specified internally or externally. In our
example, the Mediator tells the StateManager when to switch between states.
However, it is also possible that each state can decide automatically what
each successor state will be. For example, when a rectangle or circle drawing
object is created, the program could automatically switch back to the Arrow-
object State.

THOUGHT QUESTIONS

1. Rewrite the StateManager to use a Factory pattern to produce the states on demand.

2. While visual graphics programs provide obvious examples of State patterns, server programs can benefit by this approach. Outline a simple server that uses a state pattern.

Programs on the CD-ROM

\State	VB6 state drawing program
\State\Vbnet	VB7 state drawing program

CHAPTER 30

The Strategy Pattern

The Strategy pattern is much like the State pattern in outline but a little different in intent. The Strategy pattern consists of a number of related algorithms encapsulated in a driver class called the Context. Your client program can select one of these differing algorithms, or in some cases, the Context might select the best one for you. The intent is to make these algorithms interchangeable and provide a way to choose the most appropriate one. The difference between State and Strategy is that the user generally chooses which of several strategies to apply and that only one strategy at a time is likely to be instantiated and active within the Context class. By contrast, as we have seen, it is possible that all of the different States will be active at once, and switching may occur frequently between them. In addition, Strategy encapsulates several algorithms that do more or less the same thing, whereas State encapsulates related classes that each do something somewhat differently. Finally, the concept of transition between different states is completely missing in the Strategy pattern.

Motivation

A program that requires a particular service or function and that has several ways of carrying out that function is a candidate for the Strategy pattern. Programs choose between these algorithms based on computational efficiency or user choice. There can be any number of strategies, more can be added, and any of them can be changed at any time.

There are a number of cases in programs where we'd like to do the same thing in several different ways. Some of these are listed in the *Smalltalk Companion*.

- Save files in different formats.
- Compress files using different algorithms

- Capture video data using different compression schemes.
- Use different line-breaking strategies to display text data.
- Plot the same data in different formats: line graph, bar chart, or pie chart.

In each case we could imagine the client program telling a driver module (Context) which of these strategies to use and then asking it to carry out the operation.

The idea behind Strategy is to encapsulate the various strategies in a single module and provide a simple interface to allow choice between these strategies. Each of them should have the same programming interface, although they need not all be members of the same class hierarchy. However, they do have to implement the same programming interface.

Sample Code

Let's consider a simplified graphing program that can present data as a line graph or a bar chart. We'll start with an abstract PlotStrategy class and derive the two plotting classes from it, as illustrated in Figure 30-1.

Figure 30-1   Two instance of a PlotStrategy class

Our base PlotStrategy class acts as an interface containing the plot routine to be filled in in the derived strategy classes. It also contains the max and min computation code, which we will use in the derived classes by containing an instance of this class.

```
'Interface PlotStrategy
Private xmin As Single, xmax As Single
Private ymin As Single, ymax As Single
Const max = 1E+38
Public Sub plot(x() As Single, y() As Single)
'to be filled in
'in implementing classes
End Sub
'-----
```

```
Public Sub findBounds(x() As Single, y() As Single)
 Dim i As Integer
 xmin = max
 xmax = -max
 ymin = max
 ymax = -max

 For i = 1 To UBound(x())
   If x(i) > xmax Then xmax = x(i)
   If x(i) < xmin Then xmin = x(i)
   If y(i) > ymax Then ymax = y(i)
   If y(i) < ymin Then ymin = y(i)
 Next i
End Sub
'-----
Public Function getXmax() As Single
 getXmax = xmax
End Function
'-----
Public Function getYmax() As Single
 getYmax = ymax
End Function
'-----
Public Function getXmin() As Single
 getXmin = xmin
End Function
'-----
Public Function getYmin() As Single
 getYmin = ymin
End Function
```

The important part is that all of the derived classes must implement a method called *plot* with two float arrays as arguments. Each of these classes can do any kind of plot that is appropriate.

The Context

The Context class is the traffic cop that decides which strategy is to be called. The decision is usually based on a request from the client program, and all that the Context needs to do is to set a variable to refer to one concrete strategy or another.

```
'Class Context
Dim fl As vbFile
Dim x() As Single, y() As Single
Dim plts As PlotStrategy
'-----
Public Sub setLinePlot()
 Set plts = New LinePlotStrategy
End Sub
```

```
'-----
Public Sub setBarPlot()
 Set plts = New BarPlotStrategy
End Sub
'-----
Public Sub plot()
 readFile
 plts.findBounds x(), y()
 plts.plot x(), y()      'do whatever kind of plot
End Sub
'-----
Private Sub readFile()
'reads data in from data file
End Sub
```

The Context class is also responsible for handling the data. Either it obtains the data from a file or database or it is passed in when the Context is created. Depending on the magnitude of the data, it can either be passed on to the plot strategies or the Context can pass an instance of itself into the plot strategies and provide a public method to fetch the data.

The Program Commands

This simple program (Figure 30-2) is just a panel with two buttons that call the two plots. Each of the buttons is associated with a command object that sets the correct strategy and then calls the Context's plot routine. For example, here is the complete Line graph command class.

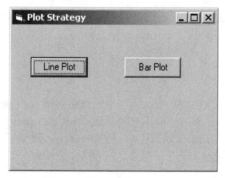

Figure 30-2   A simple panel to call two different plots

```
'Class LineCmd
Implements Command
Private contxt As Context
'-----
Public Sub init(cont As Context)
 Set contxt = cont
End Sub
```

```
'-----
Private Sub Command_Execute()
 contxt.setLinePlot
 contxt.plot
End Sub
```

The Line and Bar Graph Strategies

The two strategy classes are pretty much the same: They set up the window size for plotting and call a plot method specific for that display panel. Here is the Line graph Strategy.

```
'Class LinePlotStrategy
Implements PlotStrategy
Dim plts As PlotStrategy

Private Sub Class_Initialize()
 'base class used to compute bounds
 Set plts = New PlotStrategy
End Sub

Private Sub PlotStrategy_findBounds(x() As Single, y() As Single)
 plts.findBounds x, y
End Sub
'-----
'not used in derived classes
Private Function PlotStrategy_getXmax() As Single
End Function
Private Function PlotStrategy_getXmin() As Single
End Function
Private Function PlotStrategy_getYmax() As Single
End Function
Private Function PlotStrategy_getYmin() As Single
End Function
'-----
Private Sub PlotStrategy_plot(x() As Single, y() As Single)
Dim lplot As New LinePlot
 plts.findBounds x, y
 lplot.setBounds plts.getXmin, _
      plts.getXmax, plts.getYmin, plts.getYmax
 lplot.Show
 lplot.plot x(), y()
End Sub
```

Drawing Plots in VB

Note that both the LinePlot and the BarPlot window have plot methods that are called by the plot methods of the LinePlotStrategy and BarPlotStrategy classes. Both plot windows have a setBounds method that computes the scaling between the window coordinates and the x-y coordinate scheme.

```
Public Sub setBounds(xmn As Single, xmx As Single, ymn As Single, _
                     ymx As Single)
  xmax = xmx
  xmin = xmn
  ymax = ymx
  ymin = ymn
  h = Pic.Height
  w = Pic.Width
  xfactor = 0.9 * w / (xmax - xmin)
  xpmin = 0.05 * w
  xpmax = w - xpmin

  yfactor = 0.9 * h / (ymax - ymin)
  ypmin = 0.05 * h
  ypmax = h - ypmin
  bounds = True
End Sub
```

In VB6 you use the Line command to draw both the line and the bar plots. However, these plotting commands are immediate and do not refresh the screen if a window is obscured and needs to be redrawn. So we save the references to the x and y arrays and also call the plot method from the PictureBox's paint event.

```
Public Sub plot(xp() As Single, yp() As Single)
  Dim i As Integer, ix As Integer, iy As Integer
  'draw a line plot
  x = xp
  y = yp
  ix = calcx(x(1))
  iy = calcy(y(1))
  Pic.Cls              'clear the picture
  Pic.PSet (ix, iy)    'start the drawing point
  'draw the lines
  For i = 2 To UBound(x())
    ix = calcx(x(i))
    iy = calcy(y(i))
    Pic.Line -(ix, iy), vbBlack
  Next i
End Sub
'------
Private Function calcx(ByVal xp As Single) As Integer
  Dim ix As Integer
  ix = (xp - xmin) * xfactor + xpmin
  calcx = ix
End Function
'------
Private Function calcy(ByVal yp As Single) As Integer
  Dim iy As Integer
  yp = (yp - ymin) * yfactor
  iy = ypmax - yp
  calcy = iy
End Function
```

```
'------
Private Sub Pic_Paint()
 plot x(), y()
End Sub
```

The UML diagram showing these class relations is shown in Figure 30-3.

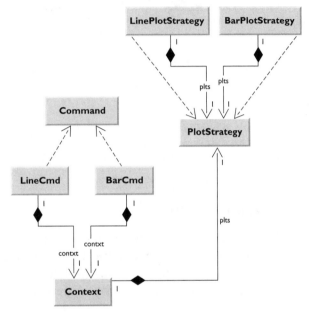

Figure 30-3   The UML Diagram for the VB6 Strategy pattern

The final two plots are shown in Figure 30-4.

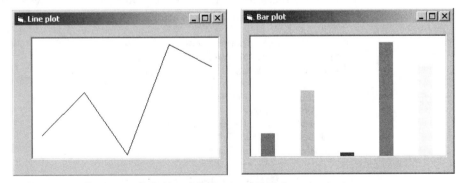

Figure 30-4   The line graph (left) and the bar graph (right)

The class diagram is given in Figure 30-5.

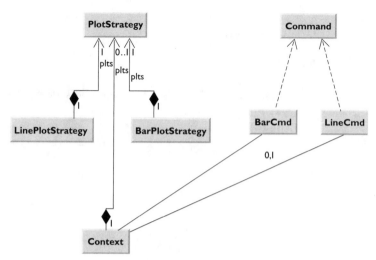

Figure 30-5   The UML class diagram for the PlotStrategy classes. Note that we again use the Command pattern.

A Strategy Pattern in VB.NET

The VB7 version of Strategy differs primarily in that we do not need to duplicate code between the two Strategies or the two windows, since we can use inheritance to make the same code work for both strategies. We define our basic PlotStrategy class as an empty class that must be overridden.

```
Public MustInherit Class PlotStrategy
    Public MustOverride Sub plot(ByVal x() As Single, _
              ByVal y() As Single)
End Class
```

The two instances for LinePlotStrategy and BarPlotStrategy differ only in the plot window they create. Here is the LinePlotStrategy.

```
Public Class LinePlotStrategy
    Inherits PlotStrategy
    Public Overrides Sub plot(ByVal x() As Single, _
                    ByVal y() As Single)
        Dim lplot As New LinePlot()
        lplot.Show()
        lplot.plot(x, y)
    End Sub
End Class
```

And here is the BarPlotStrategy.

```
Public Class BarPlotStrategy
    Inherits PlotStrategy
```

```
      Public Overrides Sub plot(ByVal x() As Single, _
                                 ByVal y() As Single)
          Dim bplot As New BarPlot()
          bplot.Show()
          bplot.plot(x, y)
      End Sub
  End Class
```

All of the scaling computations can then be housed in one of the plot window classes and inherited for the other. We chose the BarPlot window as the base class, but either one would work as well as the other as the base. This class contains the scaling routines and creates an array of SolidBrush objects for the various colors to be used in the bar plot.

```
Public Overridable Sub set_Bounds()
        findBounds()
        'compute scaling factors
        h = Pic.Height
        w = Pic.Width
        xfactor = 0.8F * w / (xmax - xmin)
        xpmin = 0.05F * w
        xpmax = w - xpmin

        yfactor = 0.9F * h / (ymax - ymin)
        ypmin = 0.05F * h
        ypmax = h - ypmin
        'create array of colors for bars
        colors = New arraylist()
        colors.Add(New SolidBrush(Color.Red))
        colors.Add(New SolidBrush(color.Green))
        colors.Add(New SolidBrush(color.Blue))
        colors.Add(New SolidBrush(Color.Magenta))
        colors.Add(New SolidBrush(color.Yellow))
    End Sub
```

The plotting amounts to copying in a reference to the x and y arrays, calling the scaling routine and then causing the Picturebox control to be refreshed, which will then call the paint routine to paint the bars.

```
      Public Sub plot(ByVal xp() As Single, _
                  ByVal yp() As Single)
          x = xp
          y = yp
          set_Bounds()      'compute scaling factors
          hasData = True
          pic.Refresh()
      End Sub
  '-----
      Public Overridable Sub Pic_Paint(_
              ByVal sender As Object, _
              ByVal e As PaintEventArgs) Handles Pic.Paint
          Dim g As Graphics = e.Graphics
```

```
            Dim i, ix, iy As Integer
            Dim br As Brush
            If hasData Then
                For i = 0 To x.Length - 1
                    ix = calcx(x(i))
                    iy = calcy(y(i))
                    br = CType(colors(i), brush)
                    g.FillRectangle(br, ix, h - iy, 20, iy)
                Next
            End If
        End Sub
```

The LinePlot window is much simpler now because we can derive it from the BarPlot window and reuse nearly all the code.

```
Public Class LinePlot
    Inherits BarPlot
    Private bPen As Pen
    Public Sub New()
        MyBase.New
        LinePlot = Me
        InitializeComponent()
        bpen = New Pen(Color.Black)
    End Sub

    Public Overrides Sub Pic_Paint(ByVal sender As Object, _
        ByVal e As PaintEventArgs) Handles Pic.Paint
        Dim g As Graphics = e.Graphics
        Dim i, ix, iy, ix1, iy1 As Integer
        Dim br As Brush
        If hasData Then
            For i = 1 To x.Length - 1
                ix = calcx(x(i - 1))
                iy = calcy(y(i - 1))
                ix1 = calcx(x(i))
                iy1 = calcy(y(i))
                g.drawline(bpen, ix, iy, ix1, iy1)
            Next
        End If
    End Sub
End Class
```

The two buttons are now command buttons whose Execute methods set the context and carry out the requisite plot. Here is the complete Line button code:

```
Public Class LineBtn
    Inherits System.Windows.Forms.Button
    Implements Command
    Private contxt As Context
```

```
'-----
Public Sub setContext(ByVal ctx As Context)
    contxt = ctx
End Sub
'-----
Public Sub Execute() Implements vbnetStrategy.Command.Execute
    contxt.setLinePlot()
    contxt.plot()
End Sub
End Class
```

The two resulting plot windows are identical to those drawn in the VB6 version
(Figure 30-4).

Consequences of the Strategy Pattern

Strategy allows you to select one of several algorithms dynamically. These algorithms can be related in an inheritance hierarchy, or they can be unrelated as long as they implement a common interface. Since the Context switches between strategies at your request, you have more flexibility than if you simply called the desired derived class. This approach also avoids the sort of conditional statements that can make code hard to read and maintain.

On the other hand, strategies don't hide everything. The client code is usually aware that there are a number of alternative strategies, and it has some criteria for choosing among them. This shifts an algorithmic decision to the client programmer or the user.

Since there are a number of different parameters that you might pass to different algorithms, you have to develop a Context interface and strategy methods that are broad enough to allow for passing in parameters that are not used by that particular algorithm. For example the *setPenColor* method in our PlotStrategy is actually only used by the LineGraph strategy. It is ignored by the BarGraph strategy, since it sets up its own list of colors for the successive bars it draws.

Programs on the CD-ROM

`\Strategy`	VB6 plot strategy
`\Strategy\VBNetStrategy`	VB7 plot strategy

CHAPTER 31

The Template Method Pattern

The Template Method pattern is a very simple pattern that you will find yourself using frequently. Whenever you write a parent class where you leave one or more of the methods to be implemented by derived classes, you are in essence using the Template pattern. The Template pattern formalizes the idea of defining an algorithm in a class but leaving some of the details to be implemented in subclasses. In other words, if your base class is an abstract class, as often happens in these design patterns, you are using a simple form of the Template pattern.

Since inheritance is a critical part of this pattern, we will develop our Template Method example exclusively in VB7.

Motivation

Templates are so fundamental, you have probably used them dozens of times without even thinking about it. The idea behind the Template pattern is that some parts of an algorithm are well defined and can be implemented in the base class, whereas other parts may have several implementations and are best left to derived classes. Another main theme is recognizing that there are some basic parts of a class that can be factored out and put in a base class so they do not need to be repeated in several subclasses.

For example, in developing the BarPlot and LinePlot classes we used in the Strategy pattern examples in the previous chapter, we discovered that in plotting both line graphs and bar charts we needed similar code to scale the data and compute the x and y pixel positions.

```
Public MustInherit Class PlotWindow
    Inherits System.Windows.Forms.Form
    'base plot window class for bar and line plots
    Protected xfactor As Single, xpmin As Single
```

```vbnet
        Protected xpmax As Single
        Protected xmin As Single, xmax As Single
        Protected ymin As Single, ymax As Single
        Protected yfactor As Single, ypmin As Single
        Protected ypmax As Single
        Protected x() As Single, y() As Single
        Protected bPen As Pen
        Protected hasData As Boolean
        Protected w As Integer, h As Integer
        Const max As Single = 1E+38

        '-----
        Public Sub setPenColor(ByVal c As Color)
            bpen = New Pen(c)
        End Sub
        '-----
        Private Sub findBounds()
            'on CD-Rom
          End Sub
        '-----
        Public Overridable Sub set_Bounds( _
                ByVal pic As PictureBox)
            findBounds()
            'on CD-Rom
        End Sub
        '-----
        Public Function calcx(ByVal xp As Single) As Integer
            Dim ix As Integer
            ix = ((xp - xmin) * xfactor + xpmin).ToInt16
            Return ix
        End Function
        '-----
        Public Function calcy(ByVal yp As Single) As Integer
            Dim iy As Integer
            yp = ((yp - ymin) * yfactor).ToInt16
            iy = (ypmax - yp).ToInt16
            Return iy
        End Function
        '-----
        Public Sub plot(ByVal xp() As Single, _
                    ByVal yp() As Single, ByVal pic As PictureBox)
            x = xp
            y = yp
            set_Bounds(pic)       'compute scaling factors
            hasData = True
            repaint()
        End Sub
        '-----
        Public MustOverride Sub repaint()
        '-----
End Class
```

Thus, these methods all belonged in a base PlotPanel class without any actual plotting capabilities. Note that the *plot* method sets up all the scaling constants and just calls *repaint*. The actual repaint method is deferred to the derived classes. It is exactly this sort of extension to derived classes that exemplifies the Template Method pattern.

Kinds of Methods in a Template Class

As discussed in *Design Patterns*, the Template Method pattern has four kinds of methods that you can use in derived classes.

1. Complete methods that carry out some basic function that all the subclasses will want to use, such as *calcx* and *calcy* in the preceding example. These are called *Concrete methods*.

2. Methods that are not filled in at all and must be implemented in derived classes. In VB7, you would declare these as *MustOverride* methods.

3. Methods that contain a default implementation of some operations but that may be overridden in derived classes. These are called *Hook* methods. Of course, this is somewhat arbitrary because in VB7 you can override any public or protected method in the derived class but Hook methods, however, are intended to be overridden, whereas Concrete methods are not.

4. Finally, a Template class may contain methods that themselves call any combination of abstract, hook, and concrete methods. These methods are not intended to be overridden but describe an algorithm without actually implementing its details. *Design Patterns* refers to these as Template methods.

Sample Code

Let's consider a simple program for drawing triangles on a screen. We'll start with an abstract Triangle class and then derive some special triangle types from it, as we see in Figure 31-1.

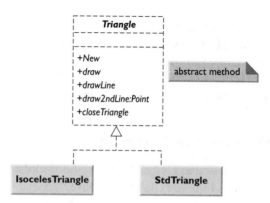

Figure 31-1   The abstract Triangle class and three of its subclasses

Our abstract Triangle class illustrates the Template pattern.

```
Public MustInherit Class Triangle
    Private p1, p2, p3 As Point
    Protected bPen As Pen
    '-----
    Public Sub New(ByVal a As Point, ByVal b As Point, _
            ByVal c As Point)
        p1 = a
        p2 = b
        p3 = c
        bPen = New Pen(Color.Black)
    End Sub
    '-----
    'draw the complete triangle
    Public Sub draw(ByVal g As Graphics)
        drawLine(g, p1, p2)
        Dim c As Point = draw2ndLine(g, p2, p3)
        closeTriangle(g, c)
    End Sub
    '-----
    'draw one line
    Public Sub drawLine(ByVal g As Graphics, _
        ByVal a As Point, ByRef b As Point)
        g.drawLine(bpen, a.x, a.y, b.x, b.y)
    End Sub
    '-----
    'method you must override in derived classes
    Public MustOverride Function draw2ndLine(_
        ByVal g As Graphics, _
        ByVal a As Point, ByVal b As Point) As Point
    '-----
    'close by drawing back to beginning
    Public Sub closeTriangle(ByVal g As Graphics, _
        ByVal c As Point)
        g.DrawLine(bpen, c.X, c.Y, p1.x, p1.y)
    End Sub
End Class
```

This Triangle class saves the coordinates of three lines, but the *draw* routine draws only the first and the last lines. The all-important *draw2ndLine* method that draws a line to the third point is left as an abstract method. That way the derived class can move the third point to create the kind of rectangle you wish to draw.

This is a general example of a class using the Template pattern. The *draw* method calls two concrete base class methods and one abstract method that must be overridden in any concrete class derived from Triangle.

Another very similar way to implement the case triangle class is to include default code for the *draw2ndLine* method.

```
Public Overridable Function draw2ndLine(_
        ByVal g As Graphics, ByVal a As point, _
        ByVal b As Point) As Point
        g.DrawLine(bpen, a.X, a.Y, b.X, b.Y)
        Return b
    End Function
```

In this case, the *draw2ndLine* method becomes a Hook method that can be overridden for other classes.

Drawing a Standard Triangle

To draw a general triangle with no restrictions on its shape, we simple implement the *draw2ndLine* method in a derived *stdTriangle* class.

```
Public Class StdTriangle
    Inherits Triangle
    '-----
    Public Sub new(ByVal a As Point, _
            ByVal b As Point, ByVal c As Point)
        MyBase.new(a, b, c)
    End Sub
    '-----
    Public Overrides Function draw2ndLine(_
        ByVal g As Graphics, ByVal a As point, _
        ByVal b As Point) As Point
        g.DrawLine(bpen, a.X, a.Y, b.X, b.Y)
        Return b
    End Function
End Class
```

Drawing an Isosceles Triangle

This class computes a new third data point that will make the two sides equal in length and saves that new point inside the class.

```
Public Class IsoscelesTriangle
    Inherits Triangle
    Private newc As Point
    Private newcx, newcy As Integer
    '-----
    Public Sub New(ByVal a As Point, ByVal b As Point, _
                   ByVal c As Point)
        MyBase.New(a, b, c)
        Dim dx1, dy1, dx2, dy2, side1, side2 As Single
        Dim slope, intercept As Single
        Dim incr As Integer
        dx1 = b.x - a.x
        dy1 = b.y - a.y
        dx2 = c.x - b.x
        dy2 = c.y - b.y

        side1 = calcSide(dx1, dy1)
        side2 = calcSide(dx2, dy2)

        If (side2 < side1) Then
            incr = -1
        Else
            incr = 1
        End If
        slope = dy2 / dx2
        intercept = c.y - slope * c.X

        'move point c so that this is an isosceles triangle
        newcx = c.X
        newcy = c.Y
        While (abs(side1 - side2) > 1)
            newcx = newcx + incr
            'iterate a pixel at a time until close
            newcy = (slope * newcx + intercept).ToInt16
            dx2 = newcx - b.x
            dy2 = newcy - b.y
            side2 = calcSide(dx2, dy2)
        End While
        newc = New Point(newcx, newcy)
    End Sub
    '-----
    Private Function calcSide(ByVal dx As Single, _
            ByVal dy As Single) As Single
        Return Sqrt(dx * dx + dy * dy).ToSingle
    End Function
```

When the Triangle class calls the *draw* method, it calls this new version of *draw2ndLine* and draws a line to the new third point. Further, it returns that new point to the *draw* method so it will draw the closing side of the triangle correctly.

```
'draw 2nd line using new saved point
    Public Overrides Function draw2ndLine( _
        ByVal g As Graphics, ByVal b As Point, _
            ByVal c As Point) As Point
        g.DrawLine(bpen, b.X, b.Y, newc.X, newc.Y)
        Return newc
    End Function
```

The Triangle Drawing Program

The main program simply creates instances of the triangles you want to draw. Then it adds them to an ArrayList in the TriangleForm class.

```
Public Class Form1
    Inherits System.Windows.Forms.Form
    Private triangles As ArrayList
    Private Sub init()
        'Create a list of triangles to draw
        triangles = New ArrayList()
        Dim t1 As New StdTriangle( _
            New Point(10, 10), New Point(150, 50), _
            New Point(100, 75))
        Dim t2 As New IsocelesTriangle( _
            New Point(150, 100), New Point(240, 40), _
            New Point(175, 150))
        triangles.Add(t1)
        triangles.Add(t2)
    End Sub
```

It is the *paint* routine in this class that actually draws the triangles.

```
Public Sub Pic_Paint(ByVal sender As Object, _
        ByVal e As System.WinForms.PaintEventArgs) _
            Handles Pic.Paint
        Dim i As Integer
        Dim g As Graphics = e.Graphics
        For i = 0 To triangles.Count - 1
            Dim t As Triangle = _
                CType(triangles(i), triangle)
            t.draw(g)
        Next
    End Sub
```

A standard triangle and an isosceles triangle are shown in Figure 31-2.

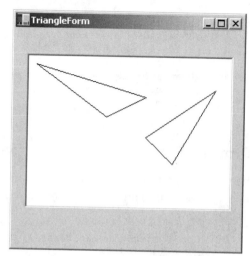

Figure 31-2   A standard triangle and an isosceles triangle

Templates and Callbacks

Design Patterns points out that Templates can exemplify the "Hollywood Principle," or "Don't call us, we'll call you." The idea here is that methods in the base class seem to call methods in the derived classes. The operative word here is *seem*. If we consider the *draw* code in our base Triangle class, we see that there are three method calls.

```
drawLine(g, p1, p2)
Dim c As Point = draw2ndLine(g, p2, p3)
closeTriangle(g, c)
```

Now *drawLine* and *closeTriangle* are implemented in the base class. However, as we have seen, the *draw2ndLine* method is not implemented at all in the base class, and various derived classes can implement it differently. Since the actual methods that are being called are in the derived classes, it appears as though they are being called from the base class.

If this idea makes you uncomfortable, you will probably take solace in recognizing that *all* the method calls originate from the derived class and that these calls move up the inheritance chain until they find the first class that implements them. If this class is the base class—fine. If not, it could be any other class in between. Now, when you call the *draw* method, the derived class moves up the inheritance tree until it finds an implementation of draw. Likewise, for each method called from within draw, the derived class starts at the current class and moves up the tree to find each method. When it gets to the *draw2ndLine* method, it finds it immediately in the current class. So it isn't "really" called from the base class, but it does seem that way.

Summary and Consequences

Template patterns occur all the time in OO software and are neither complex nor obscure in intent. They are a normal part of OO programming, and you shouldn't try to make them into more than they actually are.

The first significant point is that your base class may only define some of the methods it will be using, leaving the rest to be implemented in the derived classes. The second major point is that there may be methods in the base class that call a sequence of methods, some implemented in the base class and some implemented in the derived class. This Template method defines a general algorithm, although the details may not be worked out completely in the base class.

Template classes will frequently have some abstract methods that you must override in the derived classes, and they may also have some classes with a simple "placeholder" implementation that you are free to override where this is appropriate. If these placeholder classes are called from another method in the base class, then we call these overridable methods "Hook" methods.

Programs on the CD-ROM

\Strategy\TemplateStrategy	VB7 plot strategy using Template method pattern
\Template\Tngle	VB7 triangle drawing template

CHAPTER 32

The Visitor Pattern

The Visitor pattern turns the tables on our object-oriented model and creates an external class to act on data in other classes. This is useful when you have a polymorphic operation that cannot reside in the class hierarchy for some reason—for example, because the operation wasn't considered when the hierarchy was designed or it would clutter the interface of the classes unnecessarily. The Visitor pattern is easier to explain using VB7, since polymorphism and inheritance make the code rather simpler. We'll discuss how to implement the Visitor in VB6 at the end of this chapter.

Motivation

While at first it may seem "unclean" to put operations inside one class that should be in another, there are good reasons for doing so. Suppose each of a number of drawing object classes has similar code for drawing itself. The drawing methods may be different, but they probably all use underlying utility functions that we might have to duplicate in each class. Further, a set of closely related functions is scattered throughout a number of different classes, as shown in Figure 32-1.

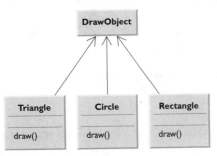

Figure 32-1   A DrawObject and three of its subclasses

Instead, we write a Visitor class that contains all the related *draw* methods and have it visit each of the objects in succession (Figure 32-2).

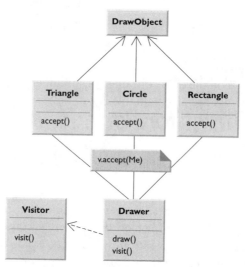

Figure 32-2   A Visitor class (Drawer) that visits each of three triangle classes

The first question that most people ask about this pattern is "What does *visiting* mean?" There is only one way that an outside class can gain access to another class, and that is by calling its public methods. In the Visitor case, visiting each class means that you are calling a method already installed for this purpose, called *accept*. The *accept* method has one argument: the instance of the visitor. In return, it calls the *visit* method of the Visitor, passing itself as an argument, as shown in Figure 32-3.

Figure 32-3   How the visit and accept methods interact

Putting it in simple code terms, every object that you want to visit must have the following method.

```
Public Sub accept(ByVal v As Visitor)
        v.visit(Me)
End Subb
```

In this way, the Visitor object receives a reference to each of the instances, one by one, and can then call its public methods to obtain data, perform calculations, generate reports, or just draw the object on the screen. Of course, if the class does not have an *accept* method, you can subclass it and add one.

When to Use the Visitor Pattern

You should consider using a Visitor pattern when you want to perform an operation on the data contained in a number of objects that have different interfaces. Visitors are also valuable if you have to perform a number of unrelated operations on these classes. Visitors are a useful way to add function to class libraries or frameworks for which you either do not have the course or cannot change the source for other technical (or political) reasons. In these latter cases, you simply subclass the classes of the framework and add the *accept* method to each subclass.

On the other hand, as we will see, Visitors are a good choice only when you do not expect many new classes to be added to your program.

Sample Code

Let's consider a simple subset of the Employee problem we discussed in the Composite pattern. We have a simple Employee object that maintains a record of the employee's name, salary, vacation taken, and number of sick days taken. The following is a simple version of this class.

```
Public Class Employee
    Dim sickDays As Integer, vacDays As Integer
    Dim salary As Single
    Dim name As String
    '-----
    Public Sub New(ByVal nm As String, ByVal sl As Single, _
                ByVal vDays As Integer, ByVal sDays As Integer)
        name = nm
        salary = sl
        vacDays = vDays
        sickDays = sDays
    End Sub
    '-----
    Public Function getName() As String
        Return name
    End Function
    '-----
    Public Function getSalary() As Single
        Return salary
    End Function
    '-----
```

```
        Public Function getSickdays() As Integer
            Return sickDays
        End Function
        '-----
        Public Function getVacDays() As Integer
            Return vacDays
        End Function
        '-----
        Public Sub accept(ByVal v As Visitor)
            v.visit(Me)
        End Sub
End Class
```

Note that we have included the *accept* method in this class. Now let's suppose that we want to prepare a report on the number of vacation days that all employees have taken so far this year. We could just write some code in the client to sum the results of calls to each Employee's *getVacDays* function, or we could put this function into a Visitor.

Since VB is a strongly typed language, our base Visitor class needs to have a suitable abstract *visit* method for each kind of class in your program. In this first simple example, we only have Employees, so our basic abstract Visitor class is just the following.

```
Public MustInherit Class Visitor
    Public MustOverride Sub visit(ByVal emp As Employee)
End Class
```

Notice that there is no indication what the Visitor does with each class in either the client classes or the abstract Visitor class. We can, in fact, write a whole lot of visitors that do different things to the classes in our program. The Visitor we are going to write first just sums the vacation data for all our employees.

```
Public Class VacationVisitor
    Inherits Visitor
    Dim totalDays As Integer
    '-----
    Public Sub new()
        totalDays = 0
    End Sub
    '-----
    Public Function getTotalDays() As Integer
        getTotalDays = totalDays
    End Function
    '-----
    Public Overrides Sub visit(ByVal emp As Employee)
        totalDays = totalDays + emp.getVacDays
    End Sub
```

```
        Public Overrides Sub visit(ByVal bos As Boss)
            totalDays = totalDays + bos.getVacDays
        End Sub
End Class
```

Visiting the Classes

Now all we have to do to compute the total vacation days taken is go through a list of the employees, visit each of them, and ask the Visitor for the total.

```
For i = 0 To empls.Length - 1
        empls(i).accept(vac)        'get the employee
Next i

List1.items.Add("Total vacation days=" & _
            vac.getTotalDays.toString)
```

Let's reiterate what happens for each visit.

1.   We move through a loop of all the Employees.

2.   The Visitor calls each Employee's *accept* method.

3.   That instance of Employee calls the Visitor's *visit* method.

4.   The Visitor fetches the vacation days and adds them into the total.

5.   The main program prints out the total when the loop is complete.

Visiting Several Classes

The Visitor becomes more useful when there are a number of different classes with different interfaces and we want to encapsulate how we get data from these classes. Let's extend our vacation days model by introducing a new Employee type called Boss. Let's further suppose that at this company, Bosses are rewarded with bonus vacation days (instead of money). So the Boss class has a couple of extra methods to set and obtain the bonus vacation day information.

```
Public Class Boss
    Inherits Employee
    Private bonusDays As Integer
    '-----
    Public Sub New(ByVal nm As String, _
                ByVal sl As Single, _
        ByVal vDays As Integer, ByVal sDays As Integer)
        MyBase.New(nm, sl, vdays, sdays)
    End Sub
    '-----
```

```
    Public Sub setBonusDays(ByVal bdays As Integer)
        bonusdays = bdays
    End Sub
    '-----
    Public Function getBonusDays() As Integer
        Return bonusDays
    End Function
    '-----
    Public Overrides Sub accept(ByVal v As Visitor)
        v.visit(Me)
    End Sub
End Class
```

When we add a class to our program, we have to add it to our Visitor as well, so that the abstract template for the Visitor is now the following.

```
Public MustInherit Class Visitor
    Public MustOverride Sub visit(ByVal emp As Employee)
    Public MustOverride Overloads Sub visit(ByVal bos As Boss)
End Class
```

This says that any concrete Visitor classes we write must provide polymorphic *visit* methods for both the Employee class and the Boss class. In the case of our vacation day counter, we need to ask the Bosses for both regular and bonus days taken, so the visits are now different. We'll write a new bVacationVisitor class that takes account of this difference.

```
Public Class bVacationVisitor
    Inherits Visitor
    Private totalDays As Integer
    '-----
    Public Overrides Sub visit( _
                    ByVal emp As Employee)
        totalDays += emp.getVacDays
    End Sub
    '-----
    Public Overrides Sub visit(ByVal bos As Boss)
        totalDays += bos.getVacDays
        totalDays += bos.getBonusDays
    End Sub
    '-----
    Public Function getTotalDays() As Integer
        Return totalDays
    End Function
End Class
```

Note that while in this case Boss is derived from Employee, it need not be related at all as long as it has an *accept* method for the Visitor class. It is quite important, however, that you implement a *visit* method in the Visitor for *every class* you will be visiting and not count on inheriting this behavior, since the *visit* method from the parent class is an Employee rather than a Boss visit method. Likewise, each of your derived classes (Boss, Employee, etc.) must have its own *accept* method rather than calling one in its parent class. This is illustrated in the class diagram in Figure 32-4.

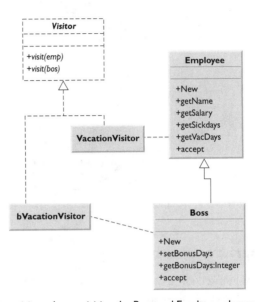

Figure 32-4   The two visitor classes visiting the Boss and Employee classes

Bosses Are Employees, Too

We show in Figure 32-5 a simple application that carries out both Employee visits and Boss visits on the collection of Employees and Bosses. The original VacationVisitor will just treat Bosses as Employees and get only their ordinary vacation data. The bVacationVisitor will get both.

```
Dim i As Integer
Dim vac As New VacationVisitor()
Dim bvac As New bVacationVisitor()
For i = 0 To empls.Length - 1
    empls(i).accept(vac)      'get the employee
    empls(i).accept(bvac)
Next i
List1.items.Add("Total vacation days=" & _
    vac.getTotalDays.toString)
List1.items.Add("Total boss vacation days=" & _
    bvac.getTotalDays.tostring)
```

The two lines of displayed data represent the two sums that are computed when the user clicks on the Vacations button.

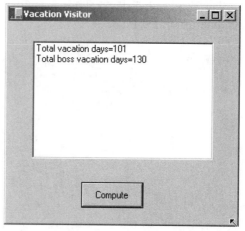

Figure 32-5   A simple application that performs the vacation visits described

Catch-All Operations with Visitors

In the preceding cases, the Visitor class has a visit method for each visiting class, such as the following.

```
Public MustOverride Sub visit(ByVal emp As Employee)
Public MustOverride Sub visit(ByVal bos As Boss)
```

However, if you start subclassing your visitor classes and adding new classes that might visit, you should recognize that some *visit* methods might not be satisfied by the methods in the derived class. These might instead "fall through" to methods in one of the parent classes where that object type is recognized. This provides a way of specifying default visitor behavior.

Now every class must override *accept(v)* with its own implementation so the return call *v.visit(this)* returns an object *this* of the correct type and not of the superclass's type.

Let's suppose that we introduce another layer of management into our company: the Manager. Managers are subclasses of Employees, and now they have the privileges formerly reserved for Bosses of extra vacation days. Bosses now have an additional reward—stock options. Now if we run the same program to compute vacation days but do not revise our Visitor to look for Managers, it will recognize them as mere Employees and count only their regular vacation and not their extra vacation days. However, the catch-all parent class is a good thing if subclasses may be added to the application from time to time and you want the visitor operations to continue to run without modification.

There are three ways to integrate the new Manager class into the visitor system. You could define a ManagerVisitor or use the BossVisitor to handle both. However, there could be conditions when continually modifying the Visitor structure is not desirable. In that case, you could simply test for this special case in the EmployeeVisitor class.

```
Public Overrides Sub visit(ByVal emp As Employee)
      totalDays += emp.getVacDays
      If TypeOf emp Is Manager Then
          Dim mgr As Manager = CType(emp, Manager)
          totaldays += mgr.getBonusDays
      End If
  End Sub
```

While this seems "unclean" at first compared to defining classes properly, it can provide a method of catching special cases in derived classes without writing whole new visitor program hierarchies. This "catch-all" approach is discussed in some detail in the book *Pattern Hatching* (Vlissides 1998).

Double Dispatching

No discussion on the Visitor pattern is complete without mentioning that you are really dispatching a method twice for the Visitor to work. The Visitor calls the polymorphic *accept* method of a given object, and the *accept* method calls the polymorphic *visit* method of the Visitor. It is this bidirectional calling that allows you to add more operations on any class that has an *accept* method, since each new Visitor class we write can carry out whatever operations we might think of using the data available in these classes.

Why Are We Doing This?

You may be asking yourself why we are jumping through these hoops when we could call the getVacationDays methods directly. By using this "callback" approach, we are implementing "double dispatching." There is no requirement that the objects we visit be of the same or even of related types. Further, using this callback approach, you can have a different visit method called in the Visitor, depending on the actual type of class. This is harder to implement directly.

Further, if the list of objects to be visited in an ArrayList is a collection of different types, having different versions of the visit methods in the actual Visitor is the only way to handle the problem without specifically checking the type of each class.

Traversing a Series of Classes

The calling program that passes the class instances to the Visitor must know about all the existing instances of classes to be visited and must keep them in a simple structure such as an array or collection. Another possibility would be to create an Enumeration of these classes and pass it to the Visitor. Finally, the Visitor itself could keep the list of objects that it is to visit. In our simple example program, we used an array of objects, but any of the other methods would work equally well.

Writing a Visitor in VB6

In VB6, we will define the Visitor as an *interface* and define only the employee visit as being required.

```
'Interface Visitor
Public Sub visit(emp As Employee)
End Sub
```

The Employee class has an accept method much the same as in our VB7 version.

```
Public Sub accept(v As Visitor)
  v.visit Me
End Sub
```

To create a VacationVisitor, we create a class that implements the Visitor interface.

```
'Class VacationVisitor
Implements Visitor
Dim totalDays As Integer
'-----
Private Sub Class_Initialize()
 totalDays = 0
End Sub
'-----
Private Sub Visitor_visit(emp As Employee)
 totalDays = totalDays + emp.getVacDays
End Sub
'-----
Public Function getTotalDays() As Integer
 getTotalDays = totalDays
End Function
```

Then, to carry out the visiting and tabulate employee vacation days, we loop through and call each employee's accept method, much as before.

```
'loop through all the employees
For i = 1 To empls.Count
   Set empl = empls(i)
   empl.accept v          'get the employee
 Next i
List1.AddItem "Total vacation days=" & Str$(vac.getTotalDays)
```

In VB6, our Boss class implements the Employee interface rather than being derived from it and *contains* an instance of the Employee class.

```
'Class Boss
Implements Employee
Private empl As Employee
Private bonusDays As Integer
'-----
Private Sub Class_Initialize()
 Set empl = New Employee
End Sub
'-----
Private Sub Employee_accept(v As Visitor)
 empl.accept v
End Sub
'-----
Private Function Employee_getName() As String
 Employee_getName = empl.getName
End Function
'-----
Private Function Employee_getSalary() As Single
 Employee_getSalary = empl.getSalary
End Function
'-----
Private Function Employee_getSickdays() As Integer
 Employee_getSickdays = empl.getSickdays
End Function
'-----
Private Function Employee_getVacDays() As Integer
 Employee_getVacDays = empl.getVacDays
End Function
'-----
Private Sub Employee_init(nm As String, sl As Single, _
        vDays As Integer, sDays As Integer)
 empl.init nm, sl, vDays, sDays
End Sub
'-----
Public Sub setBonusdays(bday As Integer)
 bonusDays = bday
End Sub
'-----
Public Function getBonusDays() As Integer
 getBonusDays = bonusDays
End Function
'-----
```

```
Public Sub accept(v As Visitor)
 v.visit Me
End Sub
```

Note that this class has two *accept* methods. One is from implementing the Employee interface.

```
Private Sub Employee_accept(v As Visitor)
 empl.accept v
End Sub
```

Another is just for the Boss class.

```
Public Sub accept(v As Visitor)
 v.visit Me
End Sub
```

The problem that VB6 introduces is that you must refer to an object as being an Employee to use the Employee methods and refer to it as a Boss to use the Boss-specific methods. Thus, there cannot be a polymorphic set of visit methods in the visitor class for each class that is to visit. Instead, you must convert each object to the correct class to call that class's methods. Since we shouldn't have to know in advance which objects are Employees and which are Bosses, we just try to convert each Employee to a Boss and catch the error that is generated for classes where this is not legal.

```
Private Sub Compute_Click()
  Dim i As Integer
  Dim vac As New VacationVisitor
  Dim bvac As New bVacationVisitor
  Dim v As Visitor
  Dim bos As Boss
  Dim empl As Employee
  Set v = vac
  'loop through all the employees
  On Local Error GoTo noboss 'trap conversion errors
  For i = 1 To empls.Count
     Set empl = empls(i)
     empl.accept v         'get the employee
     empl.accept bvac      'and in box visitor
     Set bos = empls(i)
     bos.accept bvac       'get as boss
   nexti:
  Next i
  List1.AddItem "Total vacation days=" & Str$(vac.getTotalDays)
  List1.AddItem "Total boss vacation days=" & _
        Str$(bvac.getTotalDays)
Exit Sub
```

```
'error if non-boss converted
'just skips to bottom of loop
noboss:
  Resume nexti
End Sub
```

This approach is significantly less elegant, but it does allow you to use a Visitor-like approach in VB6.

Consequences of the Visitor Pattern

The Visitor pattern is useful when you want to encapsulate fetching data from a number of instances of several classes. *Design Patterns* suggests that the Visitor can provide additional functionality to a class without changing it. We prefer to say that a Visitor can add functionality to a collection of classes and encapsulate the methods it uses.

The Visitor is not magic, however, and cannot obtain private data from classes. It is limited to the data available from public methods. This might force you to provide public methods that you would otherwise not have provided. However, it can obtain data from a disparate collection of unrelated classes and utilize it to present the results of a global calculation to the user program.

It is easy to add new operations to a program using Visitors, since the Visitor contains the code instead of each of the individual classes. Further, Visitors can gather related operations into a single class rather than forcing you to change or derive classes to add these operations. This can make the program simpler to write and maintain.

Visitors are less helpful during a program's growth stage, since each time you add new classes that must be visited, you have to add an abstract *visit* operation to the abstract Visitor class, and you must add an implementation for that class to each concrete Visitor you have written. Visitors can be powerful additions when the program reaches the point where many new classes are unlikely.

Visitors can be used very effectively in Composite systems, and the boss-employee system we just illustrated could well be a Composite like the one we used in the Composite chapter.

THOUGHT QUESTION

An investment firm's customer records consist of an object for each stock or other financial instrument each investor owns. The object contains a history of the purchase, sale, and dividend activities for that stock. Design a Visitor pattern to report on net end-of-year profit or loss on stocks sold during the year.

Programs on the CD-ROM

`\Visitor\`	VB6 Visitor
`\Visitor\VBNetVisitor`	VB7 Visitor

BIBLIOGRAPHY

Alexander, Christopher, Ishikawa, Sara, *et. al. A Pattern Language,* Oxford University Press, New York, 1977.

Alpert, S. R., Brown, K., and Woolf, B. *The Design Patterns Smalltalk Companion,* Addison-Wesley, Reading, MA, 1998.

Arnold, K., and Gosling, J. *The Java Programming Language,* Addison-Wesley, Reading, MA, 1997.

Booch, G., Jacobson, I., and Rumbaugh, J. *The Unified Modeling Language User Guide,* Addison-Wesley, Reading, MA, 1999.

Buschman, F., Meunier, R., Rohnert, H., Sommerlad, P., and Stal, M. *A System of Patterns,* John Wiley and Sons, New York, 1996.

Cooper, J. W. *Java Design Patterns: A Tutorial.* Addison-Wesley, Boston, MA, 2000.

Cooper, J. W. *Principles of Object-Oriented Programming in Java 1.1.* Coriolis (Ventana), 1997.

Coplien, James O. *Advanced C++ Programming Styles and Idioms,* Addison-Wesley, Reading, MA, 1992.

Coplien, James O., and Schmidt, Douglas C. *Pattern Languages of Program Design,* Addison-Wesley, Reading, MA, 1995.

Fowler, Martin, with Kendall Scott. *UML Distilled,* Addison-Wesley, Reading, MA, 1997.

Gamma, E., Helm, T., Johnson, R., and Vlissides, J. *Design Patterns: Abstraction and Reuse of Object Oriented Design.* Proceedings of ECOOP '93, 405–431.

Gamma, Eric, Helm, Richard, Johnson, Ralph, and Vlissides, John. *Design Patterns: Elements of Reusable Object-Oriented Software,* Addison-Wesley, Reading, MA, 1995.

Grand, Mark. *Patterns in Java,* Volume 1, John Wiley & Sons, New York 1998.

Krasner, G.E. and Pope, S.T. "A cookbook for using the Model-View-Controller user interface paradigm in Smalltalk-80." *Journal of Object-Oriented Programming* I(3)., 1988.

Kurata, Deborah. "Programming with Objects," *Visual Basic Programmer's Journal,* June, 1998.

Pree, Wolfgang. *Design Patterns for Object-Oriented Software Development,* Addison-Wesley, 1995.

Riel, Arthur J. *Object-Oriented Design Heuristics,* Addison-Wesley, Reading, MA, 1996.

Vlissides, John. *Pattern Hatching: Design Patterns Applied,* Addison-Wesley, Reading, MA, 1998.

INDEX

Also Available from Addison-Wesley:

Java™ Design Patterns: A Tutorial

By James W. Cooper

If you're a busy Java programmer who has yet to learn about design patterns and incorporate this powerful technology into your work, *Java™ Design Patterns* is exactly the tutorial resource you need. Accessible and clearly written, it helps you understand the nature and purpose of design patterns. It also serves as a practical guide to using design patterns to create sophisticated, robust Java programs.

This book presents the 23 patterns cataloged in the flagship book Design Patterns by Gamma, Helm, Johnson, and Vlissides. In *Java™ Design Patterns*, each of these patterns is illustrated by at least one complete visual Java program. This practical approach makes design pattern concepts more concrete and easier to grasp, brings Java programmers up to speed quickly, and enables you to take practical advantage of the power of design patterns.

0-201-48539-7 • Paperback • 352 pages • © 2000

www.**informit**.co

| Articles | Books | Free Library | Expert Q&A | Training | News | Downloa |

OPERATING SYSTEMS

WEB DEVELOPMENT

PROGRAMMING

NETWORKING

CERTIFICATION

AND MORE...

**Expert Access.
Free Content.**

Solutions
from experts
you know
and trust.

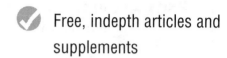

Free, indepth articles and
supplements

Master the skills you need,
when you need them

Choose from industry leadir
books, ebooks, and training
products

Achieve industry certificatio
and advance your career

Get answers when you
need them from live
experts or InformIT's
comprehensive library

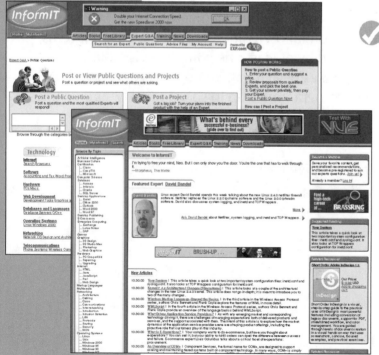

Visit **InformIT**
and get great content
from

Addison
Wesley

Addison-Wesley and InformIT
are trademarks of Pearson plc /
Copyright©2000 pearson

www.**informit**.com

Register Your Book

at www.aw.com/cseng/register

You may be eligible to receive:

- Advance notice of forthcoming editions of the book
- Related book recommendations
- Chapter excerpts and supplements of forthcoming titles
- Information about special contests and promotions throughout the year
- Notices and reminders about author appearances, tradeshows, and online chats with special guests

Contact us

If you are interested in writing a book or reviewing manuscripts prior to publication, please write to us at:

Editorial Department
Addison-Wesley Professional
75 Arlington Street, Suite 300
Boston, MA 02116 USA
Email: AWPro@aw.com

Visit us on the Web: http://www.aw.com/cseng

CD-ROM Warranty

Addison-Wesley warrants the enclosed disc to be free of defects in materials and faulty workmanship under normal use for a period of ninety days after purchase. If a defect is discovered in the disc during this warranty period, a replacement disc can be obtained at no charge by sending the defective disc, postage prepaid, with proof of purchase to:

Editorial Department
Addison-Wesley Professional
Pearson Technology Group
75 Arlington Street, Suite 300
Boston, MA 02116
Email: AWPro@awl.com

Addison-Wesley makes no warranty or representation, either expressed or implied, with respect to this software, its quality, performance, merchantability, or fitness for a particular purpose. In no event will Addison-Wesley, its distributors, or dealers be liable for direct, indirect, special, incidental, or consequential damages arising out of the use or inability to use the software. The exclusion of implied royalties is not permitted in some states. Therefore, the above exclusion may not apply to you. This warranty provides you with specific legal rights. There may be other rights that you may have that vary from state to state. The contents of this CD-ROM are intended for non-commercial use only.